Low Fertility Regimes and Demographic and Societal Change

Dudley L. Poston, Jr.
Editor

Samsik Lee • Han Gon Kim
Co-Editors

Low Fertility Regimes and Demographic and Societal Change

Springer

Korea Institute for Health and Social Affairs
KiHASA
한국보건사회연구원

Editor
Dudley L. Poston, Jr.
Department of Sociology
Texas A & M University
College Station, TX, USA

Co-Editors
Samsik Lee
Department of Policy Science and Institute for Population and Aged Society
Hanyang University
Seoul, South Korea

Han Gon Kim
Yeungnam University
Gyeongbuk, South Korea

ISBN 978-3-319-64059-4 ISBN 978-3-319-64061-7 (eBook)
DOI 10.1007/978-3-319-64061-7

Library of Congress Control Number: 2017951734

Printed on acid-free paper

This Springer imprint is published by Springer Nature
The registered company is Springer International Publishing AG
The registered company address is: Gewerbestrasse 11, 6330 Cham, Switzerland

Preface

The global community is undergoing rapid demographic and societal change. It is within this context that the 27th International Union for the Scientific Study of Population (IUSSP) International Population Conference, entitled "The Future of the World," was held in Busan, South Korea, on August 26–31, 2013. More than 2,500 demographers and population professionals from all over the world attended and participated in this very successful conference. Later, in May 2014, the Korean National Organizing Committee for the 27th IUSSP International Population Conference met in Seoul to celebrate the success of the said conference. At the meeting, Byung Ho Choe, the president of the Korea Institute of Health and Social Affairs (KIHASA), and Han Gon Kim, the president of the Population Association of Korea (PAK), agreed to hold an international symposium building on some of the issues of the IUSSP Conference, especially those pertaining to demographic dynamics in low-fertility societies. They also discussed the possibility of publishing a book based on the presentations made at the symposium.

At a later meeting convened to prepare the international symposium, President Choe and Dr. Kim made a decision that KIHASA would provide the funds for the international symposium and that Dr. Kim would be in charge of organizing it. Later, KIHASA and PAK invited Dr. Dudley L. Poston, Jr., to chair the organizing committee for the symposium and to serve as the principal editor of the proposed book. Dr. Kim and Dr. Youngtae Cho then traveled to Yokohama, Japan, on July 17–18 to meet with Dr. Poston (who was attending an international conference in Yokohama) to further discuss and begin to plan the international symposium. At the Yokohama meeting, Drs. Poston, Kim, and Cho prepared an outline for the symposium and the resulting book. Dr. Poston agreed that he would be in charge of contacting demographers to present papers at the symposium who would later write chapters for the book. Dr. Poston then prepared a book proposal and submitted it to Ms. Evelien Bakker at Springer Publishing, who then issued Dr. Poston and his colleagues a contract for a book to be entitled *Low Fertility Regimes and Demographic and Societal Change*.

The international symposium was held at the Seoul Plaza Hotel, South Korea, on December 16, 2014. Ten demographers traveled to Seoul to make their presentations, and three demographers unable to attend the symposium sent outlines. All planned to submit the first drafts of their chapters by August 2015. Most chapters were submitted on that month, and Dr. Poston then began to edit and revise the chapters for publication. Dr. Poston had an editorial meeting with Dr. Kim, Dr. Cho, and Dr. Samsik Lee in Seoul in September 13–15, 2015.

This book considers a variety of issues related to demographic dynamics and societal change in the twenty-first century. It begins with an introductory chapter by Dudley Poston that provides some context for low-fertility regimes and demographic and societal change. Four chapters follow dealing with demographic dynamics, namely, Chap. 2 on fertility by Francesco Billari; Chap. 3 on natural decrease by Nayoung Heo and Dudley Poston; Chap. 4 on mortality by Richard Rogers, Elizabeth Lawrence, and Robert Hummer; and Chap. 5 on international migration by Susan Brown, Frank Bean, and James Bachmeier. The next four chapters deal with changes in social structure, namely, Chap. 6 on aging and age dependency by Samsik Lee; Chap. 7 on issues of motherhood and gender by Nancy Riley; Chap. 8 on marital relationships by Linda Waite and Juyeon Kim; and Chap. 9 on marriage and cohabitation by Gavin Jones. The last three chapters focus on institutions and demographic change, namely, Chap. 10 on family by Daniel Lichter and Zhenchao Qian; Chap. 11 on political effects by Michael Teitelbaum; and Chap. 12 on religion by Christopher Ellison, Xiaohe Xu, and Andrea Ruiz.

We express our sincere gratitude to Dr. Bung Ho Choe, the former president of KIHASA, and to Dr. SangHo Kim, the current president of KIHASA. This book would not have been published without their financial and administrative support. We also thank Dr. Samsik Lee of KIHASA, Dr. Youngtae Cho of Seoul National University, and Dr. Joongbaek Kim, the secretary general of PAK, for their advice and support.

Finally, and most importantly, we acknowledge Dr. Dudley Poston for his extensive editorial work, his inspiration, and his dedication. This book would not have been published without his enthusiasm and sacrifice.

Gyeongbuk, South Korea Han Gon Kim

Contents

Chapter 1
The Context of Low Fertility Regimes and Demographic and Societal Change

Dudley L. Poston, Jr.

Introduction

This volume focuses on demographic and societal changes in societies experiencing low and very low fertility. In this introductory chapter I provide some demographic context for evaluating and understanding these changes. I discuss in some detail the two major theories and perspectives that best inform the demographic and social dynamics currently underway in low fertility populations. These are the classic theory of demographic transition and the theory of the second demographic transition. The book that follows this introductory chapter contains 11 chapters; four chapters deal with demographic dynamics of fertility, natural decrease, mortality, and international migration. The next four chapters deal with structural changes in societies pertaining to aging, mothering and gender, marital relationships, and marriage and cohabitation. The last three chapters deal with changing social institutions, namely, the family, the political arena, and religion. In all these chapters attention is directed to low fertility societies, and in many of them a major focus is given to the Republic of Korea. Later in this chapter I summarize briefly each of the chapters.

I turn now to a discussion and review of the classic model of demographic transition.

The Classical Theory of Demographic Transition

The most prominent explanation for the growth of human populations is the theory of demographic transition. Changes in the size of a society's population over a period of time are due entirely to changes during the same time period in fertility,

D.L. Poston, Jr. (✉)
Dept. Sociology College Station, Texas A&M University, College Station, TX 77843, USA
e-mail: d-poston@tamu.edu

D.L. Poston, Jr. (ed.), *Low Fertility Regimes and Demographic and Societal Change*, DOI 10.1007/978-3-319-64061-7_1

mortality and migration. Although there are a few exceptions (e.g., the United States, Canada, Australia and Israel), for most societies, particularly a society such as South Korea, fertility and mortality are the major agents in the changing size of the population. Over time, South Korea and most other societies have changed their size by adding persons born during the period and subtracting persons dying.

Demographic transition theory was first developed by Thompson (1929) and Notestein (1945) and later extended by Davis (1963). The theory proposes four stages of mortality and fertility change that occur in the process of societal modernization. The first stage is the pretransitional or preindustrialization stage. It lasted for thousands of years when societies were characterized by high birth rates and high death rates and stable population growth. This first stage is typically one of fluctuating mortality and high fertility. The relative instability of the mortality rates means that during this stage there were some periods of natural increase (more births than deaths) and some of natural decrease (more deaths than births), but that over the long period, there was very little change in population size (Poston and Heo 2017).

The pretransitional stage is followed by a transition to a second stage. For reasons discussed below, first mortality began to decline in many countries of the world. With the onset of industrialization and modernization, many societies transitioned to lower death rates, mainly due to lower rates of infant mortality and maternal mortality, but maintained fairly high birth rates. Rapid population growth was the result. It would take another generation or so before fertility would begin to fall. During Stage 2, population growth was intense.

The transition from Stage 1 to State 2 occurred first in several European countries in the context of the industrial revolution. In short, the Industrial Revolution eventually created a healthier society, resulting in several European countries moving from the first stage to the second stage. With better transportation, food supplies were improved and famines occurred less frequently. New foods were introduced from the colonies in the Americas and elsewhere. Also, better housing was constructed, and better clothing became available as cotton became more plentiful. In the nineteenth century, sanitary behavior began to be practiced by the population, and public-health movements were appearing. Medical improvements did not really contribute too much to declining mortality until the twentieth century. But birth rates remained high.

The rapid population growth occurring in Stage 2 was pretty much limited to Western Europe. Death rates remained high for the most part outside Europe. It was not until after World War II that there were significant improvements there in longevity. Then, death rates started falling in many non-European countries, and they fell rapidly. These areas benefited from the knowledge learned in the more advanced nations a decade or two earlier. By then, too, medical knowledge had increased, and the residents were the benefactors of this new information.

The decline in mortality in the European nations, i.e., Stage 2, was later followed by a decline in fertility, i.e., Stage 3. By the 1930s in many European countries, overall population growth rates were coming down. Whereas throughout most of history, up until the eighteenth century, population growth was very slow because of high fertility and high mortality, population growth now began to start to slow down because of lower rates of fertility and mortality.

Stage 3 was characterized by decreasing population growth due to lower birth and death rates; it was during this stage that fertility began to decline. The causal linkages are complex. Underlying the global concepts of industrialization and modernization are such factors leading to fertility reductions as women's participation in the nonagricultural labor force and the changing role of the family. In Stage 3, the normative, institutional, and economic supports for the large family started to erode, and the small family norm became predominant. The increasing importance of urbanization affects the family by altering its role in production. Also, urban families are typically met with considerably higher demands for consumption by their children, especially for education and recreation.

In the final stage (Stage 4), both fertility and mortality are very low. And it is not really possible to determine how low fertility will go. In recent years, fertility has fallen so low in many European countries and in some Asian countries that the number of deaths exceeds the number of births (Poston et al. 2016).

The decline in fertility, i.e., the movement from the second stage to the third stage, is not as easily understood as that for mortality. Individual decisions were not as important when it came to lowering mortality. The social system, for the most part, was the major contributing factor. When it came to fertility, however, individual decisions were necessary if the birth rates were to decline. But even those decisions depended on the social situation. As urbanization and industrialization continued to occur, the family became less important as an economic unit of production. When most people resided in rural areas, having large families was important. The children, as they grew up, participated in the daily household chores. Having another child was economically feasible since families lived mainly off the land. With the move to the city, impersonal systems like the factory took over the allocation of jobs. Those moving from the farm to the city often found themselves living in tenement houses, perhaps with only one or two bedrooms. It was soon concluded that children who were useful as a cheap supply of labor in farming families were not as useful in industrial working-class urban families. Furthermore, child labor laws were soon passed and formal education became mandatory. Hence, children did not contribute as much to the family economy as they did prior to the initiation of these changes (Poston and Bouvier 2010; Poston and Heo 2017).

Another factor in the process of declining fertility was the fall in infant mortality. Along with overall mortality declines, there was also a decrease in infant deaths. Prior to the Industrial Revolution, many families would often have nine or ten or more children, perhaps subconsciously realizing that only three or four would survive to adulthood. Now, most survived; the solution, thus, was to limit fertility (Poston and Bouvier 2010).

For centuries, i.e., during the first stage, the society's culture virtually dictated that women should have as many offspring as possible. Consider how dramatic this shift in sexual behavior was for those couples. It was not at all surprising that it took more than one generation for smaller families to become the norm. This was a major cultural change in familial behavior.

The demographic transition has been completed in virtually all the developed countries of the world, but not in most of the less developed countries. Most African countries are early in stage 3 of the transition, with falling, death rates and high, though falling, birth rates; some of them, however, particularly many in sub-Saharan Africa, are still in stage 2. This is also the case in much of the Middle East. Some countries in Latin America are moving towards the stage of incipient decline but are not there yet.

These variations in demographic transition between the more developed and the less developed countries are resulting in some interesting changes in population distribution. In 2014, over 83% of the world's population (almost 6 billion people) lived in the less developed countries and just under 17% in the more developed countries (just over 1.2 billion). Just one century ago, the pattern was almost reversed, with a majority of the Earth's population residing in more developed countries. "The conclusion is obvious: not only has population growth been enormous in the 20th century, it has also led to a complete reversal of population distribution with the poorer regions gaining and surpassing the richer sections in the process" (Bouvier and Bertrand 1999: 10). The share of population living in the less developed countries will increase even further during the twenty-first century given the very low fertility rates in the developed nations.

In the final stage (stage 4), called incipient decline, both fertility and mortality became very low. In stage 4, populations only grow when there are increases in fertility, such as in the baby boom in the U.S. after World War II. During this stage, however, there are slight fluctuations in fertility; thus both natural increase and decrease will occur. The term, incipient, is used because it is not really possible to determine how low fertility will go. In recent years, fertility has fallen so low in many European countries and in Japan that the number of deaths exceeds the number of births. This has led to what demographers now refer to as the Second Demographic transition (SDT), which I will discuss in more detail below.

Although the demographic transition theory is the most popular of the demographic theories of population change, there are numerous applications of the theory in European and other populations, indicating that it does not work the same way in every population (Knodel and van de Walle 1979; Hirschman 1994; Mason 1997; Poston 2000). Its major contribution is not so much its utility as a predictor of population change, but as a general description of population change (Poston et al. 2008).

The Second and Third Demographic Transitions

I mentioned above that the 4th stage of the demographic transition is referred to as that of incipient decline because fertility and mortality are both low. In this context of these very low fertility and mortality rates, there have occurred some major societal changes. These changes have led to what is now popularly known as the "second" demographic transition, which is an attempt by demographers to explain "the revolution in living arrangements and sexual behavior, and in the setting for childbearing, now transforming the lives of many inhabitants of Western societies and, it is argued, eventually in developed societies elsewhere" (Coleman 2006: 402).

van de Kaa (1987) and Ron Lesthaeghe (1995, 2010; Lesthaeghe and Neidert 2006, 2009) have discussed these societal changes in their analyses of the falling birth rates in many European countries. In the 1980s and 1990s, they noted that within the context of stage four of the demographic transition theory (DTT) in these European countries, the birth rate continued to fall, and fell considerably lower than the already low death rate.

The second demographic transition, or SDT, focuses in part on the realization that perhaps there were two different motivations behind the fertility declines observed in the first and second demographic transitions. In the former, the large amounts of emotional and monetary investment in children induced the decline, while in the latter self-realization and fulfilment seems to be the main goal.

The even lower birth rates occurring in the SDT resulted in major changes in the marriage and the family throughout much of Europe, especially in Northern and Western Europe. These countries witnessed such behaviors as increasing age at first marriage, increases in cohabitation, increases in divorce, the emergence of same-sex partnerships and marriages, increasing rates of nonmarital childbearing, and voluntary childlessness. The second demographic transition has now occurred in most of Europe and is well underway in the United States, Canada, Australia, and many other countries, including South Korea.

These behaviors of the SDT have emerged for at least two reasons. One is that ideational changes have occurred in the society, such as increases in individualism and secularism and declines in the importance and influence of traditional religions. These ideational changes have led to an increased tolerance and acceptance of many of the so-called SDT behaviors (Yu and Xie 2015) such as premarital sexual behavior, cohabitation, and nonmarital childbearing. Another explanation focuses on modernization and industrialization (Cherlin and Furstenberg Jr. 1988). Recall that these were the bases for the initiation of the mortality reduction in Stage 2 of the classic or first demographic transition and the fertility reduction in Stage 3. However, these developmental processes, it is argued, have also led to "greater gender egalitarianism, more sexual freedom, and, specifically, a reduction in the stigma attached to unmarried sexual relations" (Yu and Xie 2015: 608).

In summary, then, classic demographic transition theory (which may now be referred to as the "first" demographic transition), involved the transition or movement of societies from high levels of fertility and mortality to low levels of fertility and mortality. This transition began in 1700 and later in Europe and is still ongoing in many Latin American and Asian countries and in virtually all of sub-Saharan Africa. I mentioned above the major changes that have occurred in demographic behavior in most of the European and other countries experiencing very low levels of fertility. These changes have led to what is now popularly known as the "second" demographic transition.

Demographic transition theory has been further revised with the recognition by Coleman (Coleman 2006) of the increasing tendency, if not requirement, of low fertility countries to rely on immigration to maintain its population. This means that "the ancestry of some national populations is being radically and permanently altered by high levels of immigration of persons from remote geographic origins" and in some countries is accompanied by "accelerated levels of emigration of the domestic population" (Coleman 2006: 401). These further changes are popularly referred to as the third demographic transition (TDT).

A particularly instructive application of this perspective is Lichter's (2013: 364) observation that the "new immigration has altered America's fundamental character. Immigration has become a national political issue and not just a state or local one." Changes in the racial mix of the U.S. are first seen among the children and young people of the society (Johnson and Lichter 2008, 2010), and many of these children are the children of immigrants. He makes the point that these children are in "the vanguard of the Third Demographic Transition that will remake America" (Lichter 2013: 364).

In summary, then, classic demographic transition now referred to as the first demographic transition, involved the transition or movement of societies from high levels of fertility and mortality to low levels of fertility and mortality. This transition began in 1700 and later in Europe and is still ongoing in many Latin American and Asian countries and in virtually all of sub-Saharan Africa. I mentioned above the major changes that have occurred in demographic behavior in most of these countries with very low levels of fertility. These changes have led to what is now popularly known as the second demographic transition, which is an attempt by demographers to better understand the changing patterns of living arrangements and sexual behavior.

But given the very low levels of fertility, so low that in some societies there are occurring more deaths than births, there has been a tendency, if not a requirement to rely on international migration to maintain their populations. Neither the first nor the second demographic transitions explicitly took into account the role of international migration. This lack of attention to the crucial role assumed by international migration has resulted in what has become known as the third demographic transition. This involves bringing increasing numbers of immigrants into the low fertility countries, and in so doing, resulting in significant changes in the "composition of national populations and thereby (their) culture, physical appearance, social experiences, and self-perceived identity (Coleman 2006: 402).

Chapter Summaries

I turn now to summaries of each of the substantive chapters in this book. As I noted earlier, following this introductory chapter are 11 chapters organized in three major sections. The first section deals with demographic change and contains four chapters. Chapter 2 by Francesco Billari focuses on fertility and asks a number of questions: Where is fertility heading with many societies completing the first demographic transition? Will fertility levels stabilize around the replacement level? Will fertility differences among advanced societies persist? Billari discusses the issues of the post-transitional level of fertility in advanced societies and the differences across societies. He also outlines the conditions under which the group of countries that are now diverging to a lower level might eventually join the many countries with current fertility rates near replacement.

The subject of the next chapter, by Nayoung Heo and Dudley Poston, is what demographers refer to as "natural decrease," that is, a population having more persons dying than being born. The authors note that currently South Korea as a country is characterized by natural increase, and not natural decrease; for every nine births in 2015 in South Korea, there were five deaths. However, in the 15-year period from 2005 to 2014, just over one-half, or 81 of Korea's 161 counties had more deaths than births. They show that there are clear concentrations of natural decrease counties in the northeastern and southwestern regions of the country. This percentage of natural decrease counties in South Korea is much higher than the 34% of counties in the United States experiencing natural decrease in around the same period. Heo and Poston hold that natural decrease is likely to loom particularly large in South Korea's future. There are relatively few young women residing in the natural decrease counties to produce the next generation of Korean infants. Hence with a very low fertility rate, a diminishing population in the child-bearing ages, and an increasingly older population at a high risk of mortality, more widespread natural decrease in South Korea is almost inevitable.

In Chap. 4, Richard Rogers, Elizabeth Lawrence and Robert Hummer provide an overview of life expectancy patterns and mortality rates in the United States, with frequent comparison to other low fertility (and high-income) countries. The authors first compare life expectancy in the U.S. with that of selected countries, and then describe life expectancy and mortality changes in the U.S. across time. Next they focus on particular causes of death and health behavior patterns where the United States fares poorly when compared to other low fertility, high-income countries. Finally, they speculate on future trends in U.S. life expectancy by comparing the United States to some of the longest living countries in the world. They show that gains in U.S. life expectancy over the twentieth century have been substantial and are one of the true success stories of the society. At the same time, they note, life expectancy in the U.S. lags behind other low fertility countries; simply put, the pace of improvement has been even faster in other low fertility, high-income countries, such as South Korea. There are clear ways for the United States to improve its position in the coming decades, and the authors conclude their chapter articulating some of these possibilities.

Chapter 5 by Susan Brown, Frank Bean and James Bachmeier relates issues of low fertility with immigration, and the focus, as in the preceding chapter, is on the United States. In the first few pages of this chapter the authors present insightful and relevant reviews of the classic theory of demographic transition and the second and third demographic transitions. The authors then note that native-born workers in the U.S. often express concern that less-skilled immigrant workers are competing with them for jobs. However, the authors show, research has found that less-skilled immigrants do not harm the employment or wages of U.S.-born workers. This is so because the size of the less-skilled U.S.-born younger population has declined over the past 25 years. In their chapter the authors demonstrate how U.S. fertility declines in particular have led to a smaller less-skilled U.S.-born workforce compared with about 25 years ago, and they also show how much smaller this workforce will be over the next 15 years or so. Thus there will be a large deficit of U.S.-born persons available to do the country's less-skilled work in 2030. This fact has important implications for possible reforms of U.S. immigration policy, and the authors conclude their chapter discussing some of these issues.

Chapter 6 by Samsik Lee on aging and age dependency is the first of several chapters in the second section of this book, all dealing with structural changes in low fertility societies. The author first shows that population aging is a consequence of fertility decline and the prolonging of human life, but that the former has the major influence. He then addresses the issue of age dependency, specifically the old age dependency ratio, i.e., the number of persons in the population of age 65 or more per 100 persons in the producing ages of 15–64. He points out that South Korea is projected to be the country in the world in 2100 with the highest old age dependency ratio of 74.4; this means that in 2100 there will be almost 75 elders in the Korean population per 100 persons in the producing ages. He then discusses the impact of aging on economic growth and notes that the mechanisms through which low fertility and population aging affect economic growth are diversified and very complex. A major conclusion of his chapter is that as countries pass through the classic demographic transition from high birth and death rates to low birth and death rates, and then move on to the second demographic transition, one of the most crucial structural consequences is the aging of the population. And most relevant is the important effect of aging on economic growth.

Nancy Riley in Chap. 7 on mothering and fertility notes at the onset that with decreasing fertility, women's lives often change greatly, along with other changes that are associated with increases in education, decreases in time devoted to child-raising, and increases in female labor force participation. With women released from spending a significant portion of their lives around having and raising many children, she asks whether their family lives, and their lives in general, will be much changed compared to women living in countries with much higher fertility. She shows that because of the intractability of gender inequalities, the situation in low fertility societies tends to resemble in many ways the situation in high fertility societies. In a declining fertility or low fertility scenario, while women might gain some traction toward gender equality, fertility change certainly does not automatically lead there. One might expect that in low fertility societies with women free from many births and the rearing of many children, they would spend less time at home and in their role as mothers. But in many low fertility societies, motherhood has taken on new pressures and women can end up spending as much time raising their one or two children as mothers in earlier generations did with raising many children. Such intensive mothering takes different forms in different societies, and Riley discusses many of these in striking detail.

Linda Waite and Juyeon Kim begin Chap. 8 on sexuality and marital relationships by noting that low and very low fertility appear in many developed and in some developing countries. And when fertility falls within marriage, the roles of husbands and wives also change, and, moreover, there are fewer years of adult life in marriage devoted to raising children. Thus, societies with low and very low fertility should both enable and follow from changes in couple relationships. The authors examine changes in marriage and cohabitation in low fertility societies compared to others. They also look at differences in sexuality in these two types of societies. They discuss couple relationships among older adults in the United States as an illustration of what a low fertility regime might mean across the life course. Among their findings is the fact that among marital and cohabiting couples in the United States at the older ages, many remain sexually active and are quite satisfied with their sexual relationships. However, other couples tend to do fewer things together and have less sex. Waite and Kim note that given the importance of marital solidarity and marital quality to mental and physical health in later life, the dissatisfaction among members of many older couples is a cause for concern. Some of these implications are discussed in this most informative chapter.

In Chap. 9 on marriage and cohabitation in low fertility societies, Gavin Jones focuses on the low fertility countries of East Asia and asks whether comparisons between these countries and the European countries support the idea of convergence of family and marriage patterns toward those thought to be representative of advanced industrial societies. He is essentially asking about the importance and relevance of William Goode's argument made more than five decades ago that family patterns in developing countries will converge in the process of their development towards those of Western countries. He looks at general patterns of marriage including cohabitation and notes that a fundamental problem is that the Western family pattern to which other societies including those of East Asia are supposed to converge is itself changing in fundamental ways. Thus one wonders which societies these other societies are supposed to be converging towards. The so-called "male breadwinner" model has been greatly modified in Western countries. The idea of convergence, he notes, is also challenged by ongoing changes in partnering patterns in Western societies – a transition from companionate marriage to individualistic marriage, with emphasis on personal fulfilment, self-development and flexible roles, along the lines of the second demographic transition. This is another of the chapters in this volume noting the important degree to which East Asian societies are exhibiting many of the behaviors predicted by the second demographic transition.

Chapter 10 focuses on the family, especially diversity, living arrangements and economic inequalities. The authors Daniel Lichter and Zhenchao Qian draw on current data to examine U.S. family patterns dealing with racial change and diversity, the changing living arrangements of children, and the shifting patterns of poverty and economic inequality. They note that the second demographic transition has been linked to the "diverging destinies" of America's children. Lichter and Qian argue in this chapter that inequality is being amplified as the second demographic transition gives way to a newly-emerging third demographic transition, one characterized by unprecedented growth of racial and ethnic minority populations in the developed world. Inequality and poverty among America's children are reinforced by a new and growing intergenerational divide, one marked by an aging white population and a rapidly growing population of minority children. The authors conclude their chapter by exploring the options available to U.S. policymakers and identifying lessons from other low-fertility and aging countries in the developed world that face similar demographic challenges.

In Chap. 11 Michael Teitelbaum focuses on political behavior in low fertility societies. He first observes that political behavior in the context of low fertility societies is very important, especially for countries such as South Korea in which low fertility rates are at the lowest level. This is so because if these very low fertility rates were to continue for many years, the countries would eventually experience declines in population size – unless net immigration numbers were to increase substantially. Most would also experience rapid shifts in their age composition toward higher percentages of older age groups. He then presents an informative discussion and review of population growth and decline. In the past 2–3 centuries, human populations have mostly been increasing, and at unprecedented and accelerating rates. In his review he also discusses some of the policies that were developed in some of the European countries as a response to the demographic changes. He shows that ideological and political perspectives and policies have been important contributors to demographic change itself and to the ways it has been perceived. In a later section of his chapter he then asks to what extent demographic trends have been important factors in political perspectives and behavior. Many of his arguments and answers have direct relevance for such low fertility countries as South Korea. Along these lines, he concludes his chapter with a detailed review of policy agendas and policies developed by the government of the Republic of Korea to address issues of very low birth rates, population size and aging.

The final chapter in this book is by Christopher Ellison, Xiaohe Xu, and Andrea Ruiz and focuses on the relationship between low fertility regimes and religion and its implications. The authors note that there is an extensive body of research dealing primarily with the positive associations between fertility and religion –that is, the link between higher fertility and higher religiosity. But they note as well that the logic of these arguments also helps us to understand why declines in fertility might undermine levels of religious participation, and why long-term, large-scale reductions in fertility rates could well affect patterns of religious affiliation, participation, salience, and belief in important ways. Ellison, Xu and Ruiz build on these arguments and examine in their chapter the association between country-level fertility decline and subsequent patterns of individual religiosity.

The authors of the chapters in this book provide interesting methodological and substantive contributions to the discourse on the wealth of demographic and social behaviors in low fertility societies, especially those occurring in the context of the second demographic transition. They also underscore the implications of the various social and demographic changes occurring today in low fertility societies. The chapters in this book provide an unprecedented overview of what is known about social and demographic change in low fertility countries as well as what future research will certainly need to address.

References

Bouvier, L. F., & Bertrand, J. T. (1999). *World population: Challenges for the 21st century*. Santa Ana: Seven Locks.
Cherlin, A. J., & Furstenberg Jr., F. F. (1988). The changing European family: Lessons for the American reader. *Journal of Family Issues, 9*, 291–297.
Coleman, D. A. (2006). Immigration and ethnic change in low-fertility countries: A third demographic transition. *Population and Development Review, 32*, 401–446.
Davis, K. (1963). The theory of change and response in modern demographic history. *Population Index, 29*, 345–366.
Hirschman, C. (1994). Why fertility changes. *Annual Review of Sociology, 20*, 203–233.
Johnson, K. M., & Lichter, D. T. (2008). Natural increase: A new source of population growth in emerging Hispanic destinations. *Population and Development Review, 34*, 327–346.
Johnson, K. M., & Lichter, D. T. (2010). Growing diversity among America's children and youth: Spatial and temporal dimensions. *Population and Development Review, 36*, 151–175.
Knodel, J., & van de Walle, E. (1979). Lessons from the past: Policy implications of historical fertility studies. *Population and Development Review, 5*, 217–245.
Lesthaeghe, R. J. (1995). The second demographic transition in western countries: An interpretation. In K. O. Mason & A. M. Jensen (Eds.), *Gender and family change in industrialized countries* (pp. 17–62). Oxford: Clarendon Press.
Lesthaeghe, R. J. (2010). The unfolding story of the second demographic transition. *Population and Development Review, 36*, 211–251.
Lesthaeghe, R. J., & Neidert, L. (2006, March). *The "Second demographic transition" in the U.S.: Spatial patterns and correlates* (Population Studies Center Research Report No. 06-592). Ann Arbor: University of Michigan.
Lesthaeghe, R. J., & Neidert, L. (2009). U.S. presidential elections and the spatial pattern of the American second demographic transition. *Population and Development Review, 35*, 391–400.
Lichter, D. T. (2013). Integration or fragmentation: Racial diversity and the American future. *Demography, 50*, 359–391.
Mason, K. O. (1997). Explaining fertility transitions. *Demography, 34*, 443–454.
Notestein, F. W. (1945). Population – The long view. In T. W. Schultz (Ed.), *Food for the world* (pp. 36–57). Chicago: University of Chicago Press.
Poston, D. L., Jr. (2000). Social and economic development and the fertility transition in mainland China and Taiwan. *Population and Development Review, 26*(Supplement), 40–60.
Poston, D. L., Jr., & Bouvier, L. F. (2010). *Population and society: An introduction to demography*. New York: Cambridge University Press.
Poston, D. L., Jr., & Heo, N.. (2017). Demography. In B. S. Turner (Ed.), *The Wiley Blackwell encyclopedia of social theory*. New York: Wiley-Blackwell.
Poston, D. L., Jr., Zhang, L., & Terrell, H. K. M. (2008). Fertility. In W. A. Darity (Ed.), *International encyclopedia of the social sciences* (2nd ed., pp. 126–130). Detroit: Macmillan.
Poston, D. L., Jr., Johnson, K., & Field, L. (2016, February 15). Deaths exceed births in most of Europe, but not in the U.S., and not in Texas. *N-IUSSP, the News Magazine of the International Union for the Scientific Study of Population.*
Thompson, W. S. (1929). Population. *American Journal of Sociology, 34*, 959–975.
van de Kaa, D. J. 1987. *Europe's second demographic transition* (Population Bulletin. Vol. 42). Washington, DC: Population Reference Bureau.
Yu, J., & Xie, Y. (2015). Cohabitation in China: Trends and determinants. *Population and Development Review, 41*, 607–628.

Part I
Demographic Dynamics and Change

Chapter 2
A "Great Divergence" in Fertility?

Francesco C. Billari

Introduction

Where is fertility heading around the world as the long-term fertility transition comes to an end? Will fertility levels stabilize around the replacement level, i.e. will micro-level decisions of individuals and couples be consistent with the macro-level stationary population? Moreover, will fertility differences among advanced societies become persistent, as part of a societal, or more specifically a demographic, *régime*?

There is ample discussion in the literature about the first two related questions, as reviews on fertility in advanced societies have already made clear (Balbo et al. 2013; Morgan and Taylor 2006). Recent studies of expert-based forecasts have noted great differences among fertility scholars in terms of how they view the future of fertility (Basten et al. 2014). This heterogeneity of views is present even if one just focuses on experts of a single (low-fertility) country, like Italy (Billari et al. 2014). Uncertainty in fertility projections and forecasts is particularly relevant and is contributing to a great extent to the general uncertainty in population forecasts (UNPD 2015).

Regarding differences across societies, there is a pretty straightforward distinction between two types of positions. One position sees long-term convergence (albeit not necessarily agreeing on the outcome) due to processes shaping fertility in all countries, namely, the Second Demographic Transition (Lesthaeghe 2010, 2014; Lesthaeghe and van de Kaa 1986; van de Kaa 1987), and the Gender Revolution (Esping-Andersen and Billari 2015; Goldscheider et al. 2015). Scholars working from the Gender Revolution perspective, in particular, see the emergence of a post-transitional fertility equilibrium close to the replacement level as an outcome under

F.C. Billari (✉)
Department of Policy Analysis and Public Management and Carlo F. Dondena Centre for Research on Social Dynamics and Public Policies, Bocconi University, Milan, Italy
e-mail: francesco.billari@unibocconi.it

D.L. Poston, Jr. (ed.), *Low Fertility Regimes and Demographic and Societal Change*, DOI 10.1007/978-3-319-64061-7_2

some pre-conditions. A second position sees the emergence of distinct post-transitional fertility regimes (Reher 1998; Wilson 2013), with fertility becoming an aspect of stable differentiation across societies. If fertility is persistently different, population growth rates will be different across the countries, even if migration partially offset these differences (Billari and Dalla-Zuanna 2013).

In this chapter, I will discuss post-transitional levels of fertility in advanced societies as well as persisting or emerging differences across societies. I will focus on advanced societies in Europe, North America, Oceania and East Asia and illustrate the "great divergence" in fertility between a group of countries with fertility close to replacement and a group of countries with fertility close to one child per couple. The latter group of countries is characterized by a weaker position of young people, and relatively weaker levels of well-being and/or gender equality. My analysis will help to outline the conditions under which the group of countries that are diverging to a lower level might "join the club" of those with fertility near replacement.

The chapter is structured as follows. The next section illustrates some basic data on the "great divergence" in fertility. This is followed by a discussion of differences across countries in the position of young people as they relate to fertility. Based on the literature on the transition to adulthood, the reversal of the relationship between the age at leaving the parental home and total fertility will be seen as an indication of the emergence of common determinants for a later transition to adulthood and low fertility. The subsequent section will discuss the preconditions for the progression to higher parities, and in particular economic well-being and gender equality. It will built on the recent literature on the reversal of the relationship between well-being and fertility and illustrate an example of (still) persistent differences in the emergence of a new gendered model of work-family relationships. In the last section, I will present some general discussion and concluding remarks.

A "Great Divergence" in Fertility?

The long-term decline of fertility is usually seen as an integral part of the demographic transition, a process that, sooner or later, will be experienced by all societies (Lee 2003; Livi-Bacci 2012). The fertility decline has spread to such an extent that the fertility transition in the developed world is now seen as completed. What happens to fertility after the completion of the transition is, however, not well-defined. A naïve perspective leads one to assume that post-transitional fertility stabilizes around the replacement level, i.e. more or less two children per couple. Indeed, below-replacement fertility was a rather exceptional occurrence in the past, linked with a period of extreme distress (Livi-Bacci 2015), despite the fact that fertility fell below replacement before World War II in many Western European Countries (Van Bavel 2009). It is now evident that replacement level fertility is not a glass floor for fertility decline, not even in a mild way after allowing for fluctuations around replacement.

Fertility declines have been impressive; they have led to fertility levels closer to one child per woman than to replacement. These declines have often been "more rapid and pervasive than was expected" (Bongaarts 2002). The fertility declines in the People's Republic of China and in the Republic of Korea (hereafter referred to as Korea) have been singled out as particularly important owing to their rapidity (Poston et al. 2009). In a short but land-marking piece, Wilson noted that, since 2003–2004, for the first time in history, more than half of the world's population has lived in areas in which fertility has been below the replacement level (Wilson 2004).

If one takes a cursory look at trends in Period Total Fertility Rates (PTFR) over the last half-century, the picture seems to be consistent with a decline-with-convergence to low fertility story (Fig. 2.1), with Korea being a particularly fast decliner (I shall not delve here into the discussion on the meaning of PTFR as a measure of current fertility, as "tempo effects" hardly explain major differences between the groups of countries).

The mid-1980s, in particular, marked a discontinuity, with the emergence of exceptionally and sustained lower levels of fertility. "Lowest-low fertility" has been defined as a PTFR at or below 1.3, i.e., much closer to 1 than to 2 (Billari and Kohler 2004; Kohler et al. 2002). Given the importance of smaller differences, it makes more sense to focus on the more recent period to get a better insight on "post-transitional" fertility. After 1985, we see more of a divergence than a convergence. For instance, Fig. 2.2 shows three countries with PTFRs ending up closer to 1 than to 2, namely, Bulgaria in Eastern Europe, Italy in Southern Europe, Korea in East Asia, contrasted with three countries with PTFRs ending up closer to 2 than to 1,

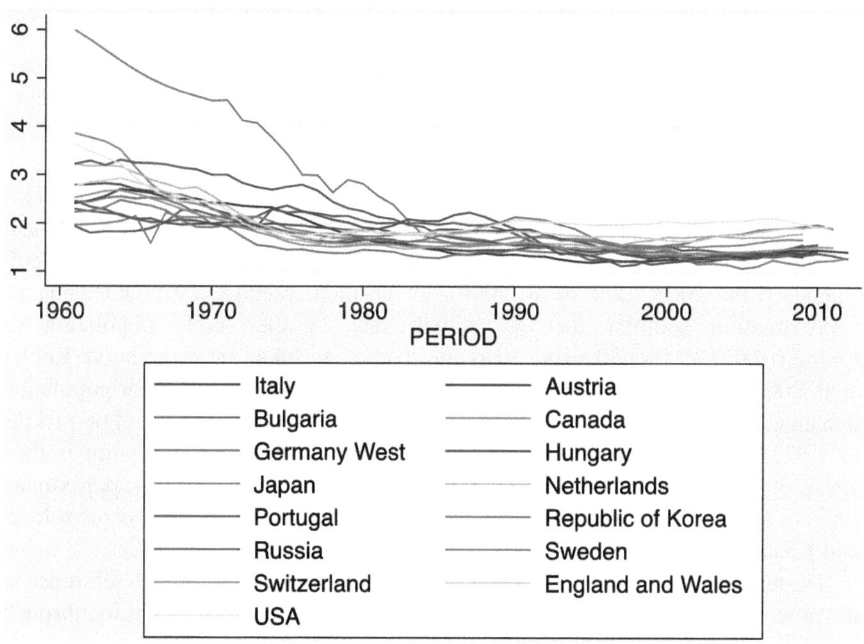

Fig. 2.1 Period Total Fertility Rate (PTFR) for a selection of countries, 1960–2013 (Sources: Human Fertility Database, Italian and Korean statistical offices)

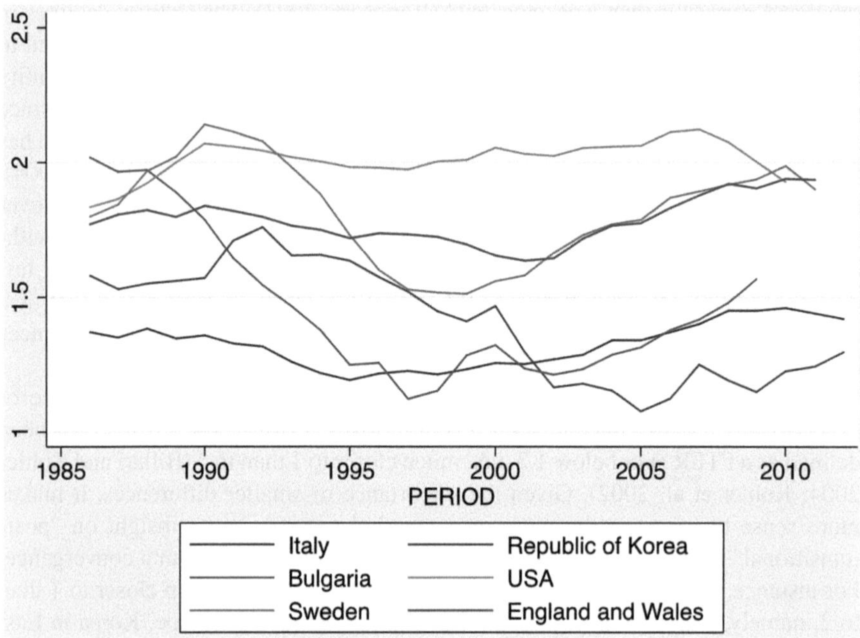

Fig. 2.2 Period Total Fertility Rate (PTFR) for a selection of countries, 1985–2013 (Sources: Human Fertility Database, Italian and Korean statistical offices)

namely, Sweden, England and Wales, and the USA. The separation of countries into two groups, one closer to a PTFR of 1 and one closer to replacement, has appeared rather stable in the last decade.

I use a PTFR of approximately 1.5 to divide the two group of countries. This corresponds to the definition of "very low fertility" given for instance by McDonald (McDonald 2008) and to the threshold for the "low fertility trap" of Lutz and colleagues (Lutz 2008; Lutz et al. 2006). To be more precise, we could using an approximation formula for the growth rate in the stable population as $r = \log(0.4886*\text{PTFR})/30$, using 30 as approximate mean age at parenthood (Kohler et al. 2002). This would allow to consider the implications of PTFR for population dynamics, giving a replacement level (with $r \approx 0$) for a PTFR of 2.045. For a PTFR of 1.0225 (i.e. half the replacement level), $r \approx -2.31\%$. The mid-point is then $r \approx -1.155\%$ and is located at 1.47. It therefore makes some sense to approximate roughly and define two as replacement-level, one as half of the replacement level and 1.5 as the mid-point.

The term "great divergence" was coined by Samuel Huntington with reference to the process of economic growth of the West during the nineteenth century, through which the West diverged from other societies with long-term consequences still visible today (Pomeranz 2009). Are we facing a "great divergence" re. below-replacement fertility, i.e. a situation in which some societies will have stable fertility not far from two, while others will have fertility not far from one? At the global level, Wilson measured a general convergence towards lower fertility (Wilson 2001), while Dorius has emphasized the growth of fertility differences between countries (Dorius 2008). I focus here, however, on advanced developed countries, with fertility around or below replacement. Simple calculations for a set of countries of indicators of between-country variability (the coefficient of variation, i.e. the ratio of the standard deviation to the mean; and the more robust ratio between the interquartile range and the median) show that variability across countries has started increasing in the early 1990s and has somehow stabilized after 2005 (Fig. 2.3).

The great divergence is consistent with some positions in the literature. For instance, Lutz and his colleagues have argued that forces might "trap" fertility when it falls below approximately a PTFR of 1.5, with a series of forces preventing fertility from a rebound above the threshold (Lutz 2008; Lutz et al. 2006). In the next part of this chapter I will discuss the theory and the evidence of a great divergence in fertility with specific reference to life course patterns, particularly (1) the situation of youth and the postponement of family formation and (2) work-family, development and gender.

Youth and the Great Divergence in Fertility

Countries with fertility rates closer to 1.0 than to 2.0 in the great divergence share a characteristic: their youth is in a relatively weaker position compared to countries with fertility closer to replacement. This weaker position of youth can be seen as a necessary, although not sufficient, condition for reaching lowest-low fertility (Kohler et al. 2002) and might be self-reinforcing through population ageing, as the relevance of youth voters becomes increasingly less significant in the electoral competition. Indeed, the postponement of family formation and of the transition to parenthood in particular has been seen as a key determinant in the emergence of lowest-low fertility (Sobotka 2004).

A New Life Course Regime in the Transition to Adulthood?

The idea of a life course regime has been used in parallel to the idea of "welfare regimes" (Kohli 2007; Mayer 2001) to indicate the intersection of welfare regimes with actual patterning of the life course in the domain of family and education. The idea of a "regime" is attractive insofar as it indicates a consistent set of policies, institutions, cultures and behavior that indicate a distinct pattern. The comparative life course literature on advanced societies has also focused, sometimes in a separate way, on the transition to adulthood and low fertility. For the transition to adulthood, the issue of the emergence of a new pattern has been extensively discussed, and includes the amount of within-society diversity that this pattern should imply

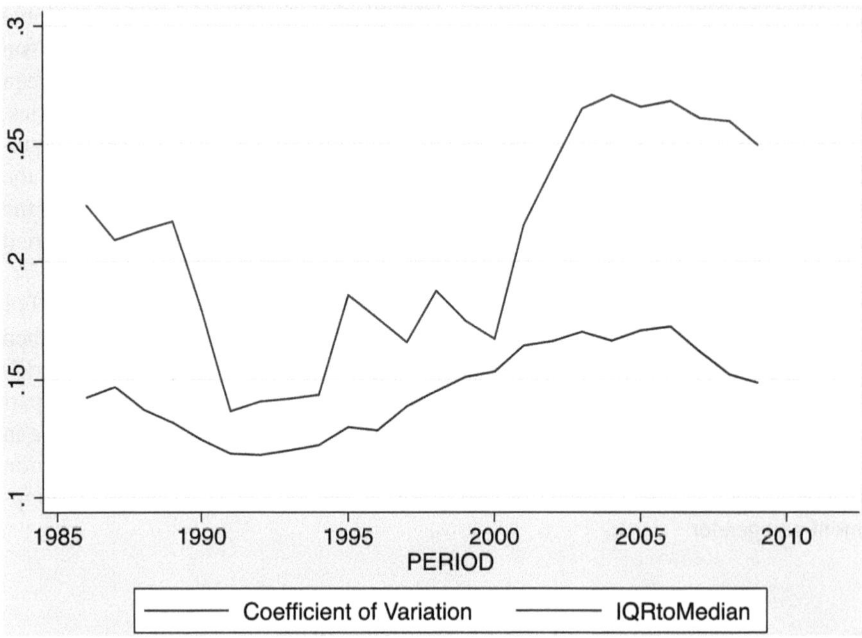

Fig. 2.3 Measures of dispersion across countries for Period Total Fertility Rate, 1985–2009 (Sources: Human Fertility Database, Italian and Korean statistical offices. Notes: countries included are Austria, Bulgaria, Canada, Czech Republic, England and Wales, Estonia, Finland, Germany, Hungary, Italy, Japan, Korea, Lithuania, Netherlands, Portugal, Russia, Scotland, Slovakia, Sweden, Switzerland, Ukraine, USA)

(Billari and Liefbroer 2010; Billari and Wilson 2001; Buchmann and Kriesi 2011; Furstenberg 2013).

What emerges with solid evidence is a generalized postponement of family formation, which is not, however, automatically linked to the postponement of youth autonomy, as indicated chiefly by one's age when leaving the parental home. The postponement of family formation is a principal explanation for the emergence of lowest-low fertility in advanced societies (Billari and Kohler 2004; Kohler et al. 2002; Suzuki 2012). Indeed, the ability to have higher rates at older ages (sometimes called "recuperation") is a chief factor to both explain cross-national differences and country-level trends showing the exit from lowest-low fertility (Goldstein et al. 2009; Lesthaeghe 2010; Sobotka 2004).

For instance, the reversal of the relationship between development and fertility at very high levels of development, which I will discuss later, is fully accounted for by the reversal of the relationship with fertility at ages 30 and above (Myrskylä et al. 2011).

Puzzles related to the reversal of traditional cross-country associations are particularly useful for analyzing the emergence of a consistent life course regime. Therefore, I now turn to a discussion of the relationship between the age at leaving home and fertility. This treatment complements discussions in the literature that focus on the relationship between (the postponement of) marriage and fertility; these are particularly relevant for low-fertility countries in East Asia (Raymo et al. 2015). My perspective here takes for granted that the delay of marriage is a common feature shared by all advanced countries, including those with fertility closer to replacement level than to 1.0. Indeed, the delay of marriage is one of the clearest and least discussed indicators of trends in the Second Demographic Transition (Lesthaeghe 2010, 2014). Some countries in Northern and Western Europe with fertility close to replacement have seen a clear upsurge, up to a complete substitution of cohabitation—with a clear majority of couples opting for cohabitation rather than direct marriage (Billari and Liefbroer 2010). What is common to lowest-low and ultra-low fertility countries is the weaker position of youth. We may take the increasingly long period spent by youth in their parental role as a key indicator of this weaker position.

A Reversal in the Cross-Country Relationship Between the Age at Leaving Home and Total Period Fertility Rates

Societies that are making it easier for youth to become independent, as signaled by an earlier age at leaving home, have become during the last decades or so the societies where it is easier to have more children. To substantiate this claim, I show in Fig. 2.4 the changing association between fertility and age at leaving home for 26 European countries, Korea, Japan and the United States (Korea and the United States only for the second period). The cross-country correlation between the median age at home leaving for the 1940–1949 birth cohort and the TFR in 1975 (i.e. approximately the TFR of that cohort) was +0.42; in other words, in countries where home leaving happened later, fertility was higher. This somehow counter-intuitive negative relationship has completely reversed later, with the emergence of very low and lowest low fertility. This indicates that the emergence of a new fertility regime in highly developed countries has been associated with a broad sweep of changes in population-related phenomena, including the transition to adulthood. The cross-country correlation between the median age at home leaving for the 1970–1979 birth cohort and the TFR in 2008 is −0.58; that is, in countries where home leaving happened later, fertility was lower. The correlation is negative even if we take into account cohort fertility; for those 24 European countries with estimates of the fertility of the 1970 birth cohort, the correlation coefficient becomes −0.61.

There can and should not be a causal interpretation of Fig. 2.4 owing to the several cases in which macro-level relationships are shifting. For instance, the cross-country correlation between the median age at home leaving and the median age at first birth has shifted from positive and low (+0.11) to negative but close to zero (−0.03), in the same time interval for European countries. What this changing relationship suggests, although does not prove, is that in the new life course regime,

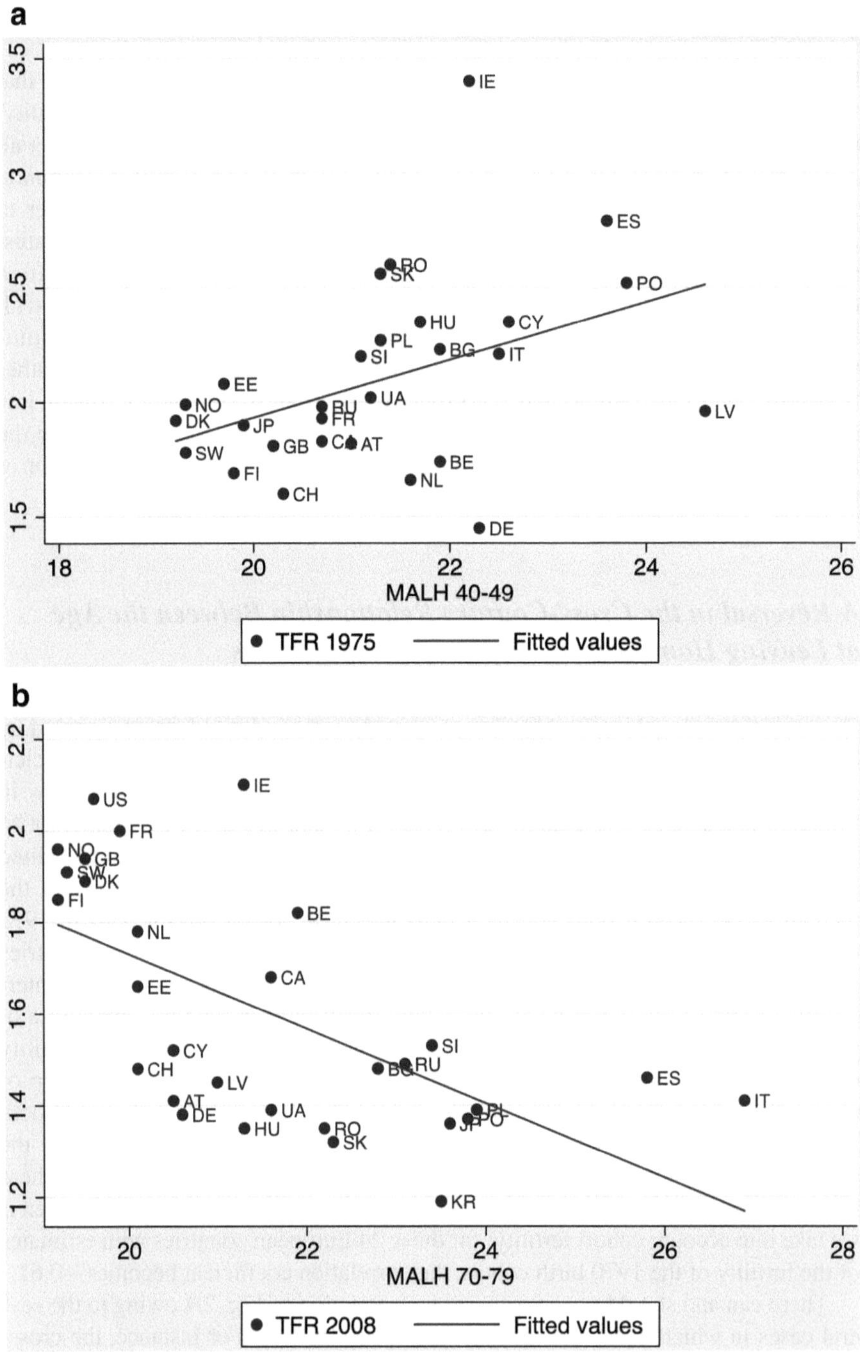

Fig. 2.4 The changing relationship between fertility and leaving the parental home: Females, in 26 European countries, Korea, Japan and the United States. (**a**) PTFR 1975 and Median Age at Leaving Home 1940–49. (**b**) PTFR 2008 and Median Age at Leaving Home 1970–79. Sources: United Nations, Billari and Liefbroer (2010), Ravanera et al. (1998), Yi et al. (1994). Note: *AT* Austria, *BE* Belgium, *BG* Bulgaria, *CA* Canada, *CH* Switzerland, *CY* Cyprus, *DE* Germany, *DK* Denmark, *EE* Estonia, *ES* Spain, *FI* Finland, *FR* France, *GB* Great Britain, *HU* Hungary, *IE* Ireland, *IT* Italy, *JP* Japan, *KR* Korea, *LV* Latvia, *NL* Netherlands, *NO* Norway, *PL* Poland, *PO* Portugal, *RO* Romania, *RU* Russia, *SI* Slovenia, *SK* Slovakia, *SW* Sweden, *UA* Ukraine, *US* United States

youth autonomy and fertility walk together. In terms of the great divergence, countries with a weaker position of youth are more likely to belong to the very low fertility group.

The connection between late home-leaving and lowest-low fertility has been noted in earlier studies, particularly those focusing on Southern Europe. This connection has been used to explain the apparent paradox that lowest-low fertility emerged in countries characterized by strong family ties (Dalla Zuanna 2001; Dalla Zuanna and Micheli 2004; Livi-Bacci 2001; Reher 1998), a paradox that Livi-Bacci vividly described as "Too few children and too much family."

Work-Family, Gender and the Great Divergence in Fertility

The weak position of young people is not the only peculiarity of societies with total period fertility rates closer to 1.0 than to 2.0 in the divergent pattern. These lowest-low and ultra-low fertility societies tend to share a situation in which the combination of work and family, and in particular work and motherhood, is more challenging than in societies with fertility closer to the replacement level. While the postponement of the transition to parenthood is more widespread than lowest-low and ultra-low fertility, what happens after parenthood, and in particular the transition to higher parities, is what distinguishes the two groups (Billari and Kohler 2004; Kohler et al. 2002). This is where the work-family nexus plays a crucial role. There is no single pathway to this difficult work-family nexus, and here I shall focus on some elements that are ingredients of the various pathways. First I look at economic resources and then at gender relationships.

(Economic) Development and the Great Divergence

The negative relationship between economic development and fertility has been one of the unchallenged empirical laws of social sciences since at least the days of Malthus, and the later idea of a demographic transition. Still in 1996, Bongaarts and Watkins (1996) were describing a world in which development trajectories for various countries were linked to fertility declines. Smaller family sizes are associated with higher development in what Thornton defines as "developmental idealism" (Thornton 2001, 2005). The level of development of a country, in the Bongaarts and Watkins study, was measured using data from United Nations' Human Development Index (HDI). The HDI is a composite index of life expectancy, years of education, and income, and has been used since the 1990s to track progress at the level of countries or regions.

The emergence of lowest-low and ultra-low fertility also changed this relationship. As documented by Myrskylä et al. (2009), we now live in a world in which, among the most developed countries, fertility is *positively* related to economic

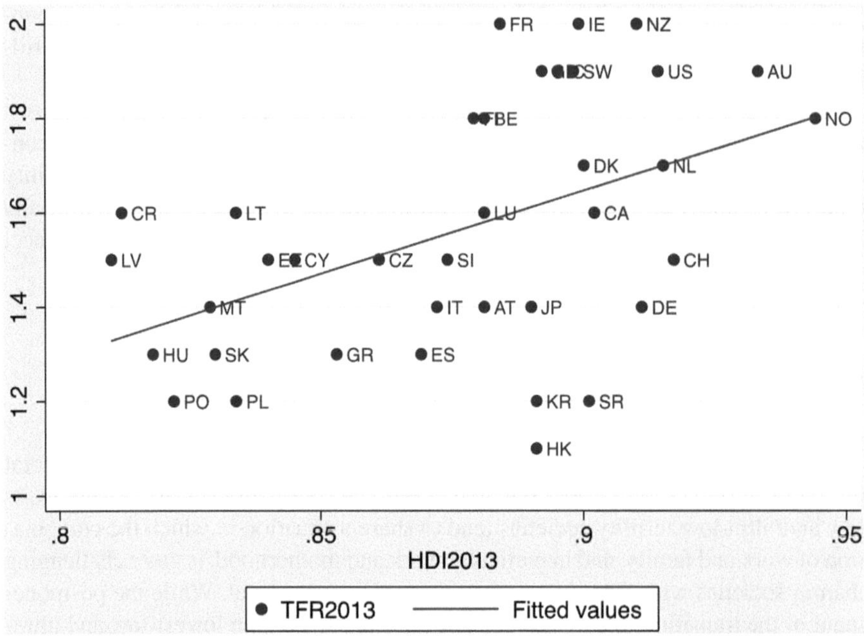

Fig. 2.5 Human development and fertility: The relationship between PTFR 2013 and the Human Development Index 2013 in the top 48 HDI countries in Europe, North America, Oceania and East Asia (Sources: UNDP and Population Reference Bureau. Note: *AT* Austria, *AU* Australia, *BE* Belgium, *BG* Bulgaria, *CA* Canada, *CH* Switzerland, *CR* Croatia, *CY* Cyprus, *CZ* Czech Republic, *DE* Germany, *DK* Denmark, *EE* Estonia, *ES* Spain, *FI* Finland, *FR* France, *GB* Great Britain, *GR* Greece, *HK* Hong Hong, *HU* Hungary, *IC* Iceland, *IE* Ireland, *IT* Italy, *JP* Japan, *KR* Korea, *LU* Luxembourg, *LV* Latvia, *MT* Malta, *NL* Netherlands, *NO* Norway, *NZ* New Zealand, *PL* Poland, *PO* Portugal, *SI* Slovenia, *SK* Slovakia, *SR* Singapore, *SW* Sweden, *US* United States. Andorra and Liechtenstein are excluded)

development. Figure 2.5 displays this cross-sectional relationship for 2013, among countries in Europe, North America, Oceania and East Asia that are among the top 48 countries according to the HDI ranking for 2013 (UNDP 2014). For the data reported in Fig. 2.5, HDI is positively related to the TPFR, with a cross-country correlation of +0.47. These cross-sectional results are consistent with earlier longitudinal analyses (Myrskylä, Kohler, and Billari 2009). They have attracted considerable attention; indeed Harttgen and Vollmer (2014) have challenged the robustness of the findings, but basically confirmed that the association between HDI and PTFR has changed over the past 20–30 years in the same countries. Luci-Greulich and Thévenon (2014), who focused only on the income component of the HDI (i.e. GDP per capita), found a reversal of the relationship between income and fertility for OECD countries in a series of models that also control for birth postponement, omitted variable bias, endogeneity and non-stationarity.

What is the link between the reversal of the relationship between development and fertility and the great divergence? First, some of the countries that diverge to a level of fertility closer to 1.0 than to 2.0 might be "stuck" at relatively lower levels of development. Among the wealthiest countries, Central and Eastern European ones and Southern European ones are located on the left side of Fig. 2.5, indicating their relatively lower levels of well-being. In this case, economic development might not be sufficient to help building a society in which parenthood (and motherhood in particular) is compatible with the realization of individual goals. This is particularly relevant if, as van de Kaa, has vividly stated, fertility becomes a "derivative": " The woman will, in a way that befits her character and circumstances, typically ask herself: 'Will my life, and the relationship with my partner, be enriched if I interrupt contraception and use my basic right to have a child, or an additional child now?" (van de Kaa 2004).

In the era of the Second Demographic Transition, once the basic material well-being issues have been solved, individuals and couples tend to search for higher-order needs, i.e. that are more subjective and individualized (Lesthaeghe 2010). In this sense, an increase in expected (subjective) well-being has to be foreseen, in order for the decision to have a (mother) child to occur (Billari 2009). This increase in expected (subjective) well-being is easier in societies in which the basic material needs are better satisfied.

Second, one can notice that in Fig. 2.5 the four East Asian countries of Hong Kong, Korea, Japan and Singapore, while having above average HDI have lower fertility, lying below the regression line. Indeed, East Asian countries are an exception to this positive relationship. If we exclude these countries, the cross-country correlation between PTFR and HDI increases significantly from +0.47 to +0.63. Indeed Myrskylä and colleagues noted the East Asian exception in their first analyses. A more recent paper (Myrskylä et al. 2011) documents the relevance of gender equality as a pre-condition for the reversal of the relationship between development and fertility. Also, it shows that the reversal is exclusively due to fertility at ages 30 and above. These findings are consistent with Luci-Greulich and Thévenon's (2014) research that what matters to explain the reversal among OECD countries is women's labor force participation. For this reason I now turn to the "gender revolution" and its role in shaping fertility in advanced societies.

The Gender Revolution and the Great Divergence

We have seen that high levels of economic development and subjective well-being have become a necessary (but not sufficient) condition for not being "trapped" in very low fertility. I now turn to another necessary (but not sufficient) condition: the "Gender Revolution." Gender has played a prime role in the study of low fertility, especially with respect to the theories developed by McDonald (McDonald 2000a, b). Here I do not build on McDonald's distinction between gender equity and gender equality, since equity is difficult to measure at the societal level (see Mills (2010)).

But it is useful to use the explicit division of the Gender Revolution in two halves as described by Goldscheider and colleagues (Goldscheider et al. 2015). The first half concerns the growth in female labor force participation, while the second half is characterized by men joining women in the domestic sphere. Put simply, the first half is about the "masculinization" of women's lives while the second half is about the "feminization" of men's lives (Esping-Andersen and Billari 2015). According to Goldscheider and her colleagues, the first half of the gender revolution "resulted in a weakening of the family" (Goldscheider et al. 2015: 210), with the rise of a second working shift (Hochschild and Machung 2012) for the market, in addition to the standard shift at home for women. The second shift brought important challenges for family formation and threats to the stability of families.

The second half of the Gender Revolution, on the contrary, is family-friendly; indeed evidence from time-use studies on 13 European countries has shown that higher educated fathers have been giving an increasing contribution to both child-care and domestic tasks (Sullivan et al. 2014).

Scholars studying family change have often contrasted the role of institutional constraints and incentives with that of cultural incentives. Those using mainly a rational-choice perspective have tended to downplay cultural explanations and to underline the role of institutions (e.g., Breen and Buchmann 2002; Esping-Andersen 1990; McDonald 2000a, b). Put simply, institutions are exogenous and culture is endogenous. Scholars who have focused on cultural explanations have tended to see institutions as mirroring long-standing differences in culture (e.g., Dalla Zuanna 2001; Reher 1998); culture here is exogenous and institutions are endogenous. "Exogenous" shocks are sometimes used to study the mechanisms triggering change, and one could assume that without a powerful exogenous shock, societies would remain in "old" equilibria (Esping-Andersen and Billari 2015). Esping-Andersen and Billari (2015) have focused in particular on the generalized increase in female educational enrolment and attainment as a key exogenous shock for the gender revolution. Goldin has given a leading role to a technological shock, the invention of modern contraception, or the "power of the pill" (Goldin et al. 2006; Goldin 2006; Goldin and Katz 2002). Other scholars have identified technological innovations in home appliances as the "engines of liberation" that allowed the Gender Revolution to start (de V. Cavalcanti and Tavares 2008; Greenwood et al. 2005).

In fact, both institutional and policy factors and cultural factors can be changing or may be stable (Billari 2004), and it is hard to disentangle what, if any, exogenous shock triggered a specific change in societal trajectories, including fertility trends. For this reason, I take here the perspective that culture and institutions are mutually evolving (Pfau-Effinger 2004, 2005), i.e. that cultural and institutional (and policy) changes are the outcome of similar processes. I thus focus on indicators permitting a long-term view of change. Indeed, it has been argued, even among scholars of family change developing a more structural-institutional explanation, that in a period of significant behavioral shifts cultural change matters importantly (Goldscheider et al. 2015; Rindfuss et al. 1996).

In what follows I present an empirical sketch of cultural change in the gendered work-family nexus in four macro-level cases. I use Google Ngram Viewer to provide a "quantitative analysis of culture" using words or combination of words (n-grams) that appear in books digitized by Google. This approach has been illustrated in general by Michel et al. (2011). Specific n-grams are normalized with respect to the total number of n-grams, so that trends are meaningful and comparisons between different n-grams in these trends can be carried out. Analyses of demographic thought using n-grams have been presented by Héran (2013) and by Bijak et al. (2014). Héran, for instance, analyzed, among other n-grams and starting around 1750, the trends in n-grams such as "de-population" and "de-natality" in French.

I consider four cases (I use the R package 'ngram' (Schmidt and Heckendorf 2016) to extract the n-gram data). A first set of cases represents societies with fertility pathways leading to the replacement level; separate analyses are undertaken of English-language publications in the United Kingdom and the United States, i.e. the upper group in the great divergence. A second set of cases represents a set of societies with fertility pathways leading to fertility closer to 1.0. Italian language publications are used to describe cultural change in Italy, the first "lowest-low" fertility country with Spain (Kohler et al. 2002). There are some Italian language publications outside Italy, notably from the Canton Ticino in Switzerland, but results should not be influenced by other societies (fertility in Ticino is basically close to the neighboring regions in Northern Italy, with a PTFR of 1.4 in 2013 (Bottinelli 2015)). German language publications are used to describe cultural change mostly taking place in Germany, Austria, and the German-speaking part of Switzerland (see Kreyenfeld et al. (2012) for an overview of fertility trends in these countries). German-speaking countries were the first ones with fertility falling under the 1.5 "trap" threshold (Lutz et al. 2006), and the first ones for which sub-replacement ideal family size was reported (Goldstein et al. 2003).

For what concerns the appearance of the n-gram "low fertility," there is a sharp contrast between the English-speaking country pair and the low-fertility one (Fig. 2.6). In the U.S., low fertility has been in steady decline since the 1980s, while in U.K.-based publications there have been fluctuation; it is not surprising that given the size of the country and of its publishing sector, that English-language publications refer to other societies more often in the U.K. than in the U.S. The emergence of low fertility in the other set of countries is, by contrast, very clear: the increase in the frequency of appearance starts in the 1980s for German-speaking countries and in the 1990s for Italy. This first analysis of n-grams reflects the idea that low fertility emerges as a cultural theme in countries that are diverging towards lower levels. The approach followed here complements the analysis of governmental positions on fertility levels, which shows an increasing influence of actual fertility levels on "state concern" for fertility (Marshall 2015).

In order to look at cultural evolution around the gender revolution and the work-family nexus, I next look at "housewife" and childcare-related n-grams (Fig. 2.7). Again, there is evidence of a contrast between the two groups of cases. The word "housewife" has been in decline since the 1970s in English-language publications, with a sharper decline for the U.S. than for the U.K. In German, the decline started during the 1990s, while there has been no significant decline in Italian. For childcare, it is hard to isolate institutionalized childcare from what happens within the house-

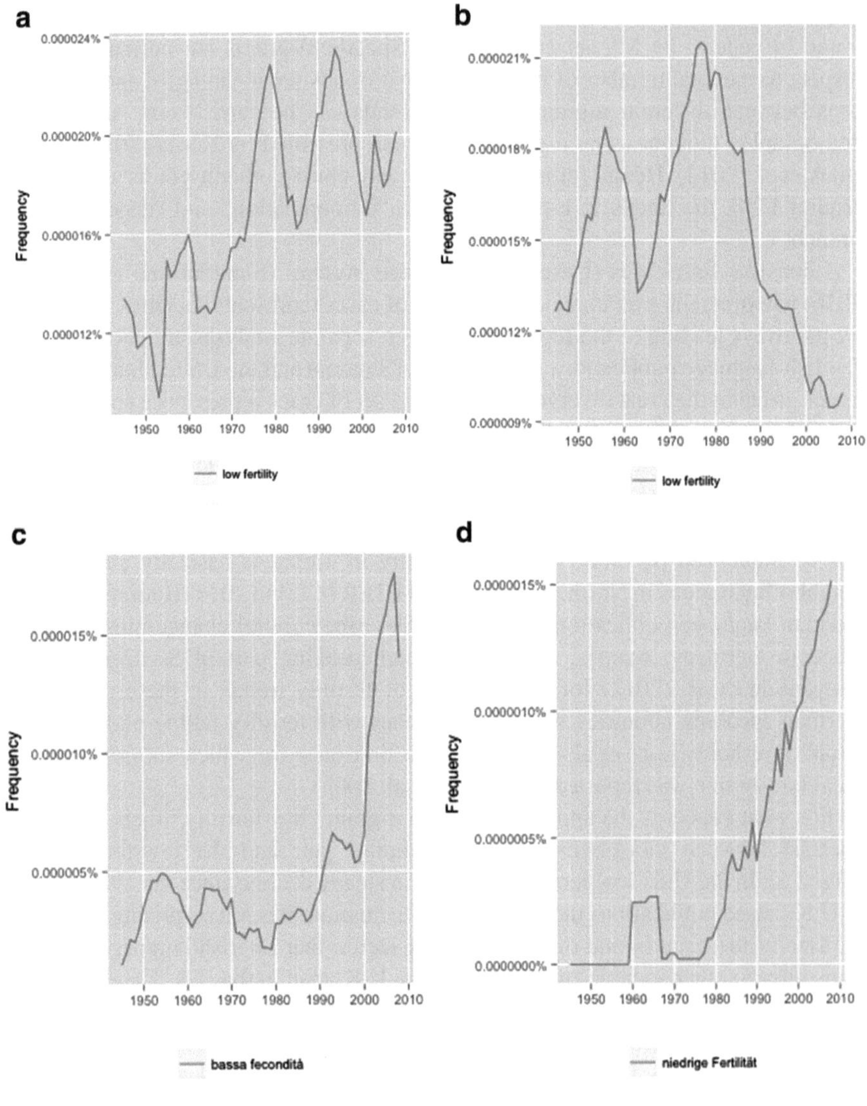

Fig. 2.6 Frequency of occurrence of "low fertility", 1945–2010. (**a**) English language (U.K. publications) (**b**) English language (U.S. publications) (**c**) Italian language ("bassa fecondità" = low fertility) (**d**) German language ("niedrige Fertilität" = low fertility) (Source: Google NGram viewer)

hold or the family at large. However, signals are consistent with ideas about the Gender Revolution, at least the first part of it. Both "childcare" and "daycare" (the latter much less used in the U.K.) have been increasing in English-speaking countries, somehow mirroring the decline of "housewife." In German and Italian, terms are more specific for institutionalized child-care (there is no standard way to define childcare in general), so the terms I used in these analysis reflect a translation of the

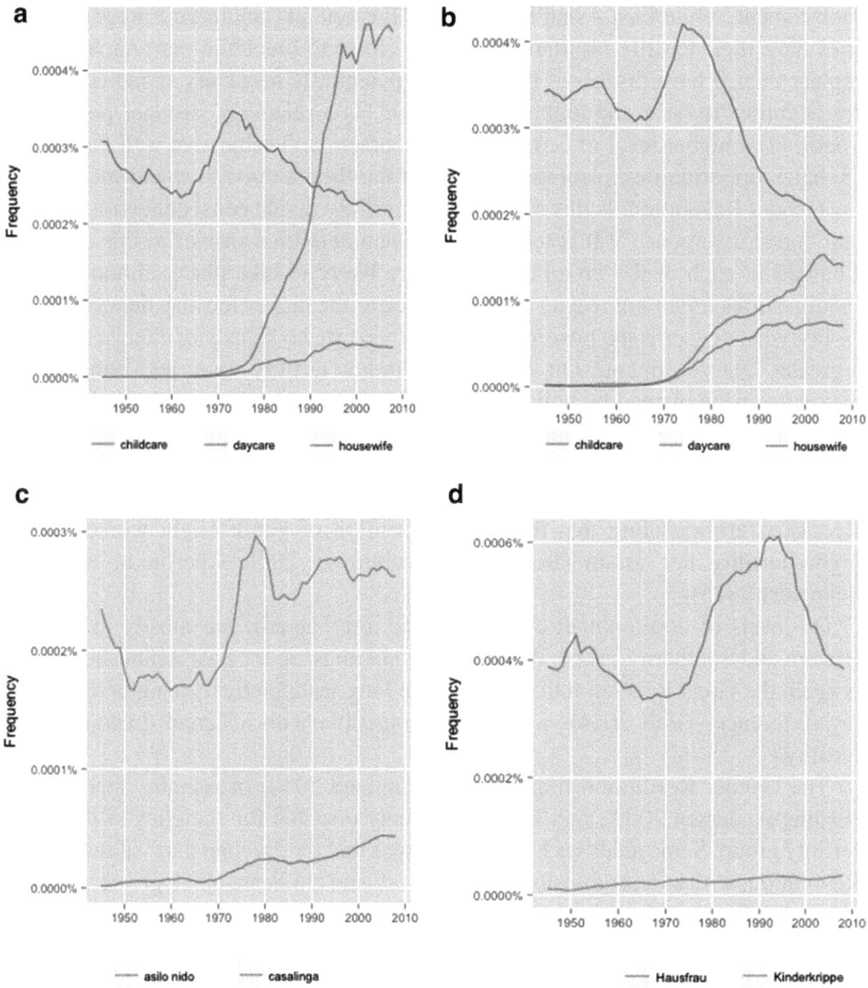

Fig. 2.7 Frequency of occurrence of work-family and childcare words, 1945–2010. (**a**) English language (U.K. publications) (**b**) English language (U.S. publications) (**c**) Italian language ("asilo nido" = daycare center; "casalinga" = housewife) (**d**) German language ("Kinderkrippe" = daycare center; "Hausfrau" = housewife) (Source: Google NGram viewer)

concept of "daycare center." Here, change is more timid, albeit in both languages there has been an increase in the frequency.

Discussion and Conclusions

In this chapter I have sketched a picture that is broadly consistent with a divide in fertility levels among advanced societies. Northern and Western European, North-American and Oceanian countries have their fertility oscillating at levels close to replacement, while East Asian and Central, Eastern and Southern European countries have their fertility oscillating at levels closer to one child per couple than to replacement. I have discussed three sets of potentially necessary broad conditions for countries to be in the higher fertility tier: (1) a relatively stronger position of youth; (2) a higher level of economic development and subjective well-being; and (3) better opportunities to combine work and family life through an advancement in the Gender Revolution. Is this evidence of a fertility divide consistent with a persistent "great divergence"? It is too early to give a definitive answer to this question. Changes in each of the broad conditions are likely to take place, although small modifications might not trigger a convergence to the higher fertility tier.

For what concerns the position of youth, there are no signals of changes towards a greater "empowerment." On the contrary, in low fertility countries young people have often been blamed by policy-makers. To illustrate, in October 2007 the Italian Minister of the Economy Padoa-Schioppa described young adults living with parents as "bamboccioni" ("big babies"). Indeed, the combined effects of population ageing (through an increasingly less relevant weight of young voters) and the Great Recession are signaling that the relative position of youth might worsen in the higher-fertility tier group (Bell and Blanchflower 2011; Cherlin et al. 2013; Schneider 2015).

On levels of development and well-being, the laggards are mostly in Central, Eastern and Southern Europe; this is clearly not an issue for East Asian societies. It is again the Great Recession that might have long-lasting effects leading to persisting differences (Ball 2014), which are compatible with a "great divergence" in fertility.

The Gender Revolution might "stall" (England 2010) or remain "incomplete" (Esping-Andersen 2009), and this is especially possible for societies in the lower fertility group. Some analyses have shown signs that the "second part" of the Gender Revolution, with a fairer division of housework and childcare and a greater involvement of fathers, might be touching the traditional laggards and members of the low fertility groups, particularly Italy and Spain (Sullivan et al. 2014), and Japan (Tsuya et al. 2005). What is crucial here is the speed of diffusion of the Gender Revolution. Esping-Andersen and Billari (2015) have identified a set of factors that enable a faster diffusion: generalized trust rather than familism (Aassve et al. 2012a) and lower levels of social stratification.

Societies in the lower fertility tier might find alternative pathways to a reversal in fertility. A first pathway is through family support, for instance from grandparents; this might increase and help parents achieve higher fertility (Aassve et al. 2012b; Harknett et al. 2014). However, given that this support is more likely to come from grandmothers, and since future grandmothers may be expected to have a higher attachment to the labor market, their availability will not necessarily increase in the future. A second pathway is through direct policy intervention; however, the evidence to date is that single policies do not seem to influence choices with long-term consequences such as becoming a parent (Gauthier 2007), compared to the broad conditions I outlined earlier. Still, policies might have a mitigating effect (McDonald

2006), but they are unlikely to be expanded in societies affected by the Great Recession.

The discussion of the broad conditions and potentially alternative pathways to fertility reversal speaks in favor of the idea of the "great divergence." In addition, some institutional and/or cultural lock-in mechanisms might prevent countries from crossing back the threshold that divides the two groups. A first example of lock-in mechanisms is the stabilization of very low fertility ideals as seen from the "low fertility trap" hypothesis (Lutz et al. 2006). A second example runs through the housing market, which has been linked to low fertility (Mulder and Billari 2010) and might adapt to smaller family sizes.

The analyses presented here have important limitations. I will touch upon four issues. First, the cross-country analysis of the relationship between leaving home and fertility needs a thorough set of robustness checks, although the lack of suitable data might prevent a more thorough investigation. Second, the analysis of cultural change using n-grams deserves extensions, replications and robustness checks, including importantly a study of East Asian, Central and Eastern European societies. Third, when I considered the implications of low fertility for population growth rates, I assumed, as is customary in the literature, a closed-population model. Higher and persistent levels of immigration can be homeostatic population responses to low fertility, and, from a policy perspective, would be both adaptive and mitigating (Billari and Dalla-Zuanna 2011, 2013). Finally, I stopped at the macro-level of analysis, albeit sketching the micro-foundations for the mechanisms I illustrated (Billari 2015). A complete discussion of the "great divergence" implies micro-founded analyses that are beyond the scope of this chapter.

References

Aassve, A., Billari, F. C., & Pessin, L. (2012a). *Trust and fertility dynamics*. Paper presented at annual meeting of the *Population Association of America*. San Franceisco, CA.

Aassve, A., Meroni, E., & Pronzato, C. (2012b). Grandparenting and childbearing in the extended family. *European Journal of Population/Revue européenne de Démographie, 28*, 499–518.

Balbo, N., Billari, F. C., & Mills, M. (2013). Fertility in advanced societies: A review of research. *European Journal of Population, 29*, 1–38.

Ball, L. (2014). Long-term damage from the great recession in OECD countries. *European Journal of Economics and Economic Policies, 11*, 149–160.

Basten, S., Sobotka, T., & Zeman, K. (2014). Future fertility in low fertility countries. In W. Lutz, W. P. Butz, & S. KC (Eds.), *World population and human capital in the twenty-first century* (pp. 39–146). Oxford: Oxford University Press.

Bell, D. N. F., & Blanchflower, D. G. (2011). Young people and the great recession. *Oxford Review of Economic Policy, 27*, 241–267.

Bijak, J., Courgeau, D., Silverman, E., & Franck, R. (2014). Quantifying paradigm change in demography. *Demographic Research, 30*, 911–924.

Billari, F. C. (2004). Becoming an adult in Europe: A macro(/micro)-demographic perspective. *Demographic Research, SC3*, 15–44.

Billari, F. C. (2015). Integrating macro- and micro-level approaches in the explanation of population change. *Population Studies, 69*, S11–S20.

Billari, F. C., & Dalla-Zuanna, G. (2011). Is replacement migration actually taking place in low-fertility countries? *Genus, 67*, 105–123.
Billari, F. C., & Dalla-Zuanna, G. (2013). Cohort replacement and homeostasis in world population, 1950–2100. *Population and Development Review, 39*, 563–585.
Billari, F. C., & Kohler, H.-P. (2004). Patterns of low and lowest-low fertility in Europe. *Population Studies, 58*, 161–176.
Billari, F. C., & Liefbroer, A. C. (2010). Towards a new pattern of transition to adulthood? *Advances in Life Course Research, 15*, 59–75.
Billari, F. C. (2009). The happiness commonality: Fertility decision in low-fertility settings. In UNECE (Ed.), *How generations and gender shape demographic change* (pp. 7–38). New York/Geneva: United Nations.
Billari, F. C., & Wilson, C. (2001). *Convergence towards diversity? Cohort dynamics in the transition to adulthood in contemporary Western Europe*. Rostock: Max Planck Institute for Demographic Research.
Billari, F. C., Graziani, R., & Melilli, E. (2014). Stochastic population forecasting based on combinations of expert evaluations within the Bayesian paradigm. *Demography*, 1–22.
Bongaarts, J. (2002). The end of the fertility transition in the developed world. *Population and Development Review, 28*, 419–443.
Bongaarts, J., & Watkins, S. C. (1996). Social interactions and contemporary fertility transitions. *Population and Development Review, 22*, 639–682.
Bottinelli, L. (2015). La natalità del Ticino nel contesto europeo. *Statistiche e Società, 15*, 53–67.
Breen, R., & Buchmann, M. (2002). Institutional variation and the position of young people: A comparative perspective. *The Annals of the American Academy of Political and Social Science, 580*, 288–305.
Buchmann, M. C., & Kriesi, I. (2011). Transition to adulthood in Europe. *Annual Review of Sociology, 37*, 23.1–23.23.
Cherlin, A., Cumberworth, E., Morgan, S. P., & Wimer, C. (2013). The effects of the great recession on family structure and fertility. *The Annals of the American Academy of Political and Social Science, 650*, 214–231.
Dalla Zuanna, G. (2001). The banquet of Aeolus: A familistic interpretation of Italy's lowest low fertility. *Demographic Research, 4*, 133–162.
Dalla Zuanna, G., & Micheli, G. A. (2004). *Strong family and low fertility : A paradox?: New perspectives in interpreting contemporary family and reproductive behaviour*. Dordrecht/London: Kluwer Academic.
de V. Cavalcanti, T. V., & Tavares, J. (2008). Assessing the "Engines of liberation": Home appliances and female labor force participation. *Review of Economics and Statistics, 90*, 81–88.
Dorius, S. F. (2008). Global demographic convergence? A reconsideration of changing intercountry inequality in fertility. *Population and Development Review, 34*, 519–537.
England, P. (2010). The gender revolution: Uneven and Stalled. *Gender and Society, 24*, 149–166.
Esping-Andersen, G. (1990). *The three worlds of welfare capitalism*. Oxford: Polity Press.
Esping-Andersen, G. (2009). *The incomplete revolution: Adapting welfare states to women's new roles*. Cambridge: Polity Press.
Esping-Andersen, G., & Billari, F. C. (2015). Re-theorizing family demographics. *Population and Development Review, 41*, 1–31.
Furstenberg, F. F. (2013). Transitions to adulthood: What we can learn from the West. *Annals of the American Academy of Political and Social Science, 646*, 28–41.
Gauthier, A. H. (2007). The impact of family policies on fertility in the industrialized countries: A review of the literature. *Population Research and Policy Review, 26*, 323–346.
Goldin, C. (2006). The quiet revolution that transformed women's employment, education, and family. *American Economic Review, 96*, 1–21.
Goldin, C., & Katz, L. F. (2002). The power of the pill: Oral contraceptives and women's career and marriage decisions. *Journal of Political Economy, 110*, 730–770.

Goldin, C., Katz, L. F., & Kuziemko, I. (2006). The homecoming of American college women: The reversal of the gender gap in college. *Journal of Economic Perspectives, 20*, 133–156.

Goldscheider, F., Bernhardt, E., & Lappegård, T. (2015). The gender revolution: A framework for understanding changing family and demographic behavior. *Population and Development Review, 41*, 207–239.

Goldstein, J., Lutz, W., & Testa, M. R. (2003). The emergence of sub-replacement family size ideals in Europe. *Population Research and Policy Review, 22*, 479–496.

Goldstein, J. R., Sobotka, T., & Jasilioniene, A. (2009). The end of "lowest-low" fertility? *Population and Development Review, 35*, 663–699.

Greenwood, J., Seshadri, A., & Yorukoglu, M. (2005). Engines of Liberation. *Review of Economic Studies, 72*, 109–133.

Harknett, K., Billari, F. C., & Medalia, C. (2014). Do family support environments influence fertility? Evidence from 20 European countries. *European Journal of Population, 30*, 1–33.

Harttgen, K., & Vollmer, S. (2014). A reversal in the relationship of human development with fertility? *Demography, 51*, 173–184.

Héran, F. (2013). La démographie et son vocabulaire au fil des siècles: une exploration numérique. *Population et Sociétés, 505*, 1–4.

Hochschild, A., & Machung, A. (2012). *The second shift: Working families and the revolution at home*. New York: Penguin.

Kohler, H.-P., Billari, F. C., & Ortega, J. A. (2002). The emergence of lowest-low fertility in Europe during the 1990s. *Population and Development Review, 28*, 641–680.

Kohli, M. (2007). The institutionalization of the life course: Looking back to look ahead. *Research in Human Development, 4*, 253–271.

Kreyenfeld, M., Zeman, K., Burkimsher, M., & Jaschinski, I. (2012). Fertility data for German-speaking countries: What is the potential? Where are the pitfalls? *Comparative Population Studies – Zeitschrift für Bevölkerungswissenschaft, 36*, 349–380.

Lee, R. (2003). The demographic transition: Three centuries of fundamental change. *Journal of Economic Perspectives, 17*, 167–190.

Lesthaeghe, R. (2010). The unfolding story of the second demographic transition. *Population and Development Review, 36*, 211–251.

Lesthaeghe, R. (2014). The second demographic transition: A concise overview of its development. *Proceedings of the National Academy of Sciences*.

Lesthaeghe, R., & van de Kaa, D. (1986). Twee demografische transities? In R. Lesthaeghe & D. van de Kaa (Eds.), *Bevolking: Groei en Krimp* (pp. 9–24). Deventer: Van Loghum Slaterus.

Livi-Bacci, M. (2001). Too few children and too much family. *Daedalus, 130*, 139–156.

Livi-Bacci, M. (2012). *A concise history of world population*. Oxford: Wiley-Blackwell.

Livi-Bacci, M. (2015). What we can and cannot learn from the history of world population. *Population Studies, 69*, S21–S28.

Luci-Greulich, A., & Thévenon, O. (2014). Does economic advancement 'cause' a re-increase in fertility? An empirical analysis for OECD countries (1960–2007). *European Journal of Population, 30*, 187–221.

Lutz, W. (2008). Has Korea's fertility reached the bottom? The hypothesis of a 'low fertility trap' in parts of Europe and East Asia. *Asian Population Studies, 4*, 1–4.

Lutz, W., Skirbekk, V., & Testa, M. R. (2006). The low-fertility trap hypothesis: Forces that may lead to further postponement and fewer births in Europe. *Vienna Yearbook of Population Research, 4*, 167–192.

Marshall, E. A. (2015). When do states respond to low fertility? Contexts of state concern in wealthier countries, 1976–2011. *Social Forces, 93*, 1541–1566.

Mayer, K. U. (2001). The paradox of global social change and national path dependencies: Life course patterns in advanced societies. In A. E. Woodward & M. Kohli (Eds.), *Inclusions and exclusions in European societies, European sociological association studies in European societies* (pp. 89–110). London: Routledge.

McDonald, P. (2000a). Gender equity in theories of fertility transition. *Population and Development Review, 26*, 427–439.
McDonald, P. (2000b). Gender equity, social institutions and the future of fertility. *Journal of Population Research, 17*, 1–16.
McDonald, P. (2006). Low fertility and the state; the efficacy of policy. *Population and Development Review, 32*, 401–510.
McDonald, P. (2008). Very low fertility: Consequences, causes and policy approaches. *Japanese Journal of Population, 6*, 19–23.
Michel, J.-B., Shen, Y. K., Aiden, A. P., Veres, A., Gray, M. K., Team The Google Books, Pickett, J. P., Hoiberg, D., Clancy, D., Norvig, P., Orwant, J., Pinker, S., Nowak, M. A., & Aiden, E. L. (2011). Quantitative analysis of culture using millions of digitized books. *Science, 331*, 176–182.
Mills, M. (2010). Gender roles, gender (in) equality and fertility: An empirical test of five gender equity indices. *Canadian Studies in Population, 37*, 445–474.
Morgan, S. P., & Taylor, M. G. (2006). Low fertility at the turn of the twenty-first century. *Annual Review of Sociology, 32*, 375–399.
Mulder, C. H., & Billari, F. C. (2010). Homeownership regimes and low fertility. *Housing Studies, 25*, 527–541.
Myrskylä, M., Kohler, H.-P., & Billari, F. C. (2009). Advances in development reverse fertility declines. *Nature, 460*, 741–743.
Myrskylä, M., Billari, F. C., & Kohler, H.-P. (2011). *High development and fertility: Fertility at older reproductive ages and gender equality explain the positive link*. Rostock: Max Planck Institute for Demographic Research.
Pfau-Effinger, B. (2004). Socio-historical paths of the male breadwinner model – An explanation of cross-national differences. *British Journal of Sociology, 55*, 377–399.
Pfau-Effinger, B. (2005). Culture and welfare state policies: Reflections on a complex interrelation. *Journal of Social Policy, 34*, 3–20.
Pomeranz, K. (2009). *The great divergence: China, Europe, and the making of the modern world economy*. Princeton: Princeton University Press.
Poston, D. L., Jr., Kincannon, H. T., & Yoon, J. (2009). Socioeconomic development and fertility in the People's Republic of China and the Republic of Korea. In G. Jones, P. T. Straughan, & A. Chan (Eds.), *Ultra-low fertility in Pacific Asia: Trends, causes and policy issues* (pp. 96–109). Abingdon: Routledge.
Ravanera, Z. R., Rajulton, F., & Burch, T. K. (1998). Early life transitions of Canadian women: A cohort analysis of timing, sequences, and variations. *European Journal of Population, 14*, 179–204.
Raymo, J. M., Park, H., Yu, X., & Wei-jun Jean Yeung. (2015). Marriage and family in East Asia: Continuity and change. *Annual Review of Sociology, 41*, 471–492.
Reher, D. S. (1998). Family ties in western Europe: Persistent contrasts. *Population and Development Review, 24*, 203–234.
Rindfuss, R. R., Brewster, K. L., & Kavee, A. L. (1996). Women, work, and children: Behavioral and attitudinal change in the United States. *Population and Development Review, 22*, 457–482.
Schmidt, D., & Heckendorf, C. (2016). *Guide to the ngram Package: Fast n-gram Tokenization*. Unpublished. Available at https://cran.r-project.org/web/packages/ngram/ngram.pdf
Schneider, D. (2015). The great recession, fertility, and uncertainty: Evidence from the United States. *Journal of Marriage and Family, 77*, 1144–1156.
Sobotka, T. (2004). Is lowest-low fertility explained by the postponement of childbearing? *Population and Development Review, 30*, 195–220.
Sullivan, O., Billari, F. C., & Altintas, E. (2014). Fathers' changing contributions to child care and domestic work in very low–fertility countries: The effect of education. *Journal of Family Issues, 35*, 1048–1065.
Suzuki, T. (2012). Low fertility and governmental intervention in Japan and Korea. *Japanese Journal of Population, 10*, 60–77.

Thornton, A. (2001). The developmental paradigm, reading history sideways, and family change. *Demography, 38*, 449–465.
Thornton, A. (2005). *Reading history sideways: The fallacy and enduring impact of the developmental paradigm on family life*. Chicago: University of Chicago Press.
Tsuya, N. O., Bumpass, L. L., Choe, M. K., & Rindfuss, R. R. (2005). Is the gender division of labour changing in Japan? *Asian Population Studies, 1*, 47–67.
UNDP. (2014). *Human development report 2014: Sustaining human progress: Reducing vulnerabilities and building resilience*. New York: United Nations Development Programme.
UNPD. (2015). *World population prospects: The 2015 revision, key findings and advance tables*. New York: United Nations, Department of Economic and Social Affairs, Population Division.
Van Bavel, J. (2009). Subreplacement fertility in the West before the baby boom: Past and current perspectives. *Population Studies, 64*, 1–18.
van de Kaa, D. J. (1987). Europe's second demographic transition. *Population Bulletin, 42*, 1–59.
van de Kaa, D. J. (2004). The true commonality: In reflexive modern societies fertility is a derivative. *Population Studies, 58*, 77–81.
Wilson, C. (2001). On the scale of global demographic convergence 1950–2000. *Population and Development Review, 27*, 155–171.
Wilson, C. (2004). Fertility below replacement level. *Science, 304*, 207–208.
Wilson, C. (2013). Thinking about post-transitional demographic regimes: A reflection. *Demographic Research, 28*, 1373–1388.
Yi, Z., Coale, A., Choe, M. K., Liang, Z., & Li, L. (1994). Leaving the parental home – Census-based estimates for China, Japan, South-Korea, United-States, France, and Sweden. *Population Studies, 48*, 65–80.

Chapter 3
Natural Decrease in the Context of Lowest-low Fertility: South Korea, 2005–2014

Nayoung Heo and Dudley L. Poston, Jr.

Introduction

Of all the countries of Asia, only Japan has more deaths than births. In 2015 Japan reported 8 births for every 10 deaths. South Korea, while currently having more births than deaths, i.e., 9 births for every 5 deaths, has a total fertility rate of 1.2 that is so low that the country will likely be following in the not too distant future the pattern of Japan, with more deaths than births. Natural decrease in the not too distant future may well characterize the country of South Korea.

Demographic research on natural decrease indicates that it is at the subnational level of a country where natural decrease (more deaths than births) first begins to appear. Research on this topic at the subnational level in South Korea, is scarce if non-existent. The research we report in this chapter is an attempt to address this void.

We begin our chapter with a very brief discussion of the Demographic Transition (DT), and then trace the progress of South Korea through the transition. We show that South Korea is now beginning stage 4 of the DT. We next trace the progress of South Korea from its high fertility rate of 6.3 in the 1950s to its very low rates of 1.1–1.2 in the years of 2005–2015.

We then focus specifically on the "counties" of South Korea, which are known in Korea as *Sis* (cities) and *Guns* (counties). There are a total of 161 *Sis* and *Guns*, and these comprise all of the country of South Korea. For each of the *Sis* and *Guns*, hereafter referred to as counties, we calculate birth/death ratios covering the 10 year

N. Heo (✉)
Asian Demographic Research Institute, Shanghai University,
Shanghai, People's Republic of China
e-mail: heon131@naver.com

D.L. Poston, Jr.
Department of Sociology, Texas A & M University, College Station, TX 77843, USA
e-mail: d-poston@tamu.edu

D.L. Poston, Jr. (ed.), *Low Fertility Regimes and Demographic and Societal Change*, DOI 10.1007/978-3-319-64061-7_3

time period of 2005–2014. We describe the patterns of natural decrease and increase among these 161 counties. We then estimate a multivariate regression equation predicting the variability in the ratios. We hypothesize that as the proportion of elderly in a county increases, the birth/death ratio will decrease, and that as the fertility rate of the county increases, the ratio will increase. We conclude our chapter with an overall discussion of natural decrease and its implications for South Korea.

The Demographic Transition

The most prominent explanation for the growth of human populations is Demographic Transition Theory (DTT). Changes in the size of the world's population over a certain period of time are due entirely to changes during the same time period in fertility and mortality (migration, obviously, does not figure into the equation when the focus is on the world). The world changes its size over a given time interval by adding persons born during the period and subtracting persons dying.

The theory proposes four stages of mortality and fertility change that occur in the process of societal modernization (see Fig. 3.1). The first stage is the pretransitional or preindustrialization stage. It lasted for thousands and thousands of years when the world was characterized by high birth and death rates and stable population growth. Stage 1 is characterized by high rates of fluctuating mortality and high fertility. The relative instability of the mortality rates means that during this stage, there were some periods of natural increase and some of natural decrease, but that over the long period of time, there was very little change in population size.

The pretransitional stage is followed by a transition to the second stage. For numerous reasons, mortality began to decline in many countries of the world (see a more detailed discussion in Chap. 1 of this volume). With the onset of industrialization and modernization, many societies transitioned to lower death rates, especially lower infant and maternal mortality rates, but maintained high birth rates; rapid population growth was the result. It would take another generation or so before fertility would begin to fall. Thus, during Stage 2, population growth was intense.

The next stage (Stage 3) was characterized by decreasing population growth due to lower birth and death rates. It was during this period that fertility began to decline. In the final stage (Stage 4), called incipient decline, both fertility and mortality are very low. In Stage 4, populations grow only when there are increases in fertility, such as in the baby boom in the United States after World War II. During this stage, however, there are slight fluctuations in fertility. Thus, both natural increase and natural decrease occur owing in Stage 4. The term incipient is used because it is not really possible to determine how low fertility will go. In recent years, fertility has fallen so low in many European countries and in Japan that the number of deaths exceeds the number of births (Johnson et al. 2015). Poston's discussion in Chap. 1 of this book of the classic theory of demographic transition provides more detail.

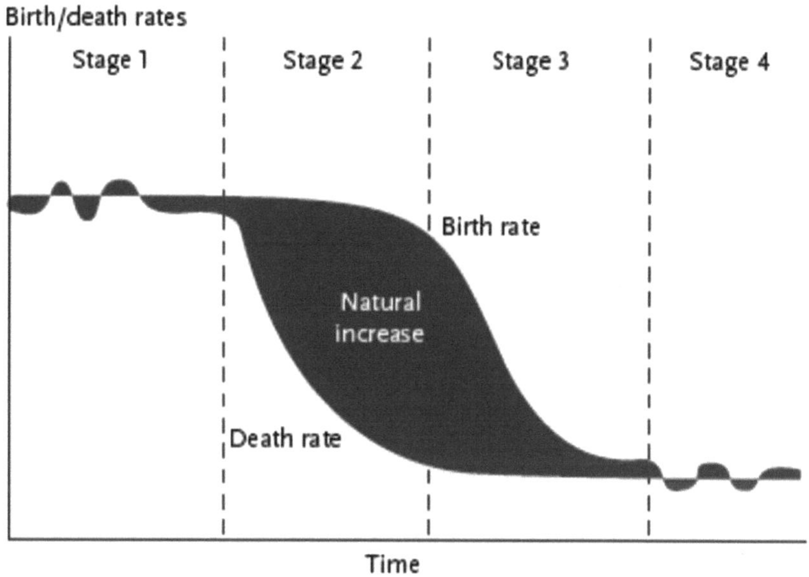

Fig. 3.1 The classic stages of demographic transitions. (Source: McFalls 2007: 27)

South Korea and the Demographic Transition

At this point in the chapter, we turn attention specifically to South Korea (also referred to as Korea). We first discuss Korea's progress through the demographic transition. We show that Korea will soon be entering the fourth stage of the transition. Although its fertility rate is considerably below the replacement level of 2.1, its birth rate is not yet at or below the level of its death rate. This is due almost entirely to population momentum. Soon, the birth rate will be lower than the death rate.

South Korea is now completing its demographic transition from high to low fertility and mortality rates, i.e., moving from Stage 3 to Stage 4 of the transition. We have plotted in Fig. 3.2 crude birth and death rates for South Korea for each year from 1970 to 2014. According to rates shown in the figure, Korea is entering the 4th and final stage of the demographic transition. Its birth rate is almost the same as its death rate.

The only reason the birth rate is slightly higher than the death rate owes to what demographers refer to as "demographic momentum." Korea's high birth rates in the 1960s and early 1970s were followed by birth rates in the mid-1980s and later that were slightly higher than the rates in the late 1970s. Although the fertility rates were on the decline, so many babies were produced in the 1960s that when those babies became adults in the mid- to late-1980s, even though their fertility was low, they still produced a lot of babies. This is an example of demographic momentum. Also, the extra babies produced in the mid- to late-1980s are having their babies in the

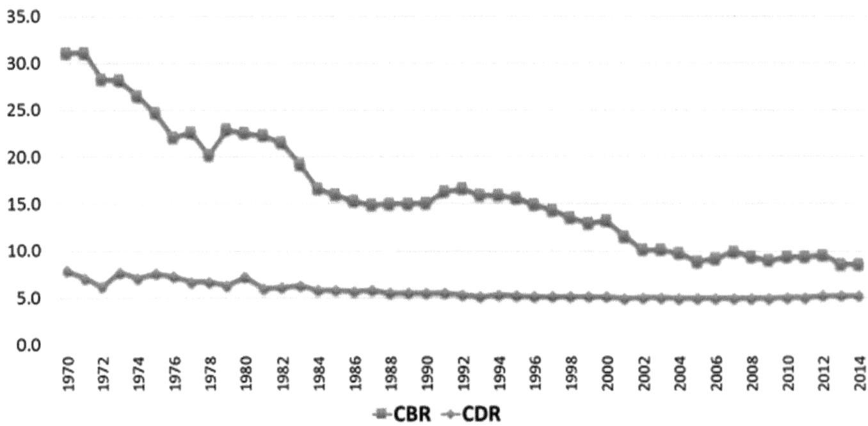

Fig. 3.2 Crude birth rates and crude death rates South Korea, 1970–2014. (Source: KOSIS 2016)

years of the current decade; and even though they have a very low fertility rate of around 1.2 children per woman, they are still producing a lot of babies. The demographic momentum will end in another 5–10 years in Korea, and it is then that the birth and death rates will be equal.

Because demographic momentum results in higher birth rates, a chart of such rates, as in Fig. 3.2, can be slightly misleading with respect to fertility change. For this reason, we will evaluate Korea's progress through the demographic transition by focusing only on changes in fertility rates, specifically total fertility rates (TFRs). The levels of the TFR are independent of any demographic momentum that may be present in the society.

We show in Fig. 3.3 total fertility rates for South Korea from 1950 to 2015, and projected to 2025. The TFRs in Fig. 3.3 show clearly that Korea has experienced a pronounced and very rapid decline in fertility, from a high of over 6.3 children per woman in the late 1950s to a level in 2015 of 1.2 children per woman (see Fig. 3.3). In this section we trace the history of population dynamics in Korea, with a special focus on fertility, since the end of the Korean War in the mid-1950s.

As we show in Fig. 3.3, the total fertility rate of South Korea reached sub-replacement levels (below 2.1) in the late 1980s. The TFR dropped rapidly from its high level of over 6 in early 1960 to 2.2 in the 1980s. In the 20 year period from 1960 to 1980, South Korea experienced one of the most rapid fertility declines in demographic history. The TFR then dropped even further to 1.7 by 1995, to 1.6 in 2000, and to 1.2 in 2010. Its recoded level in 2015 is 1.25 and is projected to reach 1.3 by 2025. We now review some of the major factors involved in this fertility reduction.

South Korea has undergone a rapid fertility decline since the government's economic planning program was adopted in 1962. The fertility decline in South Korea is due to both economic development and family planning programs (Poston and Kim 1992).

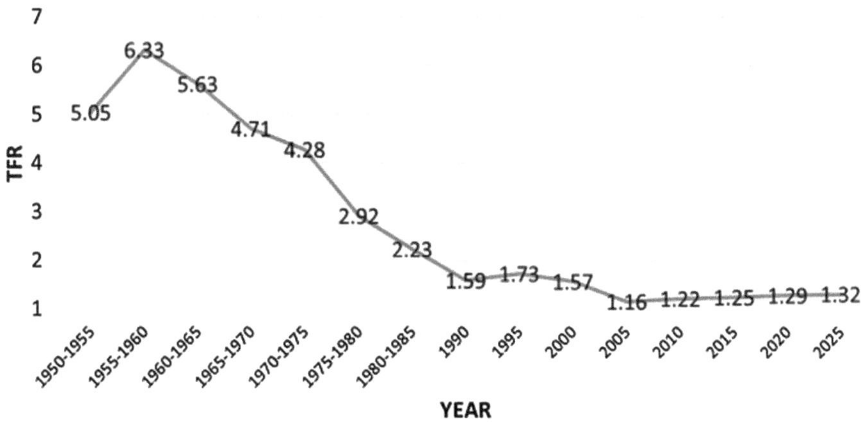

Fig. 3.3 Total fertility rates: South Korea, 1950–2025. (Source: KOSIS 2016; UNDESA 2015)

The Korean War, which broke out in 1950, had devastating effects on virtually all aspects of Korean society. From 1945 until the end of the war in 1953, most Koreans experienced a marked reduction in their reproductive behavior. The 1955 census indicated only a slight increase in population size in the country from 20.2 to 21.5 million, representing an average growth rate of around 1% per year from 1949 to 1955; the TFR in South Korea in the late 1950s was 6.3. However, as already noted, fertility began declining in the 1960s in South Korea and by 2005, South Korea had one of the lowest TFRs of any country in the world. The TFR in South Korea has been below the replacement level since the late 1980s and was just over 1.2 in 2015 (Fig. 3.3) (Poston and Davis 2009).

These actual levels of fertility are quite a bit less than the ideal levels. For instance, even though the ideal number of children reported by South Korean women in 2010 was 2.3, the actual TFR was one child less, at 1.2 (KOSIS 2016). Having reviewed and traced the progress of South Korea through the demographic transition, with a special focus on fertility, we turn next to a discussion of natural decrease and increase among the subregions of Korea.

Patterns of Natural Decrease and Increase in South Korea

We noted at the start of this chapter that presently in South Korea, the country as a whole has more births each year than deaths. In 2015 there were 9 births for every 5 deaths. Currently, South Korea is not a natural decrease country. But we also noted that demographic research on natural decrease in the countries of Europe and in the United States has indicated that natural decrease first starts to emerge in a country in several of its subregional units (Johnson et al. 2015).

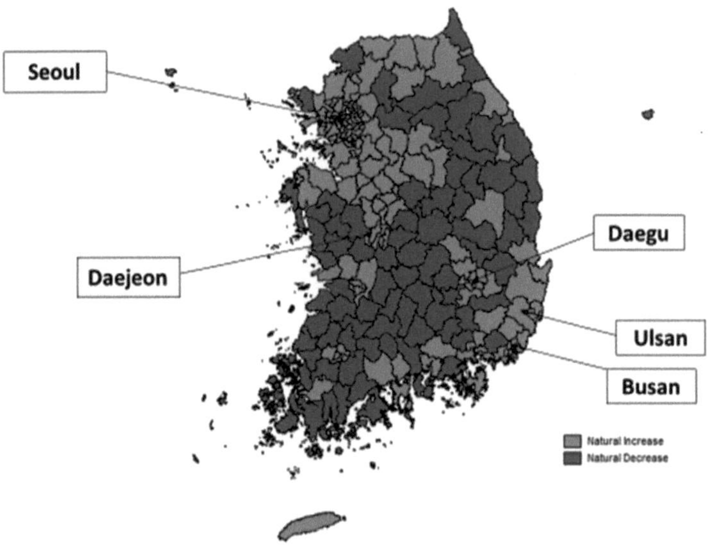

Fig. 3.4 Natural decrease and natural increase: Counties of South Korea, 2005–2014 (Source: KOSIS 2016; SGIS 2014)

In the 15-year period from 2005 to 2014, just over one-half, or 81 of the 161, of Korea's counties had more deaths than births. This percentage is between those of the United States and Europe. Poston et al. (2016) have shown that 59% of all counties in Europe had more deaths than births between 2000 and 2009 compared to 27% of the U.S. counties. These percentages of Europe and the U.S. increased to 62% and 35%, respectively, for the post-2010 period. South Korea is a bit more similar to Europe than to the U.S. with more than half of the counties in both Korea and Europe experiencing more deaths than births.

In Europe, between 2009 and 2012, three countries had percentages of natural decrease counties almost the same as the percentage of South Korea, namely, Slovakia (50%), Austria (51.4%), and Finland (52.6%). For a further comparison, we look also at their TFRs. South Korea's TFR in 2015 was 1.25. Slovakia, Austria and Finland all had higher fertility rates than South Korea, namely 1.4 for Slovakia, 1.5 for Austria, and 1.7 for Finland.

We present in Fig. 3.4 a map of all the counties of South Korea; we have marked each of the 161 counties as either natural decrease (blue) or natural increase (orange). There is clearly evidence of spatial variation in the presence of natural decrease among the counties of South Korea (Fig. 3.4). There are clear concentrations of natural decrease counties in the northeastern and southwestern regions of the country. Conversely, natural increase is mainly observed in the Seoul Capital area (the greater Seoul Metropolitan Area that includes Seoul, Incheon, and Gyeonggi Province), and in such other metropolitan areas as Busan, Daegu, and Gwangju.

Another way to measure natural decrease and natural increase is with the birth/death ratio, i.e., the number of births in a population per 1000 deaths. A ratio less than 1000 indicates natural decrease, and a ratio above 1000, natural increase. We have calculated such ratios for all the counties of South Korea for the year of 2014.

In 2014, Seoul had 1986 births per 1000 deaths, almost twice as many births as deaths. The ratios of Incheon and Daejeon, 1923 and 2127, were even higher. But these Birth/Death ratios have only been calculated for the single year of 2014. When we calculate the ratios for the 10-year period of 2005 to 2014, they become even larger. The ratios for Seoul, Incheon, and Daejeon for the 2005–14 period were 2292, 2108, and 2339, respectively. Some cities, all located in Gyeonggi province, have even higher B/D ratios, namely, Osan (4588 births per 1000 deaths), Hwaseong (3753), and Gunpo (3708).

Even though the percentage of natural decrease counties in South Korea is a little less than the percentage in Europe (50% versus 60%), the divide between metropolitan areas or big cities versus agricultural and nonmetropolitan areas is obvious. While the areas and regions adjacent to the metropolitan regions are attracting young adults owing mainly to the availability of jobs, the nonmetropolitan regions and many of the *Gun*-level regions are losing births because their young folks are moving to the big metro areas. This results in relatively larger numbers of elders in the nonmetro areas, resulting in more deaths than births. For example, nonmetro counties such as Yeoncheon-gun, Gapyeong-gun, Yangpyeong-gun, Samcheok-si, and Hongcheon-gun all experienced natural decrease during the study period (2005–2014). The wide spread of natural decrease is especially apparent in Gangwon and Jeolla Provinces, and especially more so in their *gun*s (counties) than in their *si*s (cities). The counties with the lowest B/D ratios in South Korea during the 2005–2014 period were Namhae-gun (339 births per 1000 deaths), Cheongdo-gun (340), and Guesan-gun (355); these are all nonmetro and heavily agricultural counties. The proportions of women of childbearing age in these counties were all less than 30%. Conversely, in the cities and metro areas of Osan-si and Hwaseong-si with the highest B/D ratios of 4588 and 3753, respectively, the proportions of women in the childbearing years were around 55% (KOSIS 2016). By the way, this tendency for metro areas to be more characterized by natural increase, and nonmetro areas by natural decrease, has also been found in Europe and in the U.S. (Johnson et al. 2015).

Throughout Korea, rural to urban migration, especially of younger persons, is apparent, particularly from *gun*s that are nonadjacent to the metropolitan area into metro *si*s, or into *sis* that are adjacent to metro areas. The outmigration of the young, working population from *guns* to *cis* is the major reason for the reduced size of women of reproductive age in these areas and their consequent lower births rates (Lee et al. 2014; Kim 1996).

Thus the main factor contributing to the occurrence of natural decrease in many of the nonmetro *guns* is their population structure. There seems to be a considerable difference in the proportion of older adults between counties with natural increase and counties with natural decrease. For example, in Osan-si and Hwaseong-si, the two cities with the highest B/D ratios (see our earlier discussion), the proportions of older adults in both cities were only 10%. In contrast, in the two counties, Namhae-gun and Cheongdo-gun, with the lowest ratios, their proportions of elders were over 40%. This suggests that the proportion of older adults in an area, along with its fertility rate, should be able to predict rather satisfactorily whether the area experiences natural decrease or natural increase. Later in our chapter, we subject this hypothesis to an empirical test.

Natural Decrease and Population Loss

Natural decrease in an area in a certain period of time need not necessarily lead to overall population loss in the area. It is possible for net in-migration to the area to offset the population loss due to more deaths than births, provided that the net migration gain is greater than the natural decrease loss. For instance, in Europe in the 2000–10 period, "only 55 percent of the counties with natural decrease experienced population loss … By comparison, in the U.S., 63 percent of the counties with overall natural decrease lost population" (Poston et al. 2016: 3).

The degree to which net in-migration offsets population loss in the natural decrease counties of Korea, however, is nowhere as high as it is in Europe or in the U.S. Our data indicate that about 90% of the natural decrease counties of South Korea also experienced overall reductions in their size of their populations. Specifically, 73 of the 81 counties in Korea with natural decrease in the 2005–14 period also had reductions in the size of their populations. Of the eight natural decrease counties that gained population during this period, two of them, Gapyeong and Yangpyeong, are in Gyeonggi Province, right near Seoul, thus benefitting from the large numbers of domestic migrants moving to Seoul and nearby areas from other regions in the country.

In South Korea, natural decrease and population loss over time are more highly correlated than in Europe. Migration has nowhere near as strong an influence in South Korea as an agent for offsetting population loss due to more deaths than births, as it does in Europe.

Multivariate Analysis

We now undertake a multivariate analysis of natural increase/decrease among the 161 *si*s (cities) and *gun*s (counties) of South Korea. We model natural increase/decrease occurring in the 10 year period from 2005 to 2014. The dependent variable is the birth/death ratio, i.e. the number of births per 1000 deaths occurring in the county in the 2005–14 period. We use the B/D ratio rather than the dichotomous variable indicating if the county experienced natural decrease/increase. The ratio measure is more appropriate and precise than the dichotomous indicator of whether natural decrease occurred, yes or no. Please see a more extended justification of such a ratio over a dummy variable in the recent paper by Johnson et al. (2015).

As mentioned above, the two main independent variables we have hypothesized to be related to a county's B/D ratio are the county's fertility rate measured with the

Table 3.1 Descriptive analysis

Variable	Number	Mean	Min	Max	S.D.
Dependent Variable					
Birth/Death Ratio	161	1320.5	339	4588	887.1
Independent Variables					
Percent of the population 65+	161	17.9	5.7	32.8	7.9
Child/Woman ratio	161	232.3	76.2	342	35.3

child/woman ratio, i.e., the number of persons aged 0–4 divided by the number of women aged 15–49, multiplied by 1000; and an index of the elderly population in the county measured by the ratio of persons of age 65 or greater in the population, divided by the total population, multiplied by 100. The independent variables are measured for the year of 2005. We hypothesize that the greater the elderly population in a county, the less the Birth/Death ratio; and the greater the fertility rate as measured with the child/woman ratio in a county, the greater the Birth/Death ratio.

We report in Table 3.1 descriptive data for our three variables. The B/D ratio has an average value among the 161 Korean counties of 1320. The average Korean county had 1320 births per every 1000 deaths in the 2005–14 time period. The ratios ranged from a low of 339 to a high of 4588. The elderly variable, percentage of the population 65+, had an average value among the counties of 17.9%, with a range from 5.7 to 32.8. And the child/woman ratio had a mean value across the 161 counties of 232 children per 1000 women aged 15–49, and ranged from 76 to 342.

Prior to estimating the multivariate equation, we wondered about the presence of spatial autocorrelation in the B/D ratios across the 161 counties. In the map of the South Korean counties presented earlier showing the presence of natural increase/decrease (Fig. 3.4), there is clear evidence of spatial clustering among the counties. That is, Korean counties experiencing natural decrease in the 2005–14 period are likely to be contiguous to other counties also experiencing natural decrease in the same period, and similarly for counties experiencing natural increase. Or as Waldo Tobler noted many years ago in his formulation of the "first law of geography," "Everything is related to everything else, but near things are more related than distant things" (Tobler 1970: 234).

To determine if this perceived spatial clustering is statistically significant, we computed the Moran's I spatial autocorrelation statistic (Moran 1950) for the birth/death ratio across the Korean counties. Moran's I ranges from +1.00 to −1.00 and may be interpreted much like a correlation coefficient. The higher its positive value, the greater the spatial clustering in the counties of like values of a variable; the higher its negative value, the less the degree of spatial clustering. The value of Moran's I evaluating the degree of spatial clustering of the B/D ratio across the 161 South Korean counties = 0.203, p = 0.00.

The calculated value of Moran's I indicates that there is a sizable and statistically significant amount of spatial autocorrelation among the South Korean counties, indicating the inappropriateness of ordinary least squares regression for modelling the B/D ratio (Anselin 2002; Anselin and Bera 1998). We thus opted to use a spatial

Table 3.2 Spatial error regression model estimating the Birth/Death ratio in 2005–2014 with selected independent variables in 2005: 161 Countries of South Korea

Variable	Coefficient	Standard Error	Z-value	Significance
Population 65+('00)	−81.28321	5.517266	−11.73	0.000
Child Woman Ratio('000)	3.79975	1.086531	3.50	0.000
Constant	1601.011	568.6133	2.82	0.005
Lambda	.8929609	.1040112	8.59	0.000

Variance Ratio (Pseudo R^2) = 0.604
Final log likelihood −1213.7982

error model to be able to address the spatial autocorrelation in our data. Our model thus assumes that spatial heterogeneity exists among the variables and controls for it by adding to the model a spatial error coefficient (lambda). This removes the spatial bias from the standard errors associated with the estimated regression parameters of the substantive independent variables. "Incorporating a spatial error coefficient and using maximum likelihood methods to estimate the regression parameters" leads to "multivariate analyses that are more statistically efficient and inferences from them more valid" (Johnson et al. 2015: 677; Anselin 2005).

The resulting spatial error regression model predicting the birth/death ratio is presented in Table 3.2. The metric coefficients are shown in the first data column of the table. Both of the coefficients for the elderly variable and the child/woman ratio are signed as hypothesized and are statistically significant, with b values of −81.3 for the age 65+ variable, and 3.8 for the child woman ratio. Among the 161 counties of South Korea, for every 1% increase in the percentage elderly in the population, there is an average decrease of 81 births per 1000 deaths, ceteris paribus. And for every one child increase in the ratio of children per 1000 women in the childbearing ages, there is an increase of almost 4 births per 1000 deaths.

We do not show semi-standardized regression coefficients (b*) in the table. We may calculate them by multiplying the metric b by its respective standard deviation, i.e., b* = b x's sd. The b* value for the population 65+ variable is 642.3, and is significantly larger than the b* value of 134.1 for the child woman ratio. This means that the standardized effect on the birth/death ratio of the elder population variable is quite a bit greater than the effect on the b/d ratio of the child woman ratio. This result is very consistent with the results of analyses of natural decrease conducted among the counties of Europe and the U.S. for roughly the same years (Johnson 2011; Johnson et al. 2015; Poston et al. 2016).

All in all, the results of the spatial error regression model in Table 3.2 support our hypotheses about the statistically significant effects on the birth/death ratio of the two independent variables, namely, the percent of adult population aged 65+ and the number of children per 1000 women. These two indicators of the demographic structure of the counties contribute significantly to the explanatory power of the model. The model performs very well even after controlling for spatial autocorrelation via the spatial error coefficient, lambda.

Conclusion

What might we expect for South Korea's future with regard to natural decrease? Natural decrease will not go away. Once natural decrease occurs in an area, it is likely to reoccur (Beale 1969; Johnson 2011; Johnson et al. 2015). The future for most of Korea's natural decrease counties appears to be a bleak one. Since over 90% of South Korea's natural decrease counties also experienced population loss between 2005–14, it is not likely they will be able to use net migration as an agent to offset this negative situation. It is as difficult, if not more so, to move from a situation of net out-migration to one of net in-migration, as it is to move from a situation of more deaths than births to one of more births than deaths.

Natural decrease, we hold is likely to loom particularly large in South Korea's future. There are relatively few young women residing in the natural decrease counties to produce the next generation of Korean infants. And it is very unlikely that young women will migrate from the big metro counties which are almost all natural increase counties to the small nonmetro and agricultural counties which are mainly natural decrease. With a diminishing population in the child-bearing ages in the natural decrease locations, with low fertility, and with an increasingly older population at a high risk of mortality, more widespread natural decrease is almost inevitable.

South Korea has virtually no international migration, and even if it did, the immigrants would be more likely to move to Seoul and the other large metro areas such as Busan and Daegu than to the small agricultural nonmetro counties.

Natural decrease is the end result of population aging and below replacement fertility that now characterize much of South Korea. Natural decrease is likely to become even more prevalent in Korea in future years. Natural decrease is a major policy concern because of its pronounced spatial clustering, and this is especially the case in South Korea, as we showed earlier in the map in Fig. 3.4. Research has shown that natural decrease has the potential to drain the demographic resilience of an area (Johnson et al. 2015: 651). Worries about natural decrease and its implications for South Korea, however, have been expressed very little, if at all, in Korea's media and public policy circles because, for one reason, it is relatively hidden away in the small nonmetro and mainly agricultural areas of the country. But with South Korea's very low fertility rate, aging population, and virtual lack of immigration, natural decrease is certain to become more prominent in the next few decades, and will begin to creep into the larger metro areas of the country. When this occurs, and we anticipate this trend to be well underway by the year of 2025 or so, the economic viability and the regional and international competitiveness of South Korea could well be influenced by the low birth rates and aging populations that will be characterizing increasingly larger and larger shares of the country.

References

Anselin, L. (2002). Under the hood: Issues in the specification and interpretation of spatial regression models. *Agricultural Economics, 27*(3), 247–267.

Anselin, L. (2005). *Exploring spatial data with GeoDa™ : A workbook*. Santa Barbara: Center for Spatially Integrated Social Science.

Anselin, L., & Bera, A. K. (1998). Spatial dependence in linear regression models with an introduction to spatial sconometrics. In A. Ullah & D. E. A. Giles (Eds.), *Handbook of applied economic statistics* (pp. 237–289). New York: Marcel Dekker.

Beale, C. L. (1969). Natural decrease of population: The current and prospective status of an emergent American phenomenon. *Demography, 6*, 91–99.

Johnson, K. M. (2011). The continuing incidence of natural decrease in American counties. *Rural Sociology, 76*, 74–100.

Johnson, K. M., Field, L., & Poston, D. L., Jr. (2015). More deaths than births: Subnational natural decrease in Europe and the United States. *Population and Development Review, 41*(4), 651–680.

Kim, T. (1996). The characteristics of the rural population, Korea, 1960–1995: Population composition and internal migration. *Korean Journal of Population Studies, 19*, 77–105.

Korean Statistical Information Service. (2016). *Statistics by topic* [Data file]. Available from http://kosis.kr/

Lee, C., & Kim, S. S. (2014). The transition of fertility and depopulation by stage migration: A case study of Jeollabuk-do. *Journal of the Korean Geographical Society, 49*, 728–746.

McFalls, J. A., Jr. (2007). Population: A lively introduction. *Population Bulletin, 62*(1), 1–31.

Moran, P. A. P. (1950). Notes on continuous stochastic phenomena. *Biometrika, 37*, 17–23.

Poston, D. L., Jr., & Davis, M. A. (2009). Population aging in the Koreas. Chapter 9. In P. Uhlenberg (Ed.), *International handbook of population aging* (pp. 173–190). New York: Springer.

Poston, D. L., Jr., & Kim, H. G. (1992). *Women's status and fertility in the Republic of Korea* (Final report of research grant no. RD 87056 submitted to the Rockefeller Foundation, New York). College Station: Department of Sociology, Texas A&M University.

Poston, D. L., Jr., Johnson, K., & Field, L. (2016, February 15). Deaths exceed births in most of Europe, but not in the U.S., and not in Texas. *N-IUSSP, the News Magazine of the International Union for the Scientific Study of Population.*

Statistical Geographic Information Service. (2014). *Census administrative Boundaries* [Data file]. Retrieved from http://sgis.kostat.go.kr/

Tobler, W. (1970). A computer movie simulating urban growth in the Detroit region. *Economic Geography, 46*, 234–240.

United Nations, Department of Economic and Social Affairs, Population Division. (2015). *World population prospects: The 2015 revision,* DVD Edition.

Chapter 4
A Twenty-First Century Demographic Challenge: Comparatively Low Life Expectancy in the United States

Richard G. Rogers, Elizabeth M. Lawrence, and Robert A. Hummer

Introduction

Over sixty countries today have fertility rates below the replacement level, i.e., total fertility rates (TFRs) below 2.1. Furthermore, there are 19 countries with TFRs of 1.4 or less. Although all countries with below replacement level fertility are also characterized by relatively high life expectancy, there is an imperfect association between low fertility and high life expectancy. Hong Kong, for example, reports the highest life expectancy in the world, at 84 years, and one of the very lowest TFRs, at 1.1. Other countries with exceptionally low TFRs and exceptionally high life expectancy include Singapore (at 1.2 and 83 years), Taiwan (1.1 and 80 years), and South Korea (at 1.2 and 81 years). The United States joins four other countries with a TFR of 1.9, but three of these have significantly higher life expectancies than the U.S. figure of 79: 81 for the United Kingdom, and 82 for both Sweden and Australia. Thus, while the U.S. TFR has recently declined to below replacement level and life expectancy is at an all-time high, the United States ranks neither among the lowest in fertility nor among the highest in life expectancy.

This chapter provides an overview of U.S. life expectancy patterns and mortality rates, with frequent comparison to other low fertility (and high-income) countries. We first compare life expectancy in the United States with that of selected countries. Second, we describe life expectancy and mortality changes in the United States across time. Third, we focus on particular causes of death and health behavior patterns where the United States fares poorly in comparison to other low fertility,

R.G. Rogers (✉)
University of Colorado, Boulder, CO, USA
e-mail: richard.rogers@colorado.edu

E.M. Lawrence • R.A. Hummer
University of North Carolina, Chapel Hill, NC, USA

D.L. Poston, Jr. (ed.), *Low Fertility Regimes and Demographic and Societal Change*, DOI 10.1007/978-3-319-64061-7_4

high-income countries. Fourth, we speculate on future trends in U.S. life expectancy by comparing the United States to countries with some of the highest life expectancies in the world.

Twenty-First Century Life Expectancy in the United States and Comparison Countries

Even though most countries in the world have experienced substantial increases in life expectancy at birth over the last several decades, Fig. 4.1 underscores tremendous variation across the globe (see also Rogers and Crimmins 2011). The Northern Hemisphere, including Northern America, Europe, and Asia, generally has very high life expectancies. Hong Kong boasts the highest life expectancy, at 84 years, followed by Japan, Singapore, and Switzerland, at 83 years (see Fig. 4.2). High-life-expectancy countries in the Southern Hemisphere include Australia, New Zealand, and several Latin American countries. South Korea's 81-year life expectancy at birth is tied for 11th highest in the world. The U.S. life expectancy at birth is 79 years, which places it in 28th place worldwide (tied with Chile, Puerto Rico [a commonwealth of the United States], and Cyprus). (The U.S. would fare even worse if countries with less than 1 million population were included in the comparison).

Figure 4.3 plots age-specific mortality probabilities by sex for the United States and 16 high-income peer countries selected by the Institute of Medicine and National Research Council (2013) in their recent report on international compari-

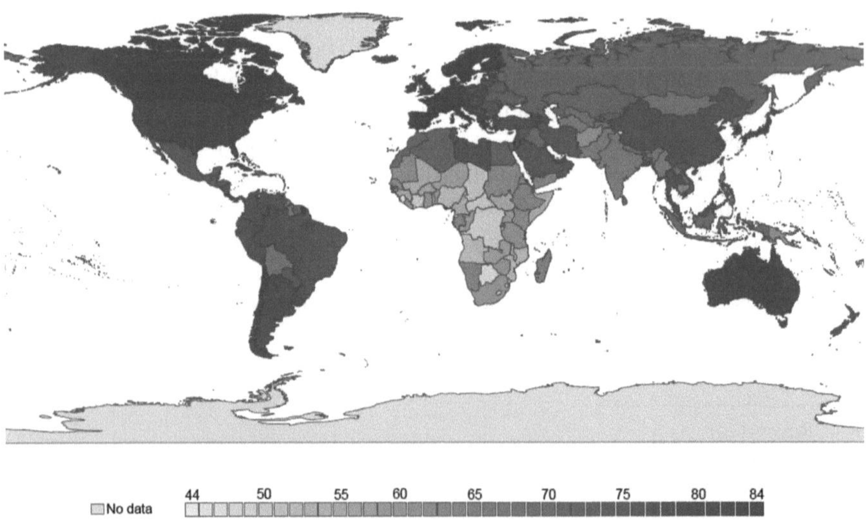

Fig. 4.1 World map of life expectancy at birth, 2013 (Source: Derived from the Population Reference Bureau 2014)

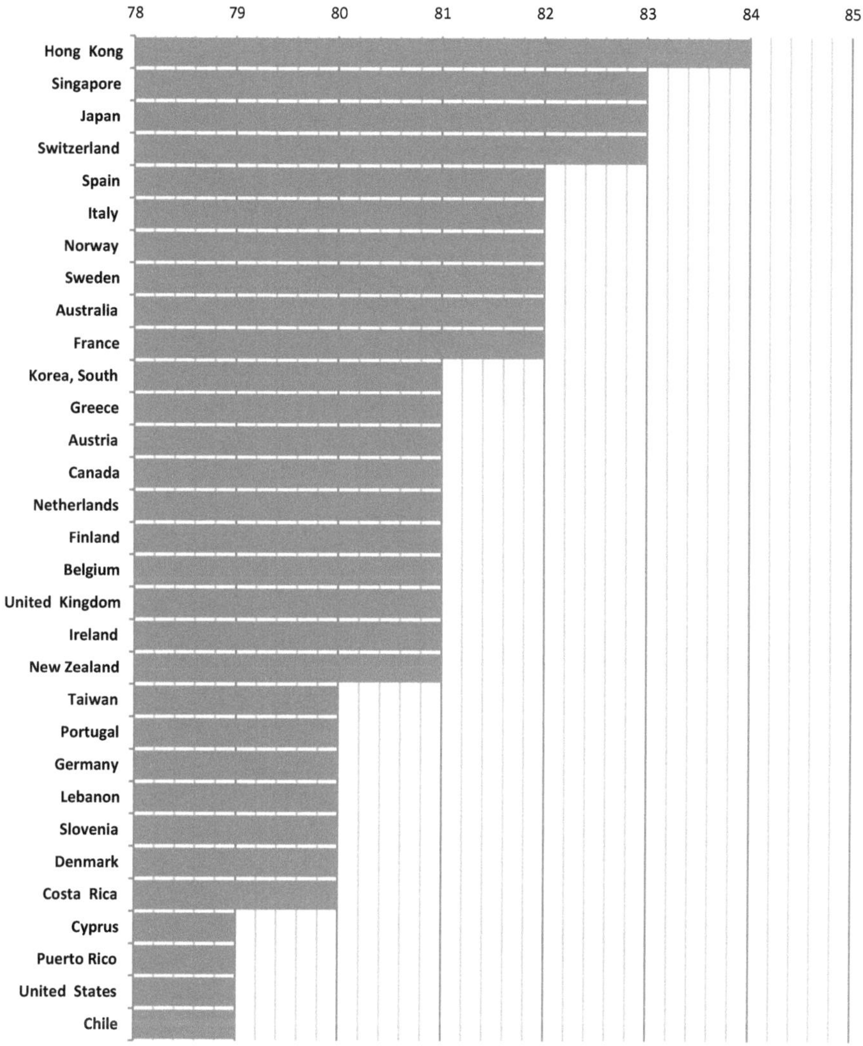

Fig. 4.2 Life expectancy at birth, selected countries, 2013 (Source: Derived from the Population Reference Bureau (2014). Note: Includes countries with at least 1 million people)

sons of health and mortality. For both sexes, the United States exhibits the highest age-specific mortality from the youngest ages through ages 50–54. That is, compared to its peer countries, the United States has higher age-specific mortality probabilities in infancy, childhood, young adolescence, young adulthood, and even into middle adulthood (Ho 2013). Infant mortality is often considered to be a central summary measure of a population's overall health and well-being. And U.S. infants fare poorly compared to those in the other countries. For example, U.S. female infant mortality (specifically, the life table value of ${}_1q_0$) is at least double that of

Panel A. Females

Rank	17th	17th	17th	17th	17th	17th	17th	17th	17th	17th	17th	17th	16th	16th	16th	16th	16th	10th	5th	4th	3rd	3rd	3rd
Age	0	1-4	5-9	10-14	15-19	20-24	25-29	30-34	35-39	40-44	45-49	50-54	55-59	60-64	65-69	70-74	75-79	80-84	85-89	90-94	95-99	100-104	105-109

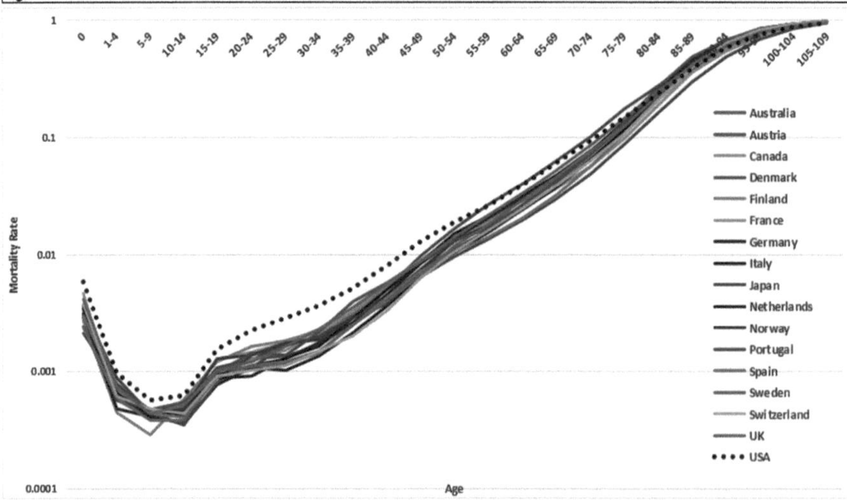

Panel B. Males

Rank	17th	17th	17th	17th	17th	17th	17th	17th	17th	17th	17th	17th	17th	14th	15th	13th	9th	6th	4th	5th	5th	5th	5th
Age	0	1-4	5-9	10-14	15-19	20-24	25-29	30-34	35-39	40-44	45-49	50-54	55-59	60-64	65-69	70-74	75-79	80-84	85-89	90-94	95-99	100-104	105-109

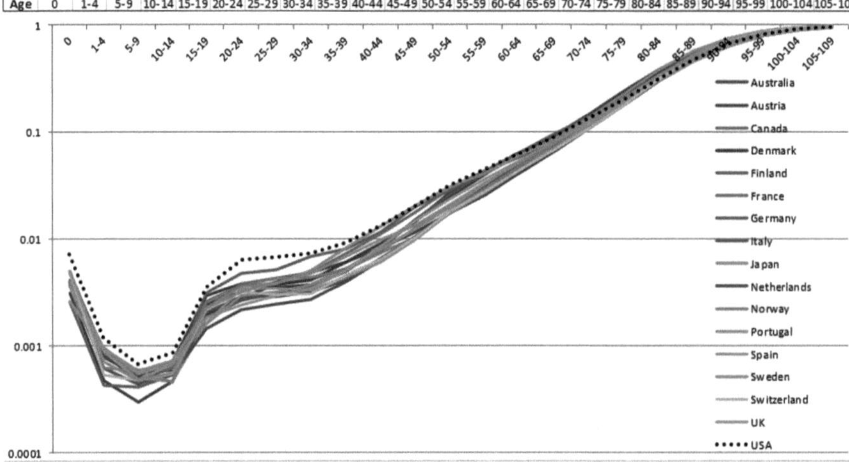

Fig. 4.3 Age-specific mortality ($_nq_x$) of the United States and peer countries, 2009 (Source: Derived from the Human Mortality Database 2014)

Denmark and Spain (2.0 times as high), Finland (2.2 times as high), Norway and Sweden (2.4 times as high), and Japan (2.8 times as high). The United States has comparatively higher infant mortality because of a relatively higher percentage of preterm births. For instance, in a comparison with 18 European countries, MacDorman et al. (2014) found that the United States had the highest percentage of preterm births. But the U.S. disadvantage does not end in infancy. Figure 4.3 shows that the largest absolute differences between the United States and its counterpart countries occur in the young adult ages. At the oldest ages, U.S. mortality probabilities for both females and males compare quite favorably. For example, U.S. males and females rank 4th and 5th lowest in age-specific mortality at ages 85–89, and 5th and 3rd lowest, respectively, at ages 95–99.

Overall, compared to people in these 16 peer countries, U.S. males and females experience proportionally more deaths at younger ages, have a less pronounced peak where deaths are concentrated, and have a greater dispersion of deaths throughout the age range. For example, over one-quarter of all American females die before age 75, compared with only 15% of Spanish and 16% of Japanese females. Likewise, U.S. males and females have relatively low life expectancy at birth (at 76.13 and 81.04, respectively), but relatively high life expectancies at older ages; U.S. females have the 3rd highest life expectancies at ages 95–99, for example. There are thus large absolute gaps in life expectancies at the younger ages and small gaps at the older ages; the life expectancy gap between Japanese and American females is 5.38 years at birth, but only 0.55 years at ages 95–99. Although U.S. life expectancy is relatively high at older ages, higher mortality at younger ages reduces the number of individuals who survive to these advanced ages. Out of a hypothetical 100,000 U.S. births, only 12,596 can expect to live to 95 and 3021 can expect to live to 100 (based on the life table l_x values). In Japan, about twice as many people can expect to live to these advanced ages: 23,919 to age 95 and 7423 to age 100.

U.S. Mortality and Life Expectancy Trends Over Time

During the twentieth century, the United States moved through the four stages of the demographic transition from high birth and death rates to today's relatively low fertility and mortality rates. There were tremendous increases during this period in U.S. life expectancy for both sexes combined and for each sex separately. Between 1900 and 2010, life expectancy at birth for both sexes increased from 47.3 to 78.7 years (see Fig. 4.4). This sharp increase in life expectancy was due to a number of factors, including advancements in public health, medicine, and technology; broader access to modern health care; improved living standards; enhanced nutrition; increased socioeconomic status; and generally healthier behaviors. The first half of the twentieth century was characterized by some wide year-to-year swings in life expectancy, due in large part to infectious and parasitic diseases. For example, life expectancy dropped an amazing 11.8 years (from 50.9 to 39.1 years) between 1917 and 1918 because of the influenza epidemic. Still, net gains were greater in earlier than in more recent periods of the century: life expectancy increased by 4.2 years per decade, on average, between 1900 and 1950, but only by 1.8 years on average per decade between 1960 and 2010. Clearly, gains in life expectancy are now harder to make than was the case a century or so ago. Further, the sex gap in life expectancy was low in the early part of the twentieth century, slowly increased to a peak of 7.8 years in 1975 and again in 1979, and then declined to just 4.8 years

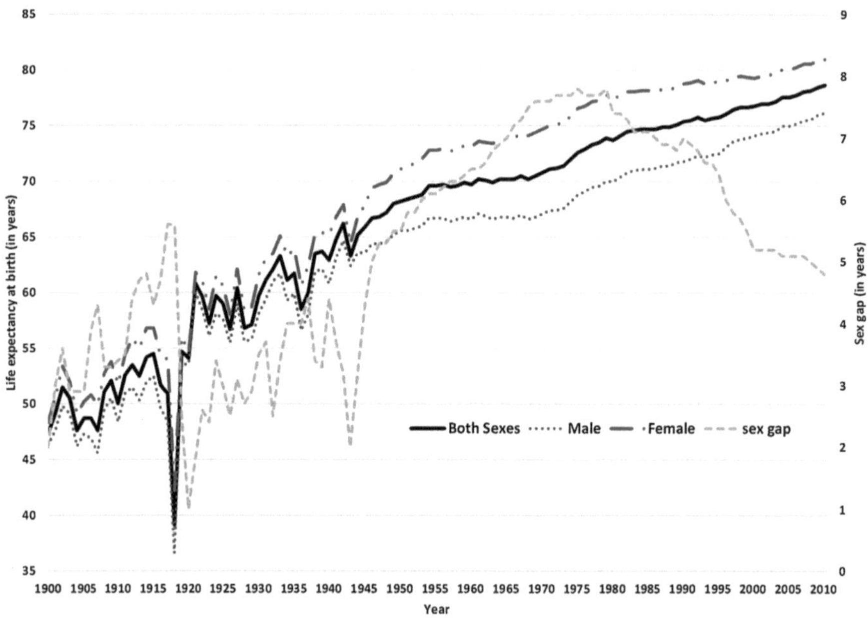

Fig. 4.4 U.S. life expectancy at birth for both sexes combined and separately, 1900–2010 (Source: Derived from Arias 2014)

in 2010. The convergence in male and female life expectancies since 1980 has been due in large part to substantial reductions in smoking among males in comparison to modest reductions among females.

Table 4.1 shows the age decomposition of U.S. life expectancies at birth by sex for selected years over the last century. We examine 20-year periods from 1900 through 2000, and the 10-year 2000–2010 period, which includes the most recent published data available. The decomposition shows the age-specific percentage contribution to changes in life expectancy. For example, between 1900 and 1920, females realized a 6.7-year increase in overall life expectancy (see Panel A, last column and row). Improvements in infant and child mortality contributed to 67.6% (42.4% + 25.2%) of this gain in life expectancy at birth. As we progress from earlier to more recent periods, the overall life expectancy gains generally decline, and the ages that contribute to gains in life expectancy tend to increase. For instance, females gained 8.5 years in life expectancy at birth between 1920 and 1940, 4.4 years between 1960 and 1980, and just 1.85 years between 1980 and 2000., Improvement in infant, child, adolescent, and young adult mortality fueled much of the life expectancy gains early in the 1900s, but it was in the middle and the older ages where life expectancy gains were the greatest in the latter half of the twentieth century. For example, infants contributed more than any other age group to life expectancy gains early in the twentieth century, but in more recent periods, they have contributed less than most age groups. In 1900–1920, decreasing infant mortality contributed to 42.4% of the female gain in life expectancy, and 41.9% of the

Table 4.1 Age decomposition of life expectancy gains by sex, selected years, United States

Age	Periods					
	2000–2010	1980–2000	1960–1980	1940–1960	1920–1940	1900–1920
A. Females						
0–1	3.8%	21.4%	20.3%	19.1%	19.9%	42.4%
1–5	0.7%	4.4%	2.7%	6.3%	16.0%	25.2%
5–15	1.4%	3.4%	2.1%	4.5%	9.4%	7.2%
15–25	2.9%	4.1%	0.7%	8.3%	14.9%	3.1%
25–35	0.6%	2.6%	3.2%	9.7%	15.5%	4.3%
35–45	3.8%	4.1%	5.4%	9.7%	9.2%	5.6%
45–55	1.5%	13.8%	7.8%	10.4%	5.4%	4.7%
55–65	18.6%	15.4%	10.5%	12.1%	4.5%	4.1%
65–75	26.6%	15.8%	17.3%	12.3%	3.8%	1.7%
75–85	31.7%	10.0%	20.4%	7.2%	1.1%	1.4%
85–95	8.1%	5.7%	9.1%	0.5%	0.2%	0.2%
95+	0.2%	–0.8%	0.5%	0.0%	0.0%	0.0%
Gain in $\dot{e}_0$ in years	1.57	1.85	4.38	7.35	8.49	6.70
B. Males						
0–1	3.6%	11.7%	32.5%	30.8%	31.9%	41.9%
1–5	1.1%	2.4%	3.5%	9.1%	22.3%	22.3%
5–15	2.1%	2.5%	3.3%	6.8%	12.2%	5.2%
15–25	4.9%	6.6%	–1.6%	6.8%	14.7%	4.2%
25–35	–0.6%	5.9%	–1.1%	10.5%	14.3%	6.4%
35–45	8.2%	4.2%	5.8%	11.3%	8.3%	6.3%
45–55	6.1%	12.3%	14.5%	9.2%	–0.3%	5.7%
55–65	14.6%	20.9%	18.7%	6.2%	–2.4%	4.3%
65–75	29.2%	22.0%	13.7%	4.7%	–0.6%	2.3%
75–85	26.3%	9.9%	7.8%	4.3%	–0.4%	1.1%
85–95	4.6%	1.6%	2.7%	0.5%	0.0%	0.2%
95+	0.1%	–0.1%	0.2%	0.0%	0.0%	0.0%
Gain in $\dot{e}_0$ in years	2.07	4.02	3.31	5.20	6.10	7.62

Source: Derived from Arias (2014)
Notes: Based on calculations in Preston et al. (2001)

male gain, but between 2000 and 2010, decreases in infant mortality contributed to just 3.8% and 3.6% of the female and male gains, respectively. Between the years 1920 and 1940, 75.8% of the gains in female life expectancy were realized between ages 0 and 34, but in the period 1980–2000 the majority of the gains were realized between ages 45 and 84. Most recently, between the years 2000 and 2010, over three-quarters of the gains were realized between ages 55 and 84.

Female and male patterns are quite similar (compare Panels A and B). But compared to females, males realized smaller gains in life expectancy during the 1920–1940, 1940–1960, and 1960–1980 periods, and larger gains during the 1980–2000 and 2000–2010 periods. In several instances, the percentage contributions were negative. For example, during the period 1920–1940, males aged 45–85 posted negative gains, indicating that mortality for these age groups was higher in 1940 than in 1920. Aside from these exceptions, most age groups contributed to increasing life expectancy for U.S. females and males over the last century or so. The most important take away point is that the older age groups are now contributing to life expectancy improvements much more so than the younger age groups (see also Cutler and Meara 2004).

Cause of Death Comparisons

The epidemiologic transition theory, developed by Omran (1971), discusses how major causes of death shift over time. Omran identified three major stages: the ages of pestilence and famine, receding pandemics, and degenerative and man-made diseases. In the first stage, mortality is high, life expectancy is low, and individuals die primarily of acute and parasitic diseases, infections, or malnutrition. When countries modernize and develop socioeconomically, they enter the second stage and experience gains in public health and nutrition. Life expectancy at birth increases to above 50 years of age and causes of death begin to shift away from infectious and parasitic diseases to chronic disease. Third, as countries continue to advance socioeconomically, they progress to the third stage of the transition; mortality declines continue, life expectancy at birth increases to around 70 years of age, and greater proportions of deaths are caused by chronic and degenerative diseases.

Olshansky and Ault (1986) called for adding a fourth stage to Omran's original theory by demonstrating that many diseases are now concentrated at the older ages, beyond 70. Over time, the distribution of deaths progressively shifts to older and older ages (Land and Yang 2006). Rogers and Hackenberg (1987) also proposed a fourth stage, in which increasing *proportions* of deaths are due to risky behaviors (including smoking, excessive drinking, drug abuse, overeating, and inactivity) and external causes of death. Unhealthy and risky behaviors at young ages, including drug use, excessive drinking, risky driving, cigarette smoking, and unprotected sex, can lead to chronic conditions in later life—including chronic alcoholism, hepatitis, HIV/AIDS, hypertension, hypercholesterolemia, heart disease, obesity, cancer, functional limitations, and disability—that can contribute to premature death. In stage four, increasing proportions of deaths are concentrated at older ages (Lutz and Butz 2014; Olshansky and Ault 1986) and due to unhealthy behaviors (Rogers and Hackenberg 1987) that are linked to chronic and degenerative diseases, some infectious diseases, and some external causes of death, including violence. The United States today finds itself in this fourth stage of the epidemiologic transition, as the cause-of-death patterns below demonstrate.

Table 4.2 displays age-standardized mortality rates for the 15 leading causes of death in the United States in 2012. Rates for these same causes are also shown for 2002, allowing for a comparison over the last decade. In accord with the epidemiological transition theory, chronic and degenerative diseases predominate.

Table 4.2 Top 15 causes of death, United States, 2012

Rank	Cause of death	(ICD-10 codes)	Age-adjusted A. 2012	Death rate B. 2002	Percentage change over decade
1	Heart disease	(I00-I09, I11, I13, I20-I51)	170.5	244.6	–30.3%
2	Malignant neoplasms	(C00-C97)	166.5	194.3	–14.3%
3	Chronic lower respiratory diseases	(J40-J47)	41.5	43.9	–5.5%
4	Cerebrovascular diseases	(I60-I69)	36.9	57.2	–35.5%
5	Accidents (unintentional injuries)	(V01-X59, Y85-Y86)	39.1	37.1	5.4%
6	Alzheimer's disease	(G30)	23.8	20.8	14.4%
7	Diabetes mellitus	(E10-E14)	21.2	25.6	–17.2%
8	Influenza and pneumonia	(J09-J18)	14.4	23.2	–37.9%
9	Nephritis, nephrotic syndrome and nephrosis	(N00-N07, N17-N19, N25-N27)	13.1	14.4	–9.0%
10	Intentional self-harm (suicide)	(*U03, X60-X84, Y87.0)	12.6	10.9	15.6%
11	Septicemia	(A40-A41)	10.3	11.9	–13.4%
12	Chronic liver disease and cirrhosis	(K70, K73-K74)	9.9	9.4	5.3%
13	Essential hypertension and hypertensive renal disease	(I10, I12, I15)	8.2	7.1	15.5%
14	Parkinson's disease	(G20-G21)	7.0	6.0	16.7%
15	Pneumonitis due to solids and liquids	(J69)	5.1	6.2	–17.7%
	All other causes		152.7	143.3	6.6%
	All causes		732.8	855.9	–14.4%

Source: Derived from Table 9, NCHS (2014)
Notes: Negative percentages indicate mortality declines between 2002 and 2012; positive percentages indicate mortality increases over the decade

Heart disease was the number one cause of death in 2012, followed by cancer (malignant neoplasms, now a very close second), and chronic lower respiratory diseases. These top three causes contributed to 52% of all deaths in 2012, and all of them had declined between 2002 and 2012 (see the last column). In fact, between 2002 and 2012, heart disease mortality declined by 30%, a major public health and medical accomplishment. Other leading chronic and degenerative diseases that declined over the decade include cerebrovascular diseases (36% decline), diabetes (17% decline), and kidney disease (or nephritis, nephrotic syndrome, and nephrosis), which declined by 9%. But several causes of death increased over the decade, including such neurodegenerative diseases as Alzheimer's disease, which increased by 14%, and Parkinson's disease, which increased by 17%. Also in accord with epidemiologic transition theory (Rogers and Hackenberg 1987), accidental mortality

Table 4.3 Top causes of death by sex, United States, 2012

		A. Females		B. Males	
Cause of death	(ICD-10 codes)	Rank	Percent of total deaths	Rank	Percent of total deaths
Heart disease	(I00-I09, I11, I13, 120-151)	1	22.6%	1	24.5%
Malignant neoplasms	(C00-C97)	2	21.8%	2	24.0%
Cerebrovascular diseases	(I60-I69)	3	6.0%	5	4.1%
Chronic lower respiratory diseases	(J40-J47)	4	6.0%	4	5.3%
Alzheimer's disease	(G30)	5	4.6%	8	2.0%
Accidents (unintentional injuries)	(V01-X59, Y85-Y86)	6	3.8%	3	6.3%
Diabetes mellitus	(E10-E14)	7	2.8%	6	3.0%
Influenza and pneumonia	(J09-J18)	8	2.1%	9	1.9%
Nephritis, nephroticsyndrome and nephrosis	(N00-N07, N17-N19, N25-N27)	9	1.8%	10	1.8%
Septicemia	(A40-A41)	10	1.5%	12	1.3%
Essential hypertension and hypertensive renal disease	(I10, I12, I15)	11	1.4%	15	0.9%
Chronic liver disease and cirrhosis	(K70, K73-K74)	12	1.0%	11	1.8%
Parkinson's disease	(G20-G21)	13	0.8%	13	1.1%
Intentional self-harm (suicide)	(*U03, X60-X84, Y87.0)	14	0.7%	7	2.5%
Pneumonitis due to solids and liquids	(J69)	15	0.6%	16	0.8%
Assault (homicide)	(*U01-*U02, X85-Y09, Y87.1)	–	0.3%	14	1.0%
All other causes			22.4%		17.6%
All causes			100.0%		100.0%

Source: Derived from Table 12, NCHS (2014)

(including motor vehicles, falls, and drug poisonings) and chronic liver disease and cirrhosis each increased by over 5%, and suicides increased by 16%. Overall, all-cause mortality declined by 14% between 2002 and 2012.

Chronic and degenerative diseases constituted the major causes of death for each sex in the United States in 2012 (see Table 4.3). Malignant neoplasms are now the second leading cause of death for each sex, just behind heart disease. Among malignant neoplasms, lung cancer is the most common specific cause; most lung cancer deaths are due to smoking. If lung cancer (malignant neoplasms of trachea, bronchus, and lung) were listed separately from all other cancers, it would be the 3rd leading cause of death among males and the 5th leading cause among females.

Table 4.4 Age-standardized death rates per 100,000 (World standard population) by cause of death for the United States and 16 peer countries, 2009

	Neoplasms	Infectious diseases	Respiratory	All external	Transport	Assault	Assault, males only
Australia	117.0	4.9	26.3	33.1	7.2	1.2	1.7
Austria	124.1	4.2	21.1	33.7	6.7	0.6	0.6
Canada	126.0	8.1	31.2	34.7	7.1	1.8	2.7
Denmark	146.7	7.0	49.2	28.1	5.5	0.8	1.1
Finland	105.3	3.8	18.3	55.7	5.8	1.9	2.8
France	131.3	7.7	20.2	37.9	6.8	0.7	0.9
Germany	125.0	8.0	29.4	24.3	5.0	0.5	0.5
Italy	127.2	6.6	21.6	23.5	7.3	0.8	1.2
Japan	109.6	7.2	39.6	35.5	3.9	0.3	0.4
Netherlands	142.4	6.2	38.9	22.4	3.8	0.9	1.3
Norway	121.8	8.5	36.6	36.3	5.1	0.6	0.8
Portugal	121.0	13.8	45.5	28.8	8.7	0.9	1.4
Spain	120.7	7.8	36.9	21.5	5.5	0.7	0.9
Sweden	113.4	7.8	22.7	32.1	3.6	0.9	1.1
Switzerland	108.9	4.2	20.9	30.0	4.5	0.7	0.7
United Kingdom	134.2	5.5	51.3	24.8	4.0	0.3	0.4
U.S.A.	120.4	14.7	43.8	50.1	11.7	5.8	9.1

Source: World Health Organization Mortality Database (2015)

Some diseases typical of old age predominate. Alzheimer's disease is the 5th leading cause among females and the 8th leading cause among males, and Parkinson's disease is the 13th leading cause for each sex. External causes of death are also still quite important for each sex: accidents are the 6th leading cause for females and the 3rd for males; suicide is the 14th leading cause for females and the 7th for males; and homicide is the 14th leading cause for males.

As we have shown above, younger Americans fare worse than older ones when compared to their international peers—in particular, because of communicable diseases and such external causes of death as accidents and homicides, which are far higher in the United States than in the peer countries. Table 4.4 displays age-standardized death rates for different causes of death for the United States and its 16 peer countries (data provided by the WHO Mortality Database). For this group of countries, the United States has a quite favorable rate of cancer (6th lowest death rate out of 17 nations), but is well below average for respiratory disease (14th), infectious diseases (17th), and external causes (16th). Deaths due to assault and transportation accidents are especially high in the United States compared to other countries. Compared to individuals in other high income countries, U.S. individuals experience similar mortality risk per mile driven, but drive greater distances on average (Avendano and Kawachi 2014). Importantly, the U.S. death rate due to assault (homicide) is three to nineteen times higher than the other countries.

Health Behaviors and Preventable Causes of Death in the United States

The recently-published report of the National Research Council and Institute of Medicine (NRC/IOM 2013) made extensive health and mortality comparisons between the United States and 16 peer high-income countries around the world. One of their major findings was "the alarming scale of health disadvantage among children and adolescents in the United States compared with their peers in other high-income countries" (NRC/IOM 2013, p. 232). And the U.S. disadvantage is increasing: the other 16 high-income countries outpaced the U.S. in reducing their early-life mortality rates over the past 25 years (NRC/IOM 2013). Why? One reason may be the high levels of racial/ethnic and socioeconomic status inequality that characterize the United States. Much research highlights the historical and continued institutional- and individual-level discrimination faced by the African American population in the United States that results in a 4–5 year life expectancy disadvantage for African Americans compared to whites (Masters et al. 2014). The United States also has high and increasing income inequality. According to the CIA World Factbook (2013), the U.S. Gini coefficient, a measure indicating the degree of inequality in the distribution of family incomes, was 45 in 2007—closer to coefficients for developing countries such as Uganda, with a Gini of 44.4, than to those of other developed countries such as Australia, with a Gini of 30.3. It is clear that U.S. life expectancies lag behind other low fertility, high-income countries in part because of its substantial levels of racial/ethnic and socioeconomic inequality. Yet even if we include in our U.S. calculations only those Americans with a college education, high income, and health insurance, the U.S. still has lower life expectancy than our peers in other low fertility, high-income nations (NRC/IOM 2013).

Thus, we need to turn to some key behavioral factors that may be in part responsible for the lower life expectancy in the United States, and focus particularly on those behaviors that contribute to excess U.S. mortality at relatively young ages. Indeed, Schroeder (2007) identifies five major sets of factors that contribute to U.S. premature mortality and identifies health behaviors (responsible for 40% of premature deaths) as the most prominent. Mokdad et al. (2004) examined what they termed "actual" causes of death, i.e., deaths that are in many instances due to risky behaviors. They found that in the year 2000, the three most common actual causes of death were tobacco consumption, poor diet and physical inactivity, and drinking. Other important causes they identified included motor vehicle accidents, firearm fatalities, and drug use. We discuss many though not all of these behavioral factors in the next paragraphs.

Tobacco Consumption is the most preventable behavioral cause of death in the United States (Mokdad et al. 2004). Cigarette consumption increased rapidly from 1900 to 1964, the year that the landmark report of the Surgeon General was released (U.S. Department of Health, Education, and Welfare 1964), but then declined nearly as rapidly as it had increased. Between 1955 and 2013, smoking prevalence declined from 57% to 21% among men, and from 34% to 15% among women (Jamal et al.

2014; Schroeder 2007). Reductions in smoking between 1964 and 2012 have increased U.S. life expectancy by 30% (U.S. Department of Health and Human Services 2014). Smoking increases the risk of death from most causes, including circulatory diseases, cancer, respiratory diseases, and accidents. Still, a sizeable proportion of the adult population continues to smoke, resulting in approximately 480,000 premature deaths per year from causes with proven links to smoking (Jamal et al. 2014). Others suggest that the yearly mortality figure is even higher if a broader array of causes of death is considered (Carter et al. 2015). Smoking is more common among the poor, those with less education (Jamal et al. 2014), those with mental illnesses, and those with other substance abuse problems (Schroeder 2007). Smoking also compromises infant health because "smoking among pregnant women is a major contributor to premature births and infant mortality" (Schroeder 2007, p. 1223). Compared to residents of other countries, U.S. adults suffer higher mortality because of the long history of high smoking prevalence and high levels of cigarette consumption among those who smoke (Pampel 2005; Preston et al. 2010).

Diet and Inactivity is the second leading preventable cause of death in the United States (Mokdad et al. 2004). Obesity, which is influenced by both diet and inactivity, contributes to diabetes, circulatory diseases, and cancer (e.g., of the breast, colon, kidney, liver, gallbladder, and pancreas) (Lutz and Butz 2014). Over the past 50 years, obesity levels have risen as smoking rates have declined. The United States has one of the highest obesity levels in the world, and, compared to its 16 peer countries, is the only country to have 30% or greater adult obesity prevalence rates (see Table 4.5). Most peer countries have age-standardized levels of obesity in the teens: 18.3% for Austria, 16.2% for Denmark, 17.2% for Italy, 16.2% for the Netherlands, 16.6% for Sweden, and 14.9% for Switzerland. Only 4.5% of Japanese adults are obese, compared to 31.8% of American adults. Preston and Stokes (2011) have shown that the exceptionally high U.S. obesity rates reduce life expectancy at age 50 by 1.54 years among women and by 1.85 years among men. Eliminating the effects of obesity would substantially close if not eliminate the life expectancy gap between the U.S. and many of its peer countries. Indeed, obesity accounts for as much as 42% of this gap among women, and 67% of the gap among men (Preston and Stokes 2011).

Alcohol Consumption contributes to about 4% of all deaths in the United States each year (Mokdad et al. 2004). However, light to moderate alcohol consumption—defined as no more than 2 drinks for men and 1 for women per day (U.S. Dept. of Agriculture and DHHS 2010)—can reduce the risk of death through increasing HDL cholesterol and reducing the risk of heart disease, blood clotting, and inflammation. On the other hand, heavy alcohol consumption affects multiple organs and increases the risks of hypertensive heart disease; stroke; alcoholism; alcohol poisoning; chronic liver disease and cirrhosis; cancer (of the liver, female breast, mouth, esophagus, larynx and pharynx, colon, and stomach); external causes of death (automobile, recreational, and industrial accidents, suicides, and homicides); disability; and reduced immune function, productivity, and physical activity (Himes 2011). The U.S. Department of Agriculture and U.S. Department of Health and

Table 4.5 Obesity prevalence rates for selected countries by sex, 2008

Country	Obesity prevalence rates		
	Male	Female	Both Sexes
Australia	25.2	24.9	25.1
Austria	19.2	17.1	18.3
Canada	24.6	23.9	24.3
Denmark	17.1	15.4	16.2
Finland	21.0	18.0	19.9
France	16.8	14.6	15.6
Germany	23.1	19.2	21.3
Italy	19.3	14.9	17.2
Japan	5.5	3.5	4.5
Netherlands	16.1	16.1	16.2
Norway	21.6	17.9	19.8
Portugal	20.4	22.3	21.6
Spain	24.9	23.0	24.1
Sweden	18.2	15.0	16.6
Switzerland	18.3	11.6	14.9
UK	24.4	25.2	24.9
USA	30.2	33.2	31.8

Source: World Health Organization http://apps.who.int/gho/data/node.main.A900
Notes: Obesity is measured as a BMI of 30 or greater for adults aged 20 and over and rates are age-standardized

Human Services define heavy or high-risk drinking as "the consumption of more than 3 drinks on any day or more than 7 per week for women and more than 4 drinks on any day or more than 14 per week for men (2010, p. 31)." Heavy episodic drinking, or binge drinking—defined as drinking at least 4 drinks for women and at least 5 drinks for men on one occasion—can contribute to a variety of problems, including accidents, sexually transmitted diseases, and uncontrolled diabetes (Johnson et al. 2014). In 2012, 27.1% of U.S. adults reported engaging in heavy episodic drinking in the past month (Johnson et al. 2014).

Compared to peer countries, the United States has slightly lower-than-average rates of alcohol consumption. For example, per capita alcohol consumption per year for both sexes is 9.2 liters for the United States, but over 12 liters for Australia, Finland, France, and Portugal (see Table 4.6). Italy has relatively low levels of alcohol consumption, at 6.7 liters per capita. Furthermore, compared to its peer countries, the United States does not stand out with respect to rates of heavy episodic drinking, alcohol use disorders, or alcohol dependence (WHO 2014). Thus, although alcohol consumption contributes to higher mortality through a variety of pathways and is the third major preventable cause of death in the United States (Mokdad et al. 2004), drinking patterns do not appear to place U.S. adults at an additional mortality disadvantage relative to other low fertility, high-income countries.

Table 4.6 Alcohol consumption, selected countries, disaggregated by sex, 2008–2010

	Alcohol consumption per capita		
Country	Male	Female	Both Sexes
Australia	17.3	7.2	12.2
Austria	15.4	6.3	10.3
Canada	15.1	5.5	10.2
Denmark	16.1	6.9	10.9
Finland	17.5	7.3	12.3
France	17.8	7.1	12.2
Germany	16.8	7.0	11.8
Italy	9.7	3.9	6.7
Japan	10.4	4.2	7.2
Netherlands	14.0	6.0	9.9
Norway	10.8	4.7	7.7
Portugal	18.7	7.6	12.9
Spain	15.9	6.7	11.2
Sweden	12.9	5.5	9.2
Switzerland	15.2	6.4	10.7
UK	15.5	6.9	11.6
USA	13.6	4.9	9.2

Source: World Health Organization http://www.who.int/substance_abuse/publications/global_alcohol_report/msb_gsr_2014_2.pdf?ua=1
Notes: Alcohol consumption per capita is measured in liters of alcohol per year for individuals aged 15 and over during the period 2008–2010

Other Major Risky Behaviors include hazardous driving, unprotected sex, drug abuse, and dangerous use of firearms (Mokdad et al. 2004). Mokdad et al. (2004) estimated that illegal drug use contributes to about 17,000 excess deaths per year in the United States, or about 1% of all deaths. But it is difficult to distinguish legal from illegal drug use, and, moreover, deaths due to prescription drug misuse are on the rise (Miech et al. 2011). Motor vehicle accidents and violence represent a small proportion of overall deaths but are particularly high among adolescents and young adults. Indeed, in the United States in 2010, deaths from accidents, homicides, and suicides contributed to almost three-quarters of all deaths among individuals aged 15–19, and 20–24 (Heron 2013). Deaths from accidents and homicide are also much higher in the United States than in peer nations (NRC/IOM 2013).

Future Trends in U.S. Life Expectancy

Speculating on future trends in life expectancy is a precarious undertaking. Before doing so, we examine the reductions in U.S. mortality that will be necessary to achieve the highest sex-specific life expectancy levels in the world. Table 4.7

Table 4.7 Age decomposition of life expectancy differences between the United States and other countries, 2009

Ages	U.S. females compared to Japanese females	U.S. males compared to Australian males
0–1	6.0%	5.3%
1–4	0.3%	0.7%
5–14	0.6%	0.8%
15–24	2.0%	7.2%
25–34	3.0%	7.5%
35–44	5.2%	8.7%
45–54	10.5%	18.7%
55–64	15.7%	23.7%
65–74	23.5%	18.3%
75–84	21.6%	7.6%
85–94	10.4%	1.4%
95–104	1.3%	0.2%
105+	0.0%	0.0%
Diff in $\mathring{e}_0$ in years	5.38	3.57

Source: Derived from Human Mortality Database (2014)
Notes: Based on calculations in Preston et al. (2001)

compares U.S. females with Japanese females, who have the highest female life expectancy in the world, and U.S. males with Australian males, who have the highest male life expectancy in the world. The 5.4 year gap in life expectancy between U.S. and Japanese females is due primarily to higher mortality among U.S. women ages 45–94, where 82% of the difference in life expectancy lies. The 3.6 year gap in life expectancy between U.S. and Australian males is due primarily to higher mortality among U.S. men ages 35–74, where 70% of the difference lies. Thus, higher U.S. mortality in infancy, childhood, and adolescence provide relatively small albeit nontrivial contributions to the life expectancy deficits currently facing the United States. For example, compared to Australian males, U.S. males aged 0–1 contribute to 5.3%, males aged 1–4 contribute to just 0.7%, and males aged 5–14 contribute to just 0.8% of the difference in life expectancy. Overall, compared to U.S. females, U.S. males display a smaller gap with the highest-life-expectancy country, and the differences arise at younger ages, especially the young adult years.

To understand the degree to which mortality would have to fall for sex-specific life expectancy in the United States to be the highest in the world, we present several scenarios in Table 4.8 for females (Panel A) and for males (Panel B). We compare current observed U.S. life expectancies for females and males to those based on: (1) various potential reductions in mortality (10, 20, 30, and 40%) across all ages, (2) 40% reductions in mortality in specific age groups (ages 0–64, 65 and over, and 0–94), (3) the current life expectancy figures for the countries with the highest sex-specific life expectancy, and (4) the current life expectancy figures for the mix of countries with the lowest age-specific mortality rates.

Table 4.8 Scenarios for future gains in sex-specific life expectancy at birth

Life expectancies	A. Females	B. Males
U.S. observed life expectancy	81.0	76.1
Reductions at all ages		
10% reductions	82.3	77.6
20% reductions	83.8	79.2
30% reductions	85.5	81.1
40% reductions	87.5	83.3
40% reductions at specific ages		
Ages 0–64	82.8	78.8
Ages 65 and over	85.5	80.3
Ages 0–94	86.4	82.6
Top performing country[a]	86.4	79.7
Contemporary ideal[b]	86.7	80.6

Source: Derived from Human Mortality Database (2014)

[a]The top performing country in life expectancy is Japan for females and Australia for males

[b]We created the contemporary ideal by using the lowest mortality rate from any of the 17 peer countries for each age group

Currently observed U.S. female life expectancy at birth lags behind that in Japan by 5.4 years (81.0 versus 86.4), so U.S. women would require a roughly 35% reduction in each age-specific mortality rate to attain Japanese life expectancy. But rather than across-the-board reductions, it might be more reasonable to expect larger reductions at specific ages. For example, 40% reductions in age-specific mortality for each U.S. age group under 65 would produce a life expectancy of 82.8 years, a 1.8 year increase over current life expectancy, but not enough to catch up to current Japanese life expectancies. Forty percent reductions at older ages (ages 65 and above) would result in a larger increase in life expectancy (to 85.5 years), but it would still not equal current Japanese life expectancy. A 40% reduction in age-specific mortality at all ages from 0 to 94 would equal current Japanese life expectancy.

The "Contemporary Ideal" for females, which combines the lowest age-specific female mortality rates for any of the 17 peer countries, yields a life expectancy very similar to current Japanese life expectancy. It is clear from any of these scenarios that major reductions in mortality across age groups would need to occur for U.S. women to achieve the current life expectancy of their long-lived Japanese or Contemporary Ideal counterparts.

The smaller 3.6-year difference between U.S. and Australian male life expectancies could close completely with across-the-board 25% reductions in U.S. age-specific mortality, or 40% reductions in U.S. mortality for ages 0–74. Although Australia enjoys the highest male life expectancy of the 17 peer countries, it does not have the lowest mortality at every age. Combining the lowest mortality rate for any of the 17 countries at each age would yield a 0.9 year increase over Australia's life expectancy (to 80.6 years). For the U.S. to attain the life expectancy of the

Contemporary Ideal for males would require a little less than a 30% reduction in each age-specific mortality rate. While these age-specific reductions in mortality for U.S. men are not as large as those for U.S. women, they are still substantial and would require major social and public health measures on the part of the United States.

How likely is the United States to experience substantial declines in mortality and increases in life expectancy in the coming decades? In considering future trends in life expectancy, researchers often contrast optimistic and pessimistic scenarios. Optimists such as James Vaupel foresee large future gains in life expectancy, for multiple reasons: we have experienced substantial mortality declines in the past, even at very old ages; there is little evidence that the human lifespan is inherently limited; there is evidence from other species that life expectancy can be extended; and biomedical developments continue. Oeppen and Vaupel (2002) found evidence of linear increases among countries at the leading edge of life expectancy increases. They find that life expectancies have been increasing on average 2.43 years per decade for women in the country at the leading edge, and slightly more slowly, at 2.22 years per decade for men over the past 160 years (from 1840 to 2000) in the country at the leading edge. They speculate that similar gains may well continue into the future.

Pessimists (or realists) suggest that future gains in life expectancy will continue, but at a slower rate than in the past. Their reasons include the following: we have already reduced mortality from causes that are relatively easy to control (e.g., infectious and parasitic diseases as polio, smallpox, and cholera) and now must grapple with more intransigent diseases (e.g., Alzheimer's disease); we have already reduced mortality in children and young adults and therefore will need to make further reductions at older ages where life expectancy gains are not nearly as great for each life that is saved; we may be approaching a limit to the human lifespan; and there may be new emerging threats (Olshansky et al. 1990, 1997; Vallin and Meslé 2009). Continuing threats include tobacco consumption; excessive alcohol consumption; HIV/AIDS; drug abuse; poor diets, inactivity, and obesity; and violence. Emerging threats may include antibiotic-resistant pathogens, greater vulnerability to some infections (such as influenza), and new or emerging infectious diseases (e.g., Ebola) (see Olshansky et al. 1997). Additionally, Vallin and Meslé (2009) reveal that the linear trend Oeppen and Vaupel describe for the 1840–2000 period does not hold for a longer time period (1750–2005) and is sensitive to the countries examined (especially Norway and New Zealand). Thus, the pessimistic/realistic camp expects future gains in life expectancy to continue, but to average significantly less than 2.4 years per decade for women (and less than 2.2 years per decade for men). For example, Bongaarts (2006) demonstrates that after removing the effects of smoking, and already low early life mortality, we can expect life expectancy gains of about 1.5 years per decade.

For the United States, we are guardedly optimistic, but we also do not expect life expectancy gains to be as substantial as the 2.0–2.5 years per decade predicted by Oeppen and Vaupel (2002). Future increases in U.S. life expectancies may depend greatly on the lowering of smoking and obesity rates (Preston et al. 2014; Stewart et al. 2009). Relatively speaking, the international life expectancy gap may begin to close as smoking prevalence increases in other countries; indeed, smoking is now more prevalent in Japan and in several European countries than in the United States (Crimmins et al. 2011). But, of course, the desideratum is not a comparative but an absolute decrease. At 17.8% in 2013, the prevalence of smoking among U.S. adults is still quite high, and one goal of the Healthy People 2020 campaign is to reduce it to 12% or less (Jamal et al. 2014). Some smoking cessation programs have been successful and could further reduce U.S. smoking prevalence rates. Because of the lagged effects between smoking cessation and reductions in the risk of death, it will take more time for the U.S. population to fully realize gains in life expectancy. Further declines in smoking prevalence could result in substantial improvement in life expectancy now and in the future, and could improve the U.S. international ranking in life expectancy (Wang and Preston 2009).

The U.S. adult obesity prevalence rate appears to have leveled off. Still, until recently, obesity had risen rapidly; it continues to have strong effects on health, disability, functional limitations, and mortality; and it may thwart efforts to reduce mortality in the United States. High rates of childhood obesity may also challenge gains in life expectancy, as individuals who are obese longer may experience poorer health throughout their life course (Reither et al. 2011). Although challenging, advancements in medical care and changes in diet and exercise could reduce obesity.

Mortality due to external causes of death, particularly accidents, could be further reduced. One of the top public health accomplishments of the twentieth century was to increase motor vehicle safety (CDC 1999). Over time, there have been tremendous increases in the numbers of drivers, automobiles, and miles driven in the United States. Yet vehicles have become safer with driver and passenger air bags, shatter-resistant laminated safety glass in windshields, head restraints, and energy-absorbing steering columns; roadways are safer with divided highways, guardrails, more extensive and improved nighttime lighting, and breakaway sign supports; and individuals are encouraged to drive safely through laws and regulations to reduce driving while impaired (CDC 1999). Additional enhancements to cars and roads—including collision warning and avoidance systems and adaptive cruise control—could further reduce motor vehicle fatalities. The high U.S. homicide rates also have a lot of room for improvement, but may require stiffer gun control laws and better treatment and control of mental health.

The United States currently spends around $3 trillion per year on health care, around 17% of our GDP (Schroeder 2007). Peer countries spend much less on health care (approximately 12% of their GDP) yet realize lower mortality risks (Bezruchka 2012). Many Americans are uninsured or underinsured, including many immigrants, individuals living in or near poverty, and the unemployed (Schroeder 2007). The Affordable Care Act (ACA) is insuring more Americans, including those with substantial health care needs, and thereby is expected to eventually result in an improvement in health and a reduction in mortality. Between 1965 and 1975, the ten years after the introduction of Medicare and Medicaid, life expectancy increased appreciably for those 65 and above, and the black-white gap in life expectancy at birth closed considerably (to 5.4 from 7.5 years) (Sickles and Taubman 1997). Because most elderly Americans were already insured through Medicare prior to the passage of the ACA, we expect that most gains due to the Affordable Care Act will be among adults less than 65 years of age, at least in the short term.

How much future gain in life expectancy can we hope for? Although we continue to see life expectancy improvements in the United States (and in other high and low income countries), our above discussions and data show that the rate of gain has decreased dramatically since the early twentieth century. Over the next 10–20 years, we expect continued but modest gains in U.S. life expectancy at birth (e.g., on the order of 1.5–2.0 years per decade). Such assessments fall below the more optimistic estimates of Oeppen and Vaupel (2002). More dramatic improvements might accompany major breakthroughs in biomedicine, including pharmacological interventions, genetic therapies, and better understanding, prevention, and treatment of carcinogenic, cardiovascular, and neurological disease processes (Lutz and Butz 2014). But because such breakthroughs are not yet on the horizon and it may take many years to implement any such breakthroughs, there may be lagged effects between interventions and reduced mortality risks, and many improvements may only benefit specific subpopulations, including, say, people who are most socioeconomically advantaged.

Conclusion

Gains in U.S. life expectancy over the twentieth century were substantial and one of the true success stories of our society. At the same time, life expectancy in the United States lags behind other low fertility countries; simply put, the pace of improvement has been even faster in other low fertility, high-income countries. There are clear ways for the United States to improve its position in the coming decades. Our examination and discussion of U.S. mortality patterns reveals the social problems that harm our health and well-being and result in lower life expectancy than peer countries. Very high levels of social and economic inequality, continued unhealthy behaviors, continued gaps in health insurance coverage and health care access, and high levels of violence all contribute to lower life expectancy in the United States compared to peer countries. Future life expectancy gains are likely, but major public health and social policy efforts will need to be focused on the issues of inequality, health behavior, health care access, and violence that we identified in this chapter. Moreover, future life expectancy gains may be slower and smaller than previous gains because deaths in the early portion of the life course have already been substantially reduced. Nevertheless, we are optimistic that with social and economic improvements and public health efforts aimed at the key factors discussed above, the United States will continue to achieve lower mortality and higher life expectancy in the future.

Acknowledgements We thank the Eunice Kennedy Shriver National Institute of Child Health and Human Development (NICHD grant R01HD082106 and F32 HD 085599) for research support, the NICHD-funded University of Colorado Population Center (Award Number P2CHD066613) and the NICHD-funded Carolina Population Center (Award Number P2CHD050924) for administrative and computing support, and Nancy Mann for editing the manuscript. The content of this manuscript is solely the responsibility of the authors and does not necessarily represent the official views of NIH or NICHD.

References

Arias, E. (2014). United States life tables, 2010. *National Vital Statistics Reports, 63*(7), 1–62.

Avendano, M., & Kawachi, I. (2014). Why do Americans have shorter life expectancy and worse health than people in other high income countries? *Annual Review of Public Health, 35*, 307–325.

Bezruchka, S. (2012). The hurrider I go the behinder I get: The deteriorating ranking of U.S. health status. *Annual Review of Public Health, 33*, 157–173.

Bongaarts, J. (2006). How long will we live? *Population and Development Review, 32*(4), 605–628.

Carter, B. D., Abnet, C. C., Feskanich, D., Freedman, N. D., Hartge, P., Lewis, C. E., Ockene, J. K., Prentice, R. L., Speizer, F. E., Thun, M. J., & Jacobs, E. J. (2015). Smoking and mortality—Beyond established causes. *The New England Journal of Medicine, 372*, 631–640.

Centers for Disease Control. (1999). Achievements in public health, 1900–1999 motor-vehicle safety: A 20th century public health achievement. *Morbidity and Mortality Weekly Report, 48*(18), 369–374.

Central Intelligence Agency (CIA). (2013). *The world factbook 2013–2014*. Washington, DC. https://www.cia.gov/library/publications/the-world-factbook/index.html

Crimmins, E. M., Preston, S. H., & Cohen, B. (Eds.). (2011). *Explaining divergent levels of longevity in high-income countries*. Washington, DC: National Academies.

Cutler, D. M., & Meara, E. (2004). Changes in the age distribution of mortality over the twentieth century. In *Perspectives on the Economics of Aging* (pp. 333–366). Chicago: University of Chicago Press.

Heron, M. (2013). Deaths: Leading causes for 2010. *National Vital Statistics Reports, 62*(6), 1–96.

Himes, C. L. (2011). Relationships among health behaviors, health, and mortality. In R. G. Rogers & E. M. Crimmins (Eds.), *International handbook of adult mortality* (pp. 289–310). New York: Springer.

Ho, J. Y. (2013). Mortality under age 50 account for much of the fact that U.S. life expectancy lags that of other high-income countries. *Health Affairs, 32*(3), 459–467.

Human Mortality Database. (2014). University of California, Berkeley (USA), and Max Planck Institute for Demographic Research (Germany). Available at www.mortality.org. Data downloaded on 12 December, 2014.

Jamal, A., Agaku, I. T., O'Connor, E., King, B. A., Kenemer, J. B., & Neff, L. (2014). Current cigarette smoking among adults—United States, 2005–2013. *Morbidity and Mortality Weekly Report, 63*(47), 1108–1112.

Johnson, N. B., Hayes, L. D., Brown, K., Hoo, E. C., & Ethier, K. A. (2014). CDC national health report: Leading causes of morbidity and mortality and associated behavioral risk and protective factors—United States, 2006–2013. *Morbidity and Mortality Weekly Report Supplement, 63*(4), 3–27.

Land, K. C., & Yang, Y. (2006). Morbidity, disability, and mortality. In R. H. Binstock, L. K. George, S. J. Cutler, J. Hendricks, & J. H. Schulz (Eds.), *Handbook of aging and the social sciences* (6th ed., pp. 41–58). San Diego: Academic.

Lutz, W., & Butz, W. P. (Eds.). (2014). *World population and human capital in the twenty-first century*. Oxford: Oxford University Press.

MacDorman, M. F., Mathews, T. J., Mohangoo, A. D., & Zeitlin, J. (2014). International comparisons of infant mortality and related factors: United States and Europe, 2010. *National Vital Statistics Reports, 63*(5), 1–6.

Masters, R. K., Hummer, R. A., Powers, D. A., Beck, A., Lin, S., & Finch, B. K. (2014). Long-term trends in adult mortality for U.S. blacks and whites: An examination of period- and cohort-based changes. *Demography, 51*(6), 2047–2073.

Miech, R., Pampel, F., Kim, J., & Rogers, R. G. (2011). The enduring association between education and mortality: The role of widening and narrowing disparities. *American Sociological Review, 76*(6), 913–934.

Mokdad, A. H., Marks, J. S., Stroup, D. F., & Gerberding, J. L. (2004). Actual causes of death in the United States, 2000. *Journal of the American Medical Association, 291*(10), 1238–1245. doi:10.1001/jama.291.10.1238.

National Center for Health Statistics. (2014). Deaths: Final data for 2012. *National Vital Statistics Reports, 63*(9), 1–85. http://www.cdc.gov/nchs/data/nvsr/nvsr63/nvsr63_09.pdf. Accessed 28 Dec 2014.

National Research Council and Institute of Medicine. (2013). U.S. health in international perspective: Shorter lives, poorer health. In S. H. Woolf & L. Aron (Eds.), *Panel on understanding cross-national health differences among high-income countries*. Washington, DC: National Academies.

Oeppen, J., & Vaupel, J. W. (2002). Broken limits to life expectancy. *Science, 296*(5570), 1029–1031.

Olshansky, S. J., & Ault, A. B. (1986). The fourth stage of the epidemiologic transition: The age of delayed degenerative diseases. *Milbank Quarterly, 64*(3), 355–391.

Olshansky, S. J., Carnes, B. A., & Cassel, C. (1990). In search of Methuselah—Estimating the upper limits to human longevity. *Science, 250*(4981), 634–640.

Olshansky, S. J., Carnes, B. A., Rogers, R. G., & Smith, L. (1997). New and ancient threats to world health. *Population Bulletin, 52*(2), 1–52.

Omran, A. R. (1971). Epidemiologic transition—Theory of epidemiology of population change. *Milbank Memorial Fund Quarterly, 49*(4), 509–538.

Pampel, F. C. (2005). Forecasting sex differences in mortality in high income nations: The contribution of smoking. *Demographic Research, 13*, 455–484.

Population Reference Bureau. (2014). 2014 world population data sheet. Washington, DC: Population Reference Bureau.

Preston, S. H., & Stokes, A. (2011). Contribution of obesity to international differences in life expectancy. *American Journal of Public Health, 101*(11), 2137–2143.

Preston, S. H., Heuveline, P., & Guillot, M. (2001). *Demography: Measuring and modeling population processes*. Oxford: Blackwell.

Preston, S. H., Glei, D. A., & Wilmoth, J. R. (2010). A new method for estimating smoking-attributable mortality in high-income countries. *International Journal of Epidemiology, 39*(2), 430–438.

Preston, S. H., Stokes, A., Mehta, N., & Cao, B. (2014). Projecting the effect of changes in smoking and obesity on future life expectancy in the United States. *Demography, 51*, 27–49.

Reither, E. N., Olshansky, S. J., & Yang, Y. (2011). New forecasting method indicates more diseases and earlier mortality for today's younger Americans. *Health Affairs, 30*(8), 1562–1568.

Rogers, R. G., & Crimmins, E. M. (Eds.). (2011). *International handbook of adult mortality*. New York: Springer.

Rogers, R. G., & Hackenberg, R. (1987). Extending epidemiologic transition theory: A new stage. *Social Biology, 34*(3–4), 234–243.

Schroeder, S. A. (2007). We can do better—Improving the health of the American people. *New England Journal of Medicine, 357*(12), 1221–1228.

Sickles, R. C., & Taubman, P. (1997). Mortality and morbidity among adults and the elderly. In M. R. Rosenzweig & O. Stark (Eds.), *Handbook of population and family economics* (Vol. 1A, pp. 559–643). Amsterdam: Elsevier.

Stewart, S. T., Cutler, D. M., & Rosen, A. B. (2009). Forecasting the effects of obesity and smoking on U.S. life expectancy. *The New England Journal of Medicine, 361*(23), 2252–2260.

U.S. Department of Agriculture and U.S. Department of Health and Human Services. (2010). *Dietary guidelines for Americans, 2010* (7th ed.). Washington, DC: U.S. Government Printing Office.

U.S. Department of Health and Human Services. (2014). *The health consequences of smoking—50 years of progress* (A report of the Surgeon General). Atlanta: U.S. Department of Health and Human Services.

U.S. Department of Health, Education, and Welfare. (1964). *Smoking and health: Report of the advisory committee to the Surgeon General of the Public Health Service* (Public Health Service Publication No. 1103). Washington, DC: U.S. Department of Health, Education, and Welfare.

Vallin, J., & Meslé, F. (2009). The segmented trend line of highest life expectancies. *Population and Development Review, 35*(1), 159–187.

Wang, H., & Preston, S. H. (2009). Forecasting United States mortality using cohort smoking histories. *Proceedings of the National Academy of Sciences, 106*(2), 393–398.

World Health Organization. (2014). Global status report on alcohol and health 2014. Geneva: WHO Press. http://www.who.int/substance_abuse/publications/global_alcohol_report/msb_gsr_2014_2.pdf?ua=1. Accessed 17 Jan 2015.

World Health Organization. 2015. *Mortality database*. http://apps.who.int/healthinfo/statistics/mortality/whodpms/. Accessed Jan 8, 2015.

Chapter 5
The Implications of Native-Born Fertility and Other Socio-Demographic Changes for Less-Skilled U.S. Immigration

Susan K. Brown, Frank D. Bean, and James D. Bachmeier

Introduction

In the United States and in many European countries, fertility has persisted at sub-replacement levels for some time. In the United States, this has been particularly true for U.S.-born women. This low fertility represents the outgrowth of demographic processes constituting integral parts of what have come to be called the *first* and *second demographic transitions*. The first transition occurred when significant improvements in health and living conditions reduced mortality, especially infant and maternal mortality, thus enabling families to escape the necessity of large numbers of offspring to ensure the survival of enough children to meet family labor and old-age needs (Davis 1963; Lee 2003). From a strictly demographic point of view, demographers described the process as one of decreasing mortality bringing about decreasing fertility, with overall population processes settling at an equilibrium and death and birth rates reaching roughly similar levels that would maintain population size (Hawley 1982). However, nothing in the dynamics of these processes required that fertility would level off at the replacement level of 2.1 children per woman, so the postulation that overall stability would emerge when the processes had run their course proved a conceptual convenience rather than a scientific prediction (Caldwell 2004; Dyson 2010).

The second demographic transition attempts to deal with the continuing fall of fertility to below-replacement levels, with no stationary population and with notable shifts toward non-marital childbearing (Coleman 2006; Lesthaeghe 2010). Some countries show total fertility rates that barely rise above a single child per woman of

S.K. Brown (✉) • F.D. Bean
University of California, Irvine, CA, USA
e-mail: skbrown@uci.edu

J.D. Bachmeier
Temple University, Philadelphia, PA, USA

D.L. Poston, Jr. (ed.), *Low Fertility Regimes and Demographic and Societal Change*, DOI 10.1007/978-3-319-64061-7_5

childbearing age, like Taiwan (1.1), South Korea (1.2), Poland (1.2), and Portugal (1.2) (Population Reference Bureau 2014). The question of how low worldwide fertility will go remains open, although some argue that the fertility decline may now have bottomed out in Europe and in East Asia (Goldstein et al. 2009).

Theorists have proposed multiple explanations for extremely low fertility (Morgan and Taylor 2006). Those who tie population growth mainly to the economy distinguish a first from a second demographic transition only loosely, and mainly in terms of economic regimes, with modern, rich industrial economies no longer needing rapid population growth to sustain income growth but nonetheless providing incentives for childbearing so as to prevent national extinction (Caldwell 2004; Galor and Weil 2000). Demographers who emphasize culture see a more pronounced distinction, with the second demographic transition showing a shift toward self-gratification, secularization, childlessness, a disconnection between marriage and procreation, and the adoption of alternative lifestyles (van de Kaa 2001; Lesthaeghe 2010). Not all countries with low fertility display all of these characteristics, however, or, if they do, they do so in polarized ways (Lesthaeghe and Neidert 2006; Kane 2013).

A variant of this theory that focuses on gender and women's equality argues that institutional equality, as in education and career opportunities, tends to lower fertility. In countries with institutional equality but where family equality remains low, i.e. where women are expected to shoulder most of the childcare and housework, fertility may fall even further. Where men help out at home, fertility may remain closer to replacement levels (McDonald 2000).

Below replacement fertility, of course, implies overall population shrinkage, at least if little else changes. Such circumstances characterize Japan, whose overall population declined from 127.8 million in 2008 to 126.9 million by 2015 (U.S. Bureau of the Census 2015). Other countries like the United States and many European ones have staved off such an outcome through immigration to sustain population growth (Brown and Bean 2005; Goldin et al. 2011; Coleman 2006) Since this immigration comes from other countries, it diversifies the national-origin composition of the receiving populations, often along ethnoracial and religious lines. Coleman (2006: 419) has termed such compositional transformations accompanying this immigration a *third demographic transition*, arguing that the changes are to a considerable extent "without precedent, irreversible, and above all of substantial social, cultural, and political significance." Although this proposition can be debated at great length, perhaps without resolution, the implications of immigration for societies with advanced economies and low fertility warrant careful attention, even if their designation as a third-demographic transition awaits consensus.

The growth in diversity caused by immigration may be mitigated by immigrant integration. Sufficient integration is likely to reduce any destabilizing effects of socio-cultural diversity that some analysts might deem inevitable byproducts of permanent demographic transitions involving composition changes. Integration is more likely to occur under certain conditions, one of which is that immigrants fulfill a need for workers. In the United States, native workers often express concern that less-skilled immigrant workers are competing with them for jobs. In fact, research on immigration's labor-market effects finds that less-skilled immigrants do not harm the employment or wages of similar natives very much (although the immigrants do compete with each other) (Holzer 2011).

One reason for the lack of competition is that the size of the less-skilled U.S.-born younger population has declined over the past 25 years. What has brought this about? This chapter focuses on the extent to which U.S. fertility and other changes have led to a smaller less-skilled U.S.-born workforce compared with about 25 years ago, as well as on how much smaller this workforce will be over the next 15 years or so. Clearly, employers over the past 30 years have been hiring ever more unauthorized labor migrants to fill less-skilled jobs (Bean et al. 2015), but it is not clear whether this occurs because employers have little alternative because comparable U.S.-born workers are becoming scarcer, or because they choose to do so because competition keeps wages down. If there were as many or more less-skilled natives available now for work as was the case 25 years ago, it might be reasonable to think that less-skilled natives have been competing a great deal with less-skilled immigrants for jobs. Such a scenario would be consistent with less-skilled migration being driven primarily by "push" factors in other countries that propel immigrant workers into the U.S. labor market. If, on the other hand, a dearth of U.S.-persons available to do low-skilled work has emerged and is growing, this would be more consistent with the idea that migrants are "pulled" into the United States rather than "pushed" out of their home countries. If they are pulled in by work, low-skilled migrants would constitute a valuable component of the country's workforce, would generate a substantial contribution to the economy, and would present the country with considerable reason to develop successful integration policies and programs.

In addition, over the past few decades, economic inequality in the United States has widened, with the wealthiest tier of Americans reaping the largest gains from economic growth (Stiglitz 2012; Wilkinson and Pickett 2010). The bottom earnings tier increasingly consists of less-skilled unauthorized migrants. The evidence we present in this chapter suggests that the growth of less-skilled migration in the United States over the past 25 years derives from declines in the size of the less-skilled U.S.-born workforce, along with the continuing availability of less-skilled jobs in the country. The presence of less-skilled immigrants thus appears driven less by push factors in other countries, a circumstance that would imply considerable labor-market competition between immigrants and natives, than it does by the pull factor of too few U.S.-born workers available to work. Thus, if the United States is to meet its workforce needs without exacerbating inequality and spurring the creation of an unstable underclass, current (and proposed) immigration policies need to do more to foster both the legal entry of less-skilled immigrants and to integrate these workers and their families better into American society.

Factors Affecting the Declines in the Less-Skilled U.S.-Born Workforce

What are the circumstances under which the number of less-skilled jobs in the United States now substantially exceeds the number of natives available to fill them? There are four: (1) U.S. population growth has usually fallen disproportionately below economic growth; (2) gains in education have reduced the number of less-skilled U.S.-born persons; (3) sub-replacement fertility has emerged among the U.S.-born that has already lowered the relative numbers of younger U.S.-born persons; and (4) an earlier very high fertility rate has resulted in a large Baby Boom group whose aging means that the cohort of those ages 25–44 is smaller than it was in 1990. This has drastically reduced the numbers of ess-skilled *younger* U.S.-born persons. And the retirement of the Baby Boomers will further reduce the size of the entire less-skilled U.S.-born workforce over the next 15–20 years. In short, fewer less-skilled younger U.S.-born workers have been available the past 25 years, and even fewer will be available in the near future.[1]

Imbalances in Economic and Population Growth

Annual U.S. population growth rates since 1980 have rarely edged past 1%, even when both unauthorized and legal immigration are included in the totals. Since 1999, population growth has fallen below 1% per year, noticeably so since 2000. Economic growth over the overall period, however, has been substantially higher. Until the recent recession, the annual percentage change in Gross Domestic Product (GDP) has averaged more than 3% annually (U.S. Department of Commerce 2010a, b). Even including periods of recession, each decade since 1970 has averaged job growth at or well above the levels needed to absorb population growth. For example, during the 1970s, economic growth generated more than 1.9 million new jobs per year, or about 50 percent *more* than the number required to absorb *both* the Baby Boomers, then coming of age, *and* the new immigrants. During the 1980s, job growth was almost as high, about 1.8 million new jobs per year, and during the

[1] The argument has also been advanced that the unauthorized Mexican population in the country grew in size after the passage of the Immigration Reform and Control Act in 1986 because that marked the beginnings of substantially increased enforcement at the U.S./Mexico border and these build-ups had the effect of encouraging migrants *not* to return to Mexico (Massey and Pren 2012; Massey, Durand and Malone 2002). While this undoubtedly has played a role in increasing the stock of migrants in the country, it seems likely that much, if not most, of the growth derives from other sources. For one thing, these increases began before IRCA was passed. For another, research has shown that the border enforcement build-up did not become large enough to become very effective until the mid-2000s, at the earliest (Bean and Lowell 2007), and growth continued before that. For still another, most migrants had been accumulating social and economic reasons not to return to their places of origin for years. This is reflected in the fact the rural-to-urban migrants in Mexico have been slow to return to their small towns and villages even though no enforcement constraints are present to discourage them from doing so (Villarreal and Hamilton 2012).

1990s, considerably higher still, averaging more than 2.1 million jobs per year (U.S. Bureau of Labor Statistics 2011). During the 2000s, until 2008, the economy would have needed to add 1.3 million new jobs each year to keep up with population expansion, a level more than half-a-million per year below the actual level of job creation (U.S. Bureau of Labor Statistics 2012; Bean et al. 2012; Federal Reserve Bank of Atlanta 2012). In short, during most years, job expansion has outstripped the levels needed to keep up with population growth, even though statistics on population growth include allowances for both legal and unauthorized immigrants.

Educational Upgrading

Changes in education have depleted the supply of less-skilled natives. The upgrading that began early in the twentieth century with the "high school completion" movement (Goldin and Katz 2008) continued after World War II with the expansion of public higher education. Notwithstanding debates about why the rate of increase in college attendance slowed in the 1990s and 2000s only to rise recently, the fraction of the population with exposure to post-secondary schooling has steeply risen for most of the last six decades. Adults age 25 and over with *more* than a high school education now comprise nearly 60 percent of the population, up from 5.3 percent in 1950 (Ruggles et al. 2010; King et al. 2010).

The number of native-born Americans with a high school diploma or less has fallen in both relative and absolute terms. In 1950, more than 88 percent of U.S. adults (ages 18+) had never finished high school (90.6 million). By 2010, only 14.7 percent had not (34.6 million). In short, by 2010, there were 62 percent *fewer* persons in the country than in 1950 without a high school diploma or its equivalent (Ruggles et al. 2010). Strikingly, this figure is for the *entire* adult population, which includes the substantial number of poorly educated immigrants who have come here over the past three decades.[2]

[2]A related question is whether the amount of less-skilled work needing to be done has similarly shrunk. In manufacturing, the answer would be yes. Since 1970, the share of manufacturing jobs in the economy has halved, dropping from more than one in four to about one in eight. The drop-off in the share of manufacturing jobs held by persons with a high school diploma or less has been similarly precipitous (also falling from approximately one in four in 1970 to approximately one in eight today). Interestingly, during this same time, the overall number of manufacturing jobs stayed at around 21 million. But because of overall job growth, a relatively smaller *share* of less-skilled persons works today in manufacturing. Also, many of today's manufacturing jobs require at least some college. Thus, the relative demand for less-skilled workers in manufacturing has declined. However, during this same period, the share of the less-skilled workforce in service jobs has grown considerably (Freeman 2007). As a result, from 1980 until today, the number of non-manufacturing jobs held by less-skilled, younger males has held steady at roughly 3.7 to 3.8 million, or approximately 45 percent of the less-skilled, male workforce ages 25 to 44. However, because service-sector work often precludes the same opportunities or pay structure as manufacturing, native low-skilled men have increasingly left the labor force altogether (Juhn and Potter 2006). Nonparticipation in the labor force by men too young to retire more than tripled between the 1960s and 1994, and that increase was concentrated among men with low skills (Murphy and Topel 1997).

Declining Native Fertility and Cohort Change

Also important, once the Baby Boom era (the years between 1946 and 1964) ended in the mid-1960s, U.S. fertility rates sharply declined. As measured by the total fertility rate (TFR), or the average number of children a woman would be expected to have if her childbearing followed the fertility pattern shown during that year, by the mid-1970s fertility rates had dropped by about half, reaching levels below 2.1, the point at which population replacement occurs. Afterward, fertility rates inched up, hovering for years around 2.0 – 2.1 children per woman (U.S. Department of Health and Human Services 2010) before falling again to 1.7 during the recent recession. Meanwhile, the size of the Baby Boom ensured that from about 1970 until 1990, the numbers of natives ages 25–44 (with high school diplomas or less) would grow appreciably, despite rising educational levels (Fig. 5.1). The expansion of the economy, more than absorbed the increase. But by 1990, when the earliest Baby Boomers started to reach age 45, the cohort of young adults aged 25–44 started to shrink. This tendency became more pronounced through the 1990s and 2000s (Fig. 5.1). In short, ever fewer young people were available to take on the less-skilled work that was being generated by the expanding economy (Figs. 5.2 and 5.3).

Thus, for a quarter of a century, the “extra” increment of persons entering the labor market from Baby Boomers coming of age has been subsiding; now the oldest Boomers have begun to retire. Today most Boomers are aged 50–64, and the labor market is experiencing the opposite dynamic from the 1970s and 1980s. As the Baby Boomers age, the number of younger U.S.-born persons entering the labor market has plummeted (in part, as noted, because the birth rate in the native-born population dropped to 1.7 births per woman by 2010, a level about 20 percent below the replacement level [Bean et al. 2012],[3] and because the very large younger Baby Boom cohorts of natives [ages 25–44] had aged into the 45–64 category). With far fewer young U.S.-born persons in the workforce, the impending retirement of Baby Boomers will further shrink the less-skilled U.S.-born working-age population in the future, opening up jobs and creating opportunities for immigrants and for upward mobility (Alba 2009). Furthermore, retiring Boomers may sell their homes, creating vacancies which may foster spatial assimilation (Myers 2007). These are looming changes. Some of the changes whose magnitude we outline below have already occurred, and others are about to occur.

[3] Roughly, a decline of this magnitude implies that every 1000 native women of childbearing age would need to have about 400 more births per year to reproduce the native population. Over a 10-year period, this would result in about six million more births. In other words, after 10 years of current levels of childbearing, the native-born population would contain almost six million fewer persons (allowing for some deaths and emigration) than would occur if a replacement TFR of 2.1 had been attained over the period. Thus, over the past 30 years, the size of new cohorts born to native-born mothers in the United States has been shrinking. A hint of this is evident in the drop in the inter-decade native growth rate, which was 21.2 percent during the 1950s, but only 7.8 percent from 2000 to 2010 (authors’ calculations from U.S. census data). Even more dramatic, the size of the younger native-born population (ages 25–34) has been shrinking since 1980. This means that the numbers of natives available to meet societal workforce needs are now in both relative and absolute decline, on account of diminished fertility alone.

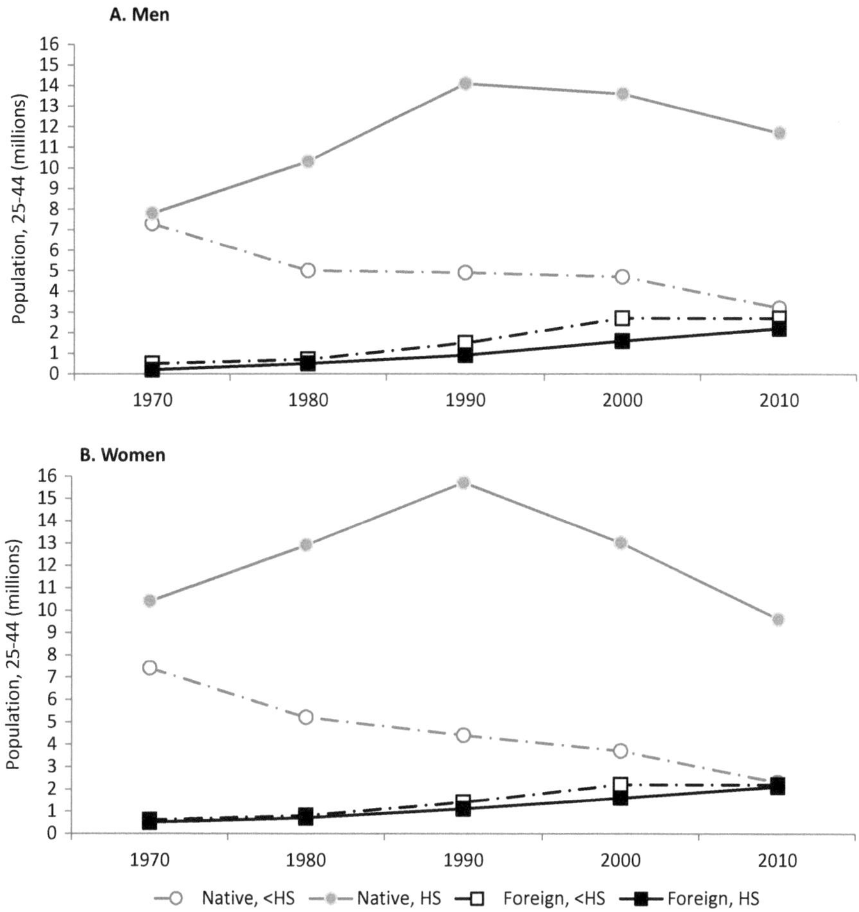

Fig. 5.1 Trends in the nativity components of the less-skilled workforce ages 25–44, by sex and educational attainment, 1970–2010. (**a**) Men. (**b**) Women. (Source: Adapted from Bean et al. (2011); Decennial U.S. Census Public-Use Micro-Data for 1970–2000 and 2010 American Community Survey Data, Ruggles et al. (2010); U.S. Bureau of the Census (2011)).

The Growth of the Working-Age Population

In assessing further the implications for immigration of the decreasing size of the native less-skilled workforce, it is useful to situate the above trends in the context of overall working-age population change over the past 40 years or so, since the end of the Baby Boom, in roughly 1964. The 1950s and 1960s, as noted above, were decades of strong economic growth and workforce expansion, as was the decade of the 1970s, although parts of that period were marred by high inflation that makes interpretation of trends difficult for those years. A recent *New York Times* article on demographic change and prospects for investment and economic growth noted a

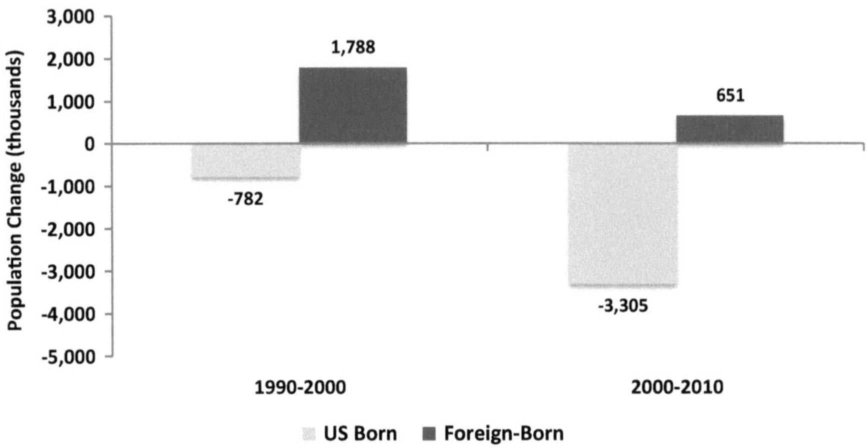

Fig. 5.2 Inter-censal change in the population of less-skilled (H.S. or less) U.S.-born and foreign-born men, Ages 25–44, 1990–2010 (Source: Adapted from Bean et al. (2011); Decennial U.S. Census Public-Use Micro-Data for 1970–2000 and 2010 American Community Survey Data, Ruggles et al. (2010))

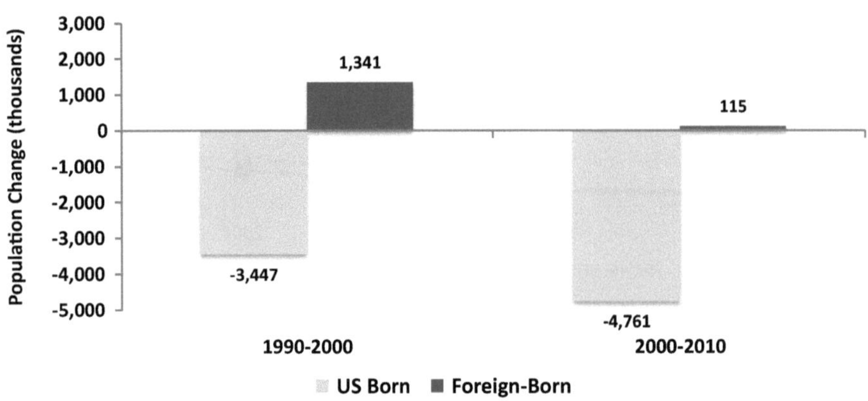

Fig. 5.3 Inter-censal change in the population of less-skilled (H.S. or less) U.S.-born and foreign-born women, ages 25–44, 1990–2010 (Source: Adapted from Bean et al. (2011); Decennial U.S. Census Public-Use Micro-Data for 1970–2000 and 2010 American Community Survey Data, Ruggles et al. (2010))

sharp drop off in the rate of expansion of the working-age population around the mid-nineteen eighties, a time when the oldest Baby Boomers (those born earliest) would have begun turning about age 40 (Sommer 2013). From 1960 to 1985, the U.S. working-age population grew at an average rate of 1.7 percent per year. But from 1986 to 2012, the growth averaged 1.1 percent per year. The main driver of this decrease is the smaller sizes of the age cohorts coming of age and entering the labor force.

Table 5.1 Annual percentage growth rates in the less-skilled working-age native-born population, by gender, selected decades and age groups, 1970–2010

Decades	Males	Females
A. Ages 25–64		
1970–2010	1.2	1.2
1970–1990	2.0	2.0
1990–2010	0.5	0.4
B. Ages 25–44		
1970–2010	–0.1	–2.0
1970–1990	1.2	0.6
1990–2010	–1.1	–2.6

Source: Calculated by the authors from the data presented in Appendix Table 5.6.

As clear-cut as this decline in growth rates would appear, when looked at in terms of the overall size of the working-age population, it does not fully reveal what it means for *less-skilled* immigration. We can see this more readily when we examine change only for the *less-skilled U.S.-born* working-age population across approximately a similar period of time. By less-skilled we mean persons with high school diplomas or less. This is the group most likely to experience competition for jobs with less-skilled immigrants. Examining trends in rates of expansion of the working-age population of *less-skilled* males and females separately from 1970 to 2010 (Table 5.1, Panel A), we see that these average about 1.2 percent per year calculated across the entire period.[4] Between only 1970 and 1990, however, they are higher (2.0 percent) than the overall expansion rate (1.2 percent) for the entire working-age population, whereas from 1990 until 2010, the rate of expansion for *less-skilled* men and women dropped to barely 0.4 percent per year, much less than the rate of 1.2 percent observed across all four decades.

These declines in the growth rates of the less-skilled populations of U.S.-born working-age men and women over the past 20 years suggest that not nearly as many less-skilled U.S.-born potential workers are now available as there were in 1990. What are the actual numbers in 1990 and 2010 and what is the size of the change? In 1990, there were 31.3 million U.S.-born males with high school diplomas or less, and 35.3 million females (compiled from data in Ruggles et al. 2010). Both of these

[4]These are calculated from Census and American Community Survey (ACS) data (Ruggles et al. 2010). Some of the numbers on schooling have been adjusted because of differences in questions across census years. In the 1990 Census long-form, the response categories for the educational attainment question do not allow us to distinguish between persons who completed less than 1 year of college and those who completed one or more years. Thus, unlike in other years, in 1990 some persons will be counted in the "some college" category even though their highest level of *completed* education is a high school diploma. In order to make counts comparable across years, it is necessary to adjust for the over-counting of the "some college" population in 1990. To do so, we calculated the proportion of the "some college" population that did not complete a full year of college in 1980 and 2000 by age, sex and nativity. We then subtracted the average of this proportion from the "some college" population in 1990 from its appropriate age, sex and nativity group and added it to the "high school" category.

Table 5.2 Components of change owing to educational upgrading and to overall population change in the U.S.-born less-skilled working-age population (Ages 25–64), by gender, 1990–2010

	Size of working-age population (000s)	
	Males	Females
1990	31,298	35,311
2010	31,026	28,276
Change	−272	−7035
% change since 1990	−0.8	−19.9
Educational-upgrading component	−3235	−9483
% change since 1990	−10.4	−26.9
Population-change component	2963	2448
% change since 1990	9.6	7.0

Source: Calculated by the authors from Census and ACS data for 1970, 1980, 1990, 2000, and 2010 (Ruggles et al. 2010)

figures declined between 1990 and 2010. For males, he drop-off was slight, only 272,000 persons, but among women it was dramatic, more than 7.0 million persons, reflecting a remarkable degree of educational upgrading among women as millions more had begun to attain levels of schooling beyond high school. In other words, considering the full age range (25–64) of U.S.-born less-skilled workers, millions fewer U.S.-born less-skilled workers, mostly women, were now available in 2010 to do less-skilled jobs than 20 years previously. Because the economy had continued to grow over the period, and because the *relative* volume of less-skilled work did not change over the period (Buera and Kaboski 2012; Blank 2009), the *absolute* number of less-skilled jobs was expanding as well, thus implying that some source of labor other than U.S.-born workers was required to fillless-skilled jobs.

The slight overall drop-off in the size of the less-skilled younger male population from 1990 to 2010 disguises large and offsetting underlying components of change. The two major factors contributing to shifts over the period are educational upgrading (the tendency for a given age range of the population to be characterized by a higher proportion with more schooling in later as opposed to earlier years) and population increase (if population growth were proportional to economic growth, more people will be needed for the labor force, all else equal). Table 5.2 shows that, for males, the number of less-skilled potential workers would have grown by nearly three million persons if growth had been proportional to overall population (the population-change component). However, because of higher educational attainment over the period, 3.2 million males "upgraded out" of the less-skilled category by 2010, meaning that the net decline in the size of the male U.S.-born less-skilled population was only slightly less in 2010 than in 1990 (272,000). But, as noted above, the economy had continued to grow and the proportion of less-skilled jobs that needed doing remained roughly the same, meaning that there were many more less-skilled jobs available than there were less-skilled U.S.-born males to fill them.

It is important to note that *overall* population change (both less- and high-skilled working-age persons) during the period was positive, even though the size of the less-skilled U.S.-born working-age population declined. The large increase in the size of the U.S.-born high-skilled population more than offset the decreases in the less-skilled U.S.-born population. The size of the component in the bottom row of Table 5.2 associated with population change (2.96 million for males and 2.45 million for females) reflects the numbers of additional male or female less-skilled potential workers respectively that would have been in the working-age population had it grown in proportion to overall population growth. In effect, since such growth roughly tracks growth in the economy, this number provides a rough estimate of the *deficit* in the number of U.S.-born less-skilled workers who were not there because this category did *not* grow at the same rate as the general population. Thus, had there been no educational upgrading among U.S.-born less-skilled males, there would have been about 3 million more U.S.-born less-skilled potential workers available. Among women, this pattern is even more pronounced. Without educational upgrading, many more U.S.-born candidates for less-skilled work (over 9 million) would have been available in 2010 than actually were so.

If we return to Table 5.1 we see that even more dramatic declines in expansion rates are evident for the *younger less-skilled* working-age population. Younger working-age persons (ages 25–44) are the ones even more likely to face competition from less-skilled immigrants because more arduous manual work tends to require younger workers, and immigrants tend to be younger. The top row of Panel D shows that the rates of change in the size of the younger less-skilled working-age population from 1970 until 2010 are actually zero or negative (0.0 and −1.0 for males and females respectively). Even more striking, from 1990 to 2010 only, the *younger* less-skilled U.S.-born male population shrank by an annualized rate of −1.2 percent. The rate of decline among females was even sharper, −2.6 percent. The two substantial reasons for these changes, in the case of both U.S.-born males and females, are educational upgrading and Baby Boomers "aging out" of the groups of younger less-skilled persons. In the analyses of 25–64 year olds discussed above, the Baby Boomers moved during the period 1970–2010 from the age category 25–44 to the age category 45–64, but they did *not* age out of the overall 25–64 age range. By 2012 they started to do so, which means that if we repeat the above components of change analyses, but now for older ages, we can obtain a window on the changes (already begun) that will further play out over the next 15–20 years for the less-skilled U.S.-born workforce.

How many fewer U.S.-born potential workers will there be in the United States in the future as a result of the aging of the Baby Boomers? The answer is shown in Table 5.3. In 1990, there were 19.0 million younger (ages 25–44) less-skilled native-born males in the country, and 20.1 million females. By 2010, the male figure had shrunk to 14.9 million, a decline of 4.1 million potential less-skilled workers. For females, the decline was more than twice as great, to 11.9 million persons, or a drop-off of 8.2 million people (see the third row of the columns in Table 5.3). In other words, between 1990 and 2010, the population of U.S.-born less-skilled persons aged 25–44 living in the United States shrank by 12.3 million (4.1 million for men plus 8.2 million for women), a very large number. This was the result of Baby Boomers entering the ages of 45–64. From now until 2030, they will continue to age

Table 5.3 Components of change owing to educational upgrading and to overall population change in the younger U.S.-born less-skilled working-age population (ages 25–44), by gender, 1990–2010

	Size of younger working-age population (000s)	
	Males	Females
1990	19,019	20,113
2010	14,931	11,906
Change	−4087	8207
% change since 1990	−21.5	−40.8
Educational-upgrading component	−872	−4338
% change since 1990	−4.6	−21.6
Population-change component	−3215	−3869
% change since 1990	−16.9	−19.2

Source: Calculated by the authors from Census and ACS data for 1970, 1980, 1990, 2000, and 2010 (Ruggles et al. 2010)

out of the working-age population altogether, portending an even larger void of U.S.-born less-skilled workers than the amount that has already occurred from 1990–2010, the magnitude of which derived more from educational upgrading than from population change.

If we turn our attention to changes in the numbers of actual workers rather than the working-age population, a similar shift appears in the actual sizes of the younger less-skilled native-born male and female workforces, that is, in the numbers of persons employed (see Table 5.4). Because of the Great Recession, these figures in 2010 may be lower than they otherwise would be, even though we roughly adjust for Great Recession effects.[5] They indicate that 1.5 million *fewer* native-born males were working in 2010 than in 1990, a drop of 6.3 percent. Again the main factors contributing to these changes were educational upgrading and overall population change. If the younger less-skilled male workforce had declined over the period at the same rate as the comparable overall population (i.e., in proportion to population change), we would expect to see only 600 thousand more U.S.-born workers in 2010 (this is the population-change component). As in the analyses of the working-age population, the biggest source of decline in all less-skilled U.S.-born workers

[5] The numbers of less-skilled U.S.-born persons working, and especially changes in those numbers as measured by differences including levels in 2010, are subject to multiple sources of influence (e.g., including the downward effects of the Great Recession on employment, declines in male labor force participation and increases in female participation stemming from long-term secular trends, as well as population dynamics and educational upgrading over the period). They are thus especially difficult to interpret with much confidence. In an effort to improve in a very rough way, we adjust the 2010 totals for the numbers of males and females working and for trends in labor force participation over the interval, seeking better to isolate the effects of educational upgrading and overall population shifts. But this adjustment is at best approximate, and in any case, problems of interpretation remain in trying to say what exactly accounts for the results involving changes in components of persons working as opposed to changes in the numbers of persons of working-age.

Table 5.4 Components of change owing to educational upgrading and to overall population change in the number of U.S.-born less-skilled employed persons (ages 25–64), by gender, 1990–2010

	Number of workers (000s)	
	Males	Females
1990	24,104	16,847
2010	22,587	13,958
Change	−1517	−2889
% change since 1990	−6.3	−17.1
Educational-upgrading component	−2124	−5196
% change since 1990	−8.8	−30.8
Population-change component	608	2307
% change since 1990	2.5	13.7

Source: Calculated by the authors from Census and ACS data for 1970, 1980, 1990, 2000, and 2010 (Ruggles et al. 2010)

Table 5.5 Components of change owing to educational upgrading and to overall population change in the number of younger U.S.-born less-skilled employed persons (ages 25–44), by gender, 1990–2010

	Number of younger workers (000s)	
	Males	Females
1990	15,524	10,034
2010	11,501	6319
Change	−4023	−4715.0
% change since 1990	−25.9	−47.0
Educational-upgrading component	−708	−2373
% change since 1990	−4.6	−23.6
Population-change component	−3315	−1342
% change since 1990	−21.4	−13.4

Source: Calculated by the authors from Census and ACS data for 1970, 1980, 1990, 2000, and 2010 (Ruggles et al. 2010)

was educational upgrading. This is even more so for women. If we focus on the younger age range (25–44), however, we see that the largest portion of the decline in workers (three-fourths) derived from population change (i.e., cohort aging) among Baby Boomers (Table 5.5). For women, the population changes and educational upgrading changes were relatively larger than for men. Cohort aging also accounted for a substantial part (one-fifth) of the decline in the size of the female workforce, dropping the size of the U.S.-born female workforce by 1.3 million persons by 2010 (Table 5.5). Similarly, educational upgrading accounted in another 2.4 million person reduction in the size of the U.S.-born female workforce. Cohort aging and educational upgrading thus were responsible for about 3.7 million fewer female workers in the younger less-skilled U.S.-born workforce in just a 20-year period and about 4.0 million fewer males.

Another way to view the magnitude of these shifts is to examine inter-decade drops in younger less-skilled native-born persons compared to interdecadal changes in younger less-skilled immigrants. Among those with less than high school diplomas, a drop occurred in the number of U.S.-born persons who would have been candidates to hold less-skilled jobs in both decades, but especially between 2000–2010. The cumulative decline across decades adds up to about 4.1 million males (Fig. 5.1). By contrast, the increase in the comparable number of foreign-born males with the same educational levels is far less, about two million. Thus, the U.S.-born male workforce of this age range and skill level shrank considerably more than the comparable immigrant workforce expanded. Note that we are talking about all less-skilled immigrants. The differences would be even more dramatic if we focused only on Mexican immigrants. A similar pattern characterizes the changes for females.

These figures illustrate a clear pattern. Because of over 20 years of higher fertility during the Baby Boom years (from 1946 until about 1969), and because of lower fertility for the past 40 years in the U.S.-born population, considerable cohort change has occurred. The aging of the Baby Boomers, along with educational upgrading, have resulted in large declines in the United States in the pool of U.S.-born persons with high school diplomas or less, especially among younger persons, the age group most needed to fill the heavy manual less-skilled jobs. In an economy that has generally continued to expand, especially during the 1990s and through 2007, this has left a sizeable void in the workforce, and immigrants, mostly from Mexico, have filled the gap. This helps to explain the growth of Mexican migration over this period (Bean et al. 2015). Mexican immigrant workers have been filling less-skilled jobs for which not enough U.S.-born less-skilled persons have been available.[6] Increasingly, most of these immigrant workers are unauthorized because they have few alternative ways to enter the country legally (Bean et al. 2015).

The figures presented and discussed in this chapter may well overstate the magnitude of the decline in the numbers of younger less-skilled U.S.-born workers since 1990. The reason is that the effects of the Great Recession have depressed employment levels in 2010. Although higher than in 2009, employment in 2010 was only beginning to recover. Thus, measures of U.S.-born decline in the numbers of less-skilled workers will be greater than they would be under conditions of full-employment recovery. However, the magnitude of the U.S.-born declines observed in the sizes of the working-age population are not so affected. These are large, running into millions of persons since 1990. Given that substantial drop-offs have not occurred in the amount of less-skilled work that has been carried out during this time, it is evident that immigrants have filled much of the void.

---

[6] One question concerns the possibility that persons with college educations could be filling jobs previously filled by those with high school diplomas or less. Since 1990, about one-third of college graduates have worked in occupations that generally have not required a college degree (Abel et al. 2014). Some research suggests that a reversal of demand for high-skilled workers has pushed educated people further down the occupational ladder and some of the less educated out of the labor force (Beaudry et al. 2013). But if the labor market were truly one big ladder and that jobs were that interchangeable, more job competition among less-skilled natives and immigrants should have emerged – and it has not.

The declines documented here would be even larger except for the presence of children of immigrants in the country. The U.S.-born children of immigrants coming to the United States before about 1975 are now adults and are included in the U.S.-born groups we have examined. The number of less-skilled U.S.-born second generation persons in 2010 exceeds the number in 1995 by about 415,000 among women and about 260,000 among men, as indicated by authors' tabulations of data from the Current Population Survey.[7] In other words, the decline in the size of the younger less-skilled U.S.-born working-age population would be at least two-thirds of a million persons *larger* were it not for prior immigration leading to offspring doing less-skilled work.

Conclusions

This chapter documents substantial declines since at least 1990 in the sizes of the less-skilled U.S.-born populations ages 25–64 and 25–44 in the United States. Specifically, our analyses show that when both males and females are considered, more than seven million *fewer* persons were in the working-age population (analyzing 25–64 year-olds), and 12.3 million fewer will be there by 2030 (analyzing 25–44 year-olds). The former translates into a deficit of U.S.-born persons available to do the country's less-skilled work in around 2010, and even a larger deficit in 2030. Not surprisingly, immigrants have been filling this void, and will continue to be needed to fill it going forward. Interestingly, the number of less-skilled immigrants coming to the country since 1970 actually falls below this figure. The availability of less-skilled work in the U.S. thus seems to constitute a major reason for unauthorized migration over the past 30 years. In regard to the future, the numbers for 25–44 year-olds, because they reflect cohort aging (i.e., the passage of younger less-skilled U.S.-born Baby Boomers into older such persons who are now starting to age out of working age altogether) provide an especially powerful indication of what is "coming down the pike" for the country insofar as the future availability of U.S.-born less-skilled workers is concerned.

The picture is stark. There will be 12 million or so fewer such persons altogether over the next 15 years or so. If unauthorized migration, especially unauthorized Mexican migration, fluctuates mostly as a result of changes in labor demand within

[7] In recent years, the magnitude of the decline of the less-skilled, younger U.S.-born workforce is understated because the increasing shares of this workforce are themselves the children of immigrants. Unlike the ACS, which distinguishes only between U.S.- and foreign-born persons, the Current Population Survey (CPS) allows one to distinguish between the first-generation (the immigrants), the second-generation (the children of the immigrants), and the third-and-later generation (the grandchildren and later of the immigrants). The tabulations here are of the second-generation population between the ages of 25–55 by level of educational attainment and gender for the years 1995 and 2010 in the CPS. While clear majorities of second-generation adults receive education beyond high school, non-trivial shares either do not complete or do not advance beyond high school and thus join what we have referred to here as the less-skilled workforce.

the United States (Hanson 2010; Holzer 2011), then it is not unreasonable to think that this demand is going to rise because of this powerful demographic reduction in supply. With the U.S.-born population increasingly obtaining college-level educations, the relative availability of less-skilled U.S.-born workers has already been seriously curtailed, and will be even more so in the future.

What are the implications of these results for possible reforms of U.S. immigration policy? They clearly imply that provision needs to be built in for low-skilled migrants as well as high-skilled migrants. For the past 30 years or so, the official population estimates of the United States have included a substantial component for international migration. The persons comprising this component include all kinds of migrants -- legal and otherwise. Even with this allowance for migration, population growth in the U.S. has not exceeded 1% per year. And except for during the recession periods, job growth has usually substantially exceeded the levels required to keep up with population growth. An important question concerns whether the United States can make do with a substantially smaller less-skilled work force. Our results in this chapter suggest no. Some claim that higher pay levels would suffice to attract more workers to the kinds of jobs less-skilled immigrants have been filling. But this overlooks the fact that many less-skilled immigrants, especially before the Great Recession, are already being paid wages above the minimum wage, often substantially so (Massey and Gentsch 2014; Massey and Sanchez R. 2010). The demographic changes causing the declines in the numbers of natives who might potentially fill less-skilled jobs are sizeable and are only now beginning to exert their full force. Their effects are not likely to be compensated for easily by other adjustments in the economy if less-skilled immigration were to disappear.

These findings imply that in a full-employment U.S. economy, shortages of less-skilled workers will develop, just as they did in the strong economy of the mid-to late-1990s. And if immigration policy fails to provide enough slots for less-skilled workers, either these shortages will be severe or unauthorized migration is likely to continue, despite any improvements in enforcement at the U.S./Mexico border. Opportunities for unauthorized entry exist through other routes. It would thus be preferable to develop policies that provide sufficient allowance for legal less-skilled migration and then seek to forestall illegal entries through other means, including employment verification systems and bilateral emigration-control mechanisms. Given the current low levels of population growth (which incorporate existing levels of immigration), it now takes slightly less than 100,000 new jobs a month to keep up with population growth. The economy, although widely viewed as still not back to full strength, has been exceeding that level for nearly 2 years now. If levels of less-skilled immigration, however, are further restricted by policy reforms, either of two alternatives are likely to develop: (1) labor shortages will emerge that will require the U.S. economy to adjust sharply, causing unforeseen hardships and disruptions (including farmer bankruptcies and restaurant closings) or (2) unauthorized migration will continue, but in the context of an even larger and more underground informal economy and even more widespread employer exploitation of workers.

Such workforce circumstances pertain to only one country, but they reflect the emergence of the conditions (low fertility and high immigration) suggested to generate a third demographic transition (Coleman 2006). Coleman implies that when growth in immigration and diversity crosses a threshold, it constitutes an actual demographic transition. He suggests that one criterion for such a threshold might be the decline of former majority populations to below 50 percent of the total, again depending on how distinctive the new populations are and how they self-identify. Another criterion would be when the electoral system ensures that migration is permanent. For now, such a transition does not appear to be universal, since some countries with aging populations have resisted large-scale immigration. But the need for immigrant labor in low-fertility countries is likely to persist, and labor migrants will ensure population diversity along some lines. Unlike the first and second demographic transitions, which might be affected by state policies but which largely seem to have occurred despite them, the consequences of a third demographic transition may be more affected by state-level action or even inaction. Social tensions resulting from migration may be alleviated by policies fostering immigrant integration and the provision of opportunities for mobility for both immigrants and citizens.

Appendix

Table 5.6 Annual percentage growth rates in the less-skilled U.S.-born working-age population, by gender, selected decades and age groups, 1970–2010

Decade	Males		Females		Both	
A. All skill levels (ages 25–64)						
1970–2010	1.2		1.1		1.2	
1970–1990		2.0		1.9		2.0
1990–2010		0.5		0.3		0.4
B. Less-skilled (ages 25–64)						
1970–2010	0.1		−0.5		−0.2	
1970–1990		2.9		0.1		0.1
1990–2010		−0.9		−1.1		−0.6
C. All skill levels (ages 25–44)						
1970–2010	1.0		0.9		0.9	
1970–1990				2.9		2.9
1990–2010				−1.1		−1.0
D. Less-skilled (ages 25–44)						
1970–2010	0.0		−1.0		−0.5	
1970–1990		1.2		0.6		0.9
1990–2010		−1.2		−2.6		−1.9

Source: Calculated by the authors from ACS and Census data (Ruggles et al. 2010)

References

Abel, Jaison R., Richard Deitz, and Yaqin Su. 2014. Are recent college graduates finding good jobs?" Current Issues in Economics and Finance 20(1). http://www.newyorkfed.org/research/current_issues/ci20-1.html. Accessed 6 July 2015.

Alba, R. (2009). *Blurring the color line: The new chance for a more integrated America*. Cambridge/London: Harvard University Press.

Bean, F. D., Brown, S. K., Bachmeier, J. D., Van Hook, J., & Leach, M. A. (2015). Unauthorized Mexican migration and the socioeconomic attainment of Mexican Americans. In J. R. Logan (Ed.), *Diversity and disparities: America enters a new century* (pp. 341–375). New York: Russell Sage Foundation Press.

Bean, F. D., Brown, S. K., Bachmeier, J. D., Gubernskaya, Z., & Smith, C. D. (2012). Luxury, necessity and anachronistic workers: Does the United States need unskilled immigrant labor? *American Behavioral Scientist, 56*, 1008–1028.

Bean, F. D., Leach, M., Brown, S. K., Bachmeier, J. D., & Hipp, J. (2011). The educational legacy of unauthorized migration: Comparisons across U.S. immigrant groups in how parent's status affects their offspring. *International Migration Review, 45*(2), 348–385.

Bean, F. D., & Lowell, B. L. (2007). Unauthorized migration. In M. Waters & R. Ueda (Eds.), *The new Americans: A guide to immigration since 1965* (pp. 70–82). Cambridge/London: Harvard University Press.

Beaudry, P., Green, D. A., & Sand, B. M. (2013). *The great reversal in the demand for skill and cognitive tasks* (National Bureau of Economic Research, Working Paper) http://www.nber.org/papers/w18901. Accessed 6 July 2015.

Blank, R. M. (2009). Economic change and the structure of opportunity for less-skilled workers. In M. Cancian & S. Danziger (Eds.), *Changing poverty, changing policies*. New York: Russell Sage Foundation.

Brown, S. K., & Bean, F. D. (2005). International migration. In D. L. Poston Jr. & M. Micklin (Eds.), *Handbook of population* (pp. 347–382). New York: Kluwer Academic Publishers.

Buera, F. J., & Kaboski, J. P. (2012). The rise of the service economy. *American Economic Review, 102*(6), 2540–2569.

Caldwell, J. C. (2004). Demographic theory: A long view. *Population and Development Review, 30*(2), 297–316.

Coleman, D. (2006). Immigration and ethnic change in low-fertility countries: A third demographic transition. *Population and Development Review, 32*(3), 401–446.

Davis, K. (1963). The theory of change and response in modern demographic history. *Population Index, 29*(4), 345–366.

Dyson, T. (2010). *Population and development: The demographic transition*. London: Zed Books.

Federal Reserve Bank of Atlanta. (2012, December 31). *Jobs calculator*. Center for Human Capital Studies. http://www.frbatlanta.org/chcs/calculator/index.cfm

Freeman, R. B. (2007). *America works: Critical thoughts on the exceptional U.S. labor market*. New York: Russell Sage Foundation.

Galor, O., & Weil, D. N. (2000). Population, technology, and growth: From Malthusian stagnation to the demographic transition and beyond. *American Economic Review, 90*(4), 806–828.

Goldin, C., & Katz, L. F. (2008). *The race between education and technology*. Cambridge/London: The Belknap Press\Harvard University Press.

Goldin, I., Cameron, G., & Balarajan, M. (2011). *Exceptional people: How migration shaped our world and will define our future*. Princeton: Princeton University Press.

Goldstein, J. R., Sobotka, T., & Jasilioniene, A. (2009). The end of lowest-low fertility? *Population and Development Review, 35*, 663–699.

Hanson, G. H. (2010). *Regulating low-skilled immigration in the United States*. Washington, DC: The American Enterprise Press.

Hawley, A. H. (1982). Ecology. In J. A. Ross (Ed.), *International encyclopedia of population* (Vol. 1, pp. 159–163). New York: Free Press.
Holzer, H. J. (2011). *Immigration policy and less-skilled workers in the United States: Reflections on future directions for reform*. Washington, DC: Migration Policy Institute.
Juhn, C., & Potter, S. (2006). Changes in labor force participation in the United States. *Journal of Economic Perspectives, 20*(3), 27–46.
Kane, J. B. (2013). A closer look at the second demographic transition in the US: Evidence of bidirectionality from a cohort perspective (1982–2006). *Population Research and Policy Review, 32*(1), 47–80.
King, M., Steven, R., Trent Alexander, J., Flood, S., Genadek, K., Schroeder, M. B., Trampe, B., & Vick, R. (2010). *Integrated public use microdata series, current population survey: Version 3.0. [Machine-readable database]*. Minneapolis: University of Minnesota.
Lee, R. (2003). The demographic transition: Three centuries of fundamental change. *Journal of Economic Perspectives, 17*(4), 167–190.
Lesthaeghe, R. (2010). The unfolding story of the second demographic transition. *Population and Development Review, 36*, 211–251.
Lesthaeghe, R., & Neidert, L. J. (2006). The second demographic transition in the United States: Exception or textbook example? *Population and Development Review, 32*, 660–698.
McDonald, P. (2000). Gender equity in theories of fertility transition. *Population and Development Review, 26*(3), 427–439.
Massey, D. S., & Gentsch, K. (2014). Undocumented migration and the wages of Mexican immigrants. *International Migration Review, 48*(2), 482–499.
Massey, D. S., & Pren, K. A. (2012). Origins of the new Latino underclass. *Race and Social Problems, 4*(1), 5–17.
Massey, D. S., & Sánchez R, M. (2010). *Brokered boundaries: Creating immigrant identity in anti-immigrant times*. New York: Russell Sage Foundation.
Morgan, S. P., & Taylor, M. G. (2006). Low fertility at the turn of the twenty-first century. *Annual Review of Sociology, 32*, 375–399.
Murphy, K. M., & Topel, R. (1997). Unemployment and nonemployment. *The American Economic Review, 87*(12), 295–300.
Myers, D. (2007). *Immigrants and boomers: Forging a new social contract for the future of America*. New York: Russell Sage Foundation.
Population Reference Bureau. (2014). *World data sheet 2014*. Washington, DC: Population Reference Bureau.
Ruggles, S., Trent Alexander, J., Genadek. K., Goeken, R., Schroeder, M. B., & Sobek, M. (2010). *Integrated public use microdata series: Version 5.0* [Machine-readable database]. Minneapolis: University of Minnesota.
Sommer, J. (2013, May 5). Dow 15,000, and the big disconnect. *The New York Times*, p. 6.
Stiglitz, J. E. (2012). *The price of inequality: How Today's divided society endangers our future*. New York: W.W. Norton and Company.
U.S. Bureau of Labor Statistics. (2011). *Current population survey*. Washington, DC: U.S. Government Printing Office. Retrieved from http://www.bls.gov/cps/#data
U.S. Bureau of Labor Statistics. (2012). *B-1. Employees on Nonfarm Payrolls by Major Industry Sector, 1962 to Date*. Washington, DC: Establishment Data, Historical Employment. Accessed on-line at ftp://ftp.bls.gov/pub/suppl/empsit.ceseeb1.txt
U.S. Bureau of the Census. (2015). International programs, country rank. Washington, DC. http://www.census.gov/population/international/data/countryrank/rank.php
U.S. Bureau of the Census. (2011). American community survey 5-year estimates, 2007–2011, Table B15001. http://factfinder2.census.gov. 14 May, 2013.
U.S. Department of Commerce. (2010a). *Gross domestic product*. Retrieved from http://www.bea.gov/national/index.htm#gdp
U.S. Department of Commerce. (2010b). *Population estimates*. Retrieved from http://www.census.gov/popest/data/historical/index.html

U.S. Department of Health and Human Services. (2010). Centers for Disease Control and Prevention. National Center for Health Statistics. Vital Stats. http://www.cdc.gov/nchs/vitalstats.htm and http://www.cdc.gov/nchs/data/statab/natfinal2003.annvoll_07.pdf. 26 January, 2012.

van de Kaa, D. J. (2001). Postmodern fertility preferences: From changing value orientation to new behavior. *Population and Development Review*, 27(Supplement: Global Fertility Transition), 290–331.

Villarreal, A., & Hamilton, E. R. (2012). Rush to the border? Market liberalization and urban- and rural-origin internal migration in Mexico. *Social Science Research, 41*, 1275–1291.

Wilkinson, R. G., & Pickett, K. (2010). *The spirit level: Why equality is better for everyone*. New York: Viking Press.

Part II
Structural Change

Chapter 6
Issues of Aging and Age Dependency in Post-industrial Societies

Samsik Lee

Introduction

The demographic transition has been underway in the Western world for the last two centuries. Prior to the onset of industrialization, high rates of mortality and fertility characterized all the countries of the world. The transition involved the death and birth rates moving from high levels to low levels. The European countries first went through the transition, and later the other countries.

However, when the Western and many Asian countries reached the final stage, Stage 4, in the transition that was characterized by low birth rates and low death rates, the transition was expected to end. But the fertility rates in many countries continued to fall below their respective death rates, and this became known as the second demographic transition. Demographers have theorized about its mechanisms in a series of different models such as the new home economics model of fertility (Namboodiri and Luying 1997), the theory of demographic change and response (Davis 1963), the wealth-flows theory of fertility (Caldwell 1976), the relative income hypothesis (Easterlin 1987), the socio-economic theory of fertility (Easterlin 1983), and the ideational theory of fertility change (Preston 1987).

It is inevitable that the demographic regime of low mortality-low fertility will lead to population aging. This phenomenon is a product of industrialization and economic growth, and may in turn, threaten economic growth. Given this situation of population aging, we ask in this chapter how best to respond. What are the ways societies may respond and react to the aging of the population?

S. Lee (✉)
Department of Policy Science and Institute for Population and Aged Society, Hanyang University, Seoul, South Korea
e-mail: lss2323@hanyang.ac.kr

D.L. Poston, Jr. (ed.), *Low Fertility Regimes and Demographic and Societal Change*, DOI 10.1007/978-3-319-64061-7_6

Industrialization, Economic Growth and Population Growth

Populations grew rapidly in the course of the transition from a traditional society centered on agriculture to an industrial society. The demographic changes resulted from industrialization and the economic growth which reduced mortality via increased food and subsistence, improved hygiene, increased medical technology and medicines, improved nutrition, and change in lifestyles. Fertility declines followed the mortality declines, although there was a time-lag and it varied from country to country. Poston provides more detail about the classic model of demographic transition and its stages in the first chapter of this volume.

In Europe, France was one of the first countries to experience a fertility decline, starting around 1830. Other European countries also started to experience fertility declines during the First World War or immediately after the Great Depression in 1929. Around this time, many European countries adopted pro-natalist policies, which prohibited contraception and induced abortion, although in some countries these policies were not very effective.

Demographic transition theory is based mainly on the experiences of the more developed countries, although it has also characterized many of the so-called less developed countries. For instance, the Republic of Korea is now in the final stage of the transition, with very low fertility. Some countries in Western Asia and sub-Saharan Africa are still in the early stages of the transition.

In many countries, fertility has fallen to very low levels (see Table 6.1 and Fig. 6.1). This has led some demographers to consider a second demographic transition that follows the first, when fertility continues to decline, well below replacement levels. This inevitably leads to population decline and population aging. According to van de Kaa (1987), the second demographic transition was influenced in part by increases in individuals' interests in their rights and self-fulfillment.

The timing of the fertility decline varies from one country to another (Reher 2004). Most of the OECD countries experienced fertility declines to below replacement levels in the latter part of the twentieth century (see Table 6.1). The rates in four countries fell below replacement levels in the late 1960s, namely, Sweden in 1968, and Finland, Denmark and Luxembourg in 1969. The fertility rates in 15 more countries dropped below replacement levels starting in 1970, as follows: Germany in 1970; Switzerland in 1971; the United States, Canada and Austria in 1972; the United Kingdom, Netherlands and Belgium in 1973; Japan in 1974; France and Norway in 1975; Australia in 1976; Italy in 1977; and Hungary and New Zealand in 1978. See Table 6.1 for the patterns of the other OECD countries.

In the Republic of Korea, the fertility rate dropped dramatically from 6.0 in 1960 to 2.06 in 1983 and to 1.08 in 2005. This was one of the most dramatic fertility declines in demographic history. It was due to increased family planning under the country's anti-natalist policy, accompanied by socio-economic development. Koreans were stimulated and encouraged to have smaller families. The fertility decline in Korea from 1997 to 2005 was also accounted for by the financial crises in 1997 and the global financial crisis after the turn of the century.

Table 6.1 Fertility rates in 1960 and 2011, the year the fertility rate first dropped below replacement level, and the year the fertility rate reached its lowest level: OECD countries

		Year fertility first dropped below replacement		Year fertility reached its lowest level		
	1960	Year	TFR	Year	TFR	2011
Australia	3.45	1976	2.01	2001	1.73	1.88
Austria	2.69	1972	2.08	2001	1.33	1.43
Belgium	2.54	1973	1.95	1985	1.51	1.87
Canada	3.90	1792	2.02	2000	1.49	1.61
Chile		1999	2.08	2006	1.83	1.91
Czech Republic	2.11	1981	2.02	1999	1.13	1.43
Denmark	2.54	1969	2.00	1983	1.38	1.76
Estonia	2.02(1980)	1990	2.05	1998	1.28	1.52
Finland	2.71	1969	1.94	1973	1.50	1.83
France	2.74	1975	1.93	1993	1.66	2.00
Germany	2.37	1970	2.03	1994	1.24	1.36
Greece	2.23	1982	2.03	1999	1.24	1.42
Hungary	2.02	1978	2.08	2011	1.24	1.24
Iceland	4.27	1997	2.04	2002	1.93	2.02
Ireland	3.76	1989	2.08	1995	1.85	2.04
Israel				2005	2.84	3.00
Italy	2.41	1977	1.97	1995	1.19	1.42
Japan	2.00	1974	2.05	2005	1.26	1.39
Korea	6.00	1983	2.06	2005	1.08	1.24
Luxembourg	2.28	1969	2.02	1985	1.38	1.51
Mexico	7.25	2009	2.08	2011	2.03	2.03
Netherlands	3.12	1973	1.90	1983	1.47	1.76
New Zealand	4.24	1978	2.07	1998	1.89	2.06
Norway	2.91	1975	1.98	1983	1.66	1.88
Poland	2.98	1989	2.07	2003	1.22	1.30
Portugal	3.10	1982	2.07	2009	1.32	1.36
Slovak Republic	3.07	1989	2.08	2002	1.19	1.45
Slovenia	2.18	1981	1.96	2003	1.20	1.56
Spain	2.86	1981	2.04	1998	1.16	1.36
Sweden	2.20	1968	2.07	1999	1.50	1.90
Switzerland	2.44	1971	2.04	2001	1.38	1.52
Turkey	6.40	2009	2.07	2011	2.02	2.02
United Kingdom	2.72	1973	2.04	2001	1.63	1.97
United States	3.65	1972	2.01	1976	1.74	1.89

Source of data: http://www.mhlw.go.jp/

Note: In the case of Japan, the fertility rate was below replacement for a while during 1957 ~ 1964. In the case of Iceland, the TFR was below replacement during 1984–1987 but thereafter increased slightly

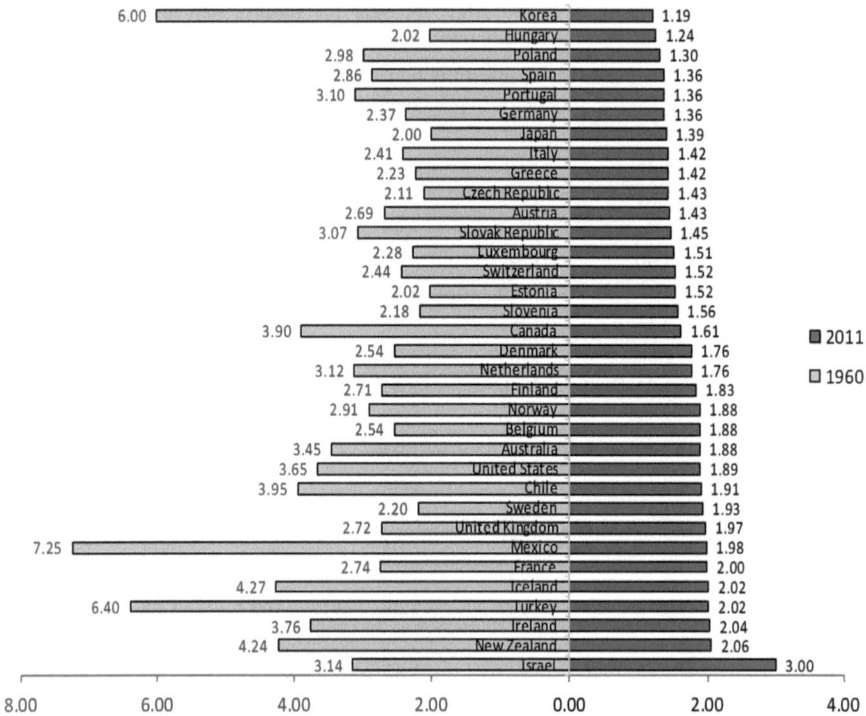

Fig. 6.1 Total fertility rates in 1960 and 2011: OECD countries

Having reviewed the dynamics of fertility change and below replacement levels within the context of the first and second demographic transitions, we turn next to a more detailed consideration of population aging. This is one of the major features of low fertility societies.

Population Aging

A common measure of population aging is the percentage of persons in the population aged 65 years and older. Population aging is a consequence of fertility decline and the prolonging of human life. Demographers have shown that fertility decline has a more important and significant effect on aging than does mortality decline. As an example, in the Republic of Korea, fertility decline has been shown to account for over two-thirds of the change in the level of population aging, and mortality decline, just over one-third (Lee et al. 2004).

Although population aging is becoming more and more a significant feature of a country's demographic structure, its prevalence varies from country to country, owing to the speed and duration of fertility decline, the extent of mortality improvement, and the current age structure formed by the present generation. For most of the countries in the developed world, which were the first to experience the second demographic transition, population aging is well underway.

According to the United Nations (2015), the percentage of the elderly to the total population in the developed world will likely increase from 17.5% in 2015, to 25.8% in 2050, and then to 28.7% in 2100 (see Table 6.2). In the less developed countries, the percentage elderly is projected to increase from 6.3% in 2015 to 14.0% in 2050, and then to 21.0% in 2100.

In 2015, population aging was the highest in Western Europe (19.8%), followed by Southern Europe (19.4%), Northern Europe (18.0%), Northern America (14.8%), Eastern Europe (14.4%), Oceania (11.9%), East Asia (10.9%), and Africa (3.5%). As of 2050, the level of population aging is projected to be the highest in Southern Europe (32.7%), followed by Western Europe (28.4%), Eastern Asia (25.2%), Northern Europe (24.3%), Northern America (21.8%), Eastern Europe (23.3%), Latin America & the Caribbean (19.3%), and Oceania (17.9%). By 2100, the percentage of elders in the population is projected to be the highest in Southern Europe (32.9%), followed by Western Europe (31.4%), Australia and New Zealand (30.1%), Northern Europe (29.1%), East Asia (29.1%), Northern America (27.0%), and Eastern Europe (24.1%) (see Table 6.2 and Fig. 6.2).

In countries already experiencing the second demographic transition, the population will age rapidly within three or four decades because the working-age population will be decreasing and will not be replaced by equal numbers of younger persons. Moreover, the numbers of persons born during the baby-boom years will be starting to join the ranks of the elders and will be living longer than the previous generations. We look now at the actual levels of population aging in countries now in the midst of the second demographic transition.

According to UN (2015) data and projections (see Table 6.2), the percentage level of population aging in 2015 is the highest in Japan (26.4%), followed by Sweden (20.0%), Italy (21.7%), Germany (21.4%), France (18.7%), Spain (18.3%), the United Kingdom (18.1%), Canada (16.0%), Australia (15.0%), the USA (14.7%), the Russian Federation (13.2%), the Republic of Korea (13.0%), China (9.5%) and India (6.3%). In 2050, the percentage of elders is projected to still be the highest in Japan (36.5%), followed by the Republic of Korea (34.9%), Spain (34.5%), Italy (33.0%), Germany (32.7%), France (25.5%), the United Kingdom (24.7%), Canada (24.7%), China (23.9%), Sweden (22.8%), the USA (21.4%), Australia (22.0%), the Russian Federation (20.5%), and India (14.0%).

By 2100, the UN projections indicate that the Republic of Korea will have overtaken Japan as the "oldest" country in the world, with an elderly percentage of 37.0%, followed by Japan at 35.7%. The countries following Japan are projected to be Germany (34.2%), Spain (33.3%), Italy (32.9%), France (30.0%), Australia (29.9%), the United Kingdom (29.6%), Canada (29.5%), China (28.2%), Sweden (28.0%), the USA (26.7%), the Russian Federation (21.7%), and India (21.0%) (see Fig. 6.3).

Another issue in any discussion of population is age dependency. This refers to the ratio of the number of young persons (0–14 years of age) and old persons (ages

Table 6.2 Percentage elderly, the world, major regions, and OECD countries, 1950–2100, and rates of change from 1950–2000, 2000–2050, and 2050–2100

	1950	2000	2015	2050	2100	1950 ~ 2000	2000 ~ 2050	2050 ~ 2100
WORLD	5.1	6.9	8.2	15.6	21.9	1.8	8.7	6.3
More developed regions	7.7	14.3	17.5	25.8	28.7	6.6	11.5	2.9
Less developed regions	3.8	5.1	6.3	14.0	21.0	1.3	8.9	7.0
Africa	3.2	3.3	3.5	5.9	14.0	0.1	2.5	8.2
Asia	4.1	5.8	7.5	17.4	26.0	1.8	11.6	8.5
Eastern Asia	4.4	7.8	10.9	25.2	29.1	3.3	17.5	3.8
China	4.5	6.9	9.5	23.9	28.2	2.4	17.1	4.3
Japan	4.9	17.2	26.4	36.5	35.7	12.2	19.4	−0.9
Republic of Korea	2.9	7.3	13.0	34.9	37.0	4.5	27.5	2.1
Southern Asia								
India	3.1	4.4	6.3	14.0	21.0	1.2	9.6	7.0
EUROPE	8.0	14.7	17.3	26.9	29.0	6.8	12.2	2.1
Eastern Europe	5.9	12.9	14.4	23.3	24.1	7.0	10.4	0.7
Russian Federation	4.8	12.4	13.2	20.5	21.7	7.6	8.1	1.2
Northern Europe	10.4	15.5	18.0	24.3	29.1	5.1	8.8	4.8
Sweden	10.2	17.3	20.0	22.8	28.0	7.1	5.5	5.2
United Kingdom	10.8	15.8	18.1	24.7	29.6	5.0	8.9	4.9
Southern Europe	7.5	16.5	19.4	32.7	32.9	9.0	16.3	0.2
Italy	8.1	18.3	21.7	33.0	32.9	10.2	14.8	−0.1
Spain	7.2	16.9	18.3	34.5	33.3	9.6	17.7	−1.3
Western Europe	10.1	15.9	19.8	28.4	31.4	5.9	12.4	3.0
France	11.4	16.0	18.7	25.5	30.0	4.6	9.4	4.5
Germany	9.6	16.3	21.4	32.7	34.2	6.8	16.4	1.5
Latin America & the Caribbean	3.5	5.7	7.6	19.3	30.5	2.2	13.6	11.2
Northern America	8.2	12.4	14.8	21.8	27.0	4.2	9.4	5.2
Canada	7.7	12.5	16.0	24.7	29.5	4.9	12.2	4.8
USA	8.3	12.4	14.7	21.4	26.7	4.1	9.1	5.3
Oceania	7.4	9.9	11.9	17.9	25.7	2.5	8.0	7.8
Australia	8.2	12.4	15.0	22.0	29.9	4.2	9.6	7.9

Source: United Nations Population Division, Department of Economic and Social Affairs, World Population Prospects: The 2015 Revision, 2015

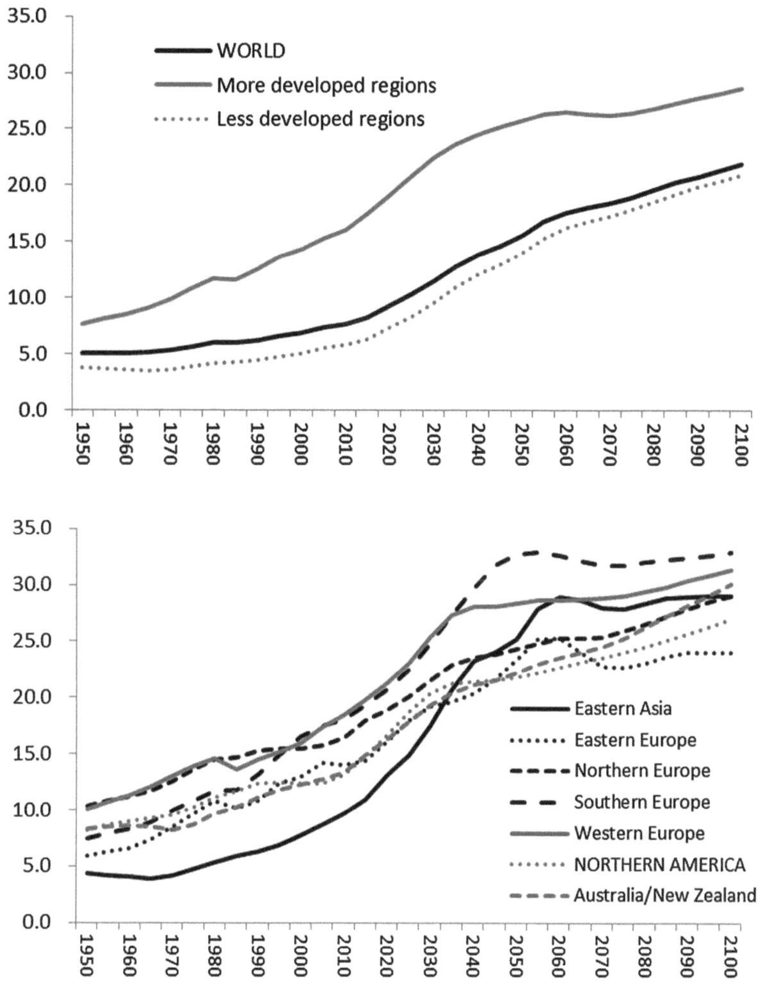

Source: United Nations Population Division, Department of Economic and Social Affairs, World Population Prospects: The 2015 Revision.

Fig. 6.2 Percentage elderly in the world and major regions, 1950–2100 (Source: United Nations Population Division, Department of Economic and Social Affairs, *World Population Prospects: The 2015 Revision*)

65 and older) per 100 persons in the producing ages (15–64). Age dependency is usually separated into youth dependency (young persons per 100 producers) and aged dependency (old persons per 100 producers). The age dependency ratio is a sum of the youth dependency ratio and the old dependency ratio. The ratios represent the burden experienced by the working age population to support the young members and the old members of the population. The continuation of low fertility will eventually result in fewer members in the working age population and increased numbers of elders.

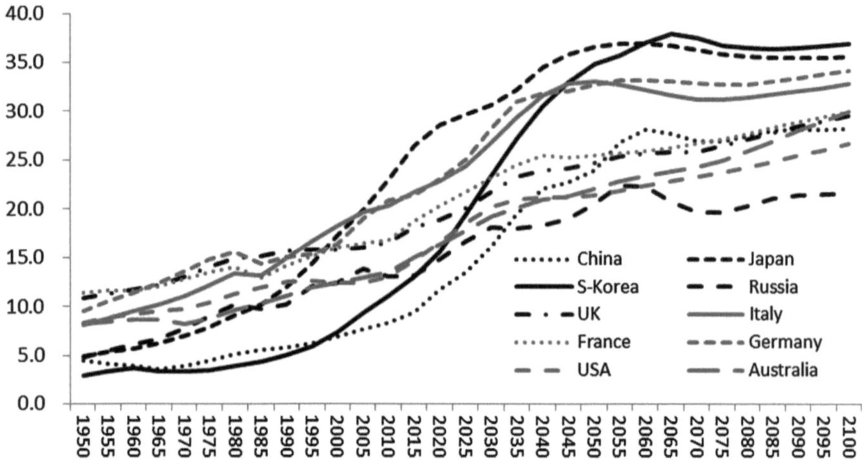

Source: United Nations Population Division, Department of Economic and Social Affairs, World Population Prospects: The 2015 Revision, 2015.

Fig. 6.3 Proportion of the elderly to total population for selected countries (Source: United Nations Population Division, Department of Economic and Social Affairs, World Population Prospects: The 2015 Revision, 2015)

Changes in old age dependency occur along with increases in overall aging, and the ratio changes along with the speed of population aging. For the World as a whole, the ratio of elders per 100 producers in 1950 was 8.4; it increased to 12.5 by 2015, and is projected to be 24.7 in 2050 and 36.4 in 2011 (United Nations 2015). Focusing only on the less developed countries, the old dependency ratio was 9.6 in 2015, and is projected to be 21.9 in 2050 and 34.5 in 2100. In contrast, the values for respective ratios for the developed countries are 26.4 in 2015, 44.4 in 2050, and 51.5 in 2100 (see Fig. 6.4).

We show in Fig. 6.5 that in 2015, the old age dependency ratio is reported to be the highest for Western Europe at 30.5, followed by Southern Europe (29.4), Northern Europe (28.0), Northern America (22.4), Eastern Europe (20.6), Oceania (18.4), Eastern Asia (15.3), Asia as a whole (11.0), and Africa (6.2). By 2050, Southern Europe is projected to have the highest ratio, 61.1, followed by Western Europe (50.1), Eastern Asia (41.8), Northern Europe (41.3), Eastern Europe (38.5), Northern America (36.2), Oceania (29.0), Asia as a whole (27.0), and Africa (9.5). By 2100, the projected ratio value will be the highest in Southern Europe (62.2), followed by Western Europe (58.5), Northern America (52.6), Eastern Asia (52.0), Northern Europe (47.8), Asia as a whole (44.4), Oceania (44.3), Eastern Europe (40.4), and Africa (21.8).

Regarding the individual countries in the year of 2100, we show in Table 6.3 and Fig. 6.6 that the projected old age dependency ratio will be the highest in the Republic of Korea (74.4), followed by Japan (70.2), Germany (65.3), Spain (63.0),

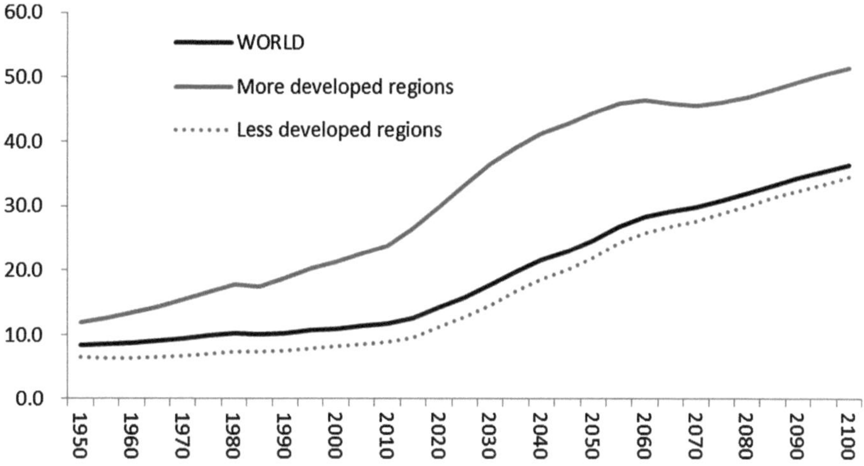

Source: United Nations Population Division, Department of Economic and Social Affairs, World Population Prospects: The 2015 Revision, 2015.

Fig. 6.4 Old dependency ratios for the world, 1950 to 2100 (Source: United Nations Population Division, Department of Economic and Social Affairs, World Population Prospects: The 2015 Revision, 2015)

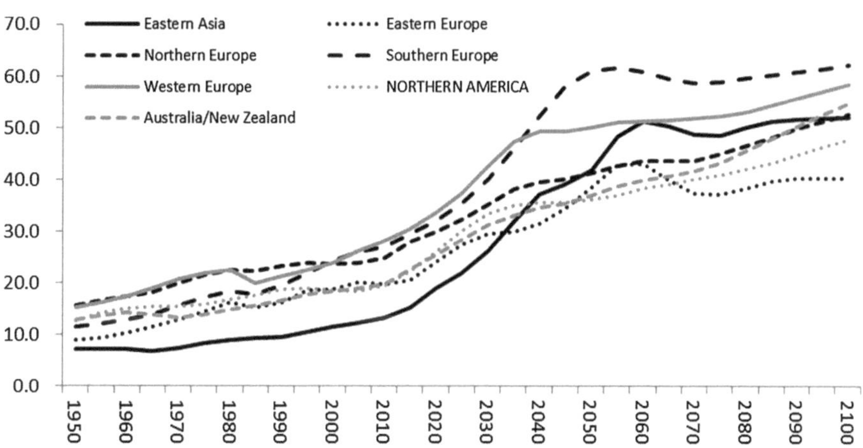

Source: United Nations Population Division, Department of Economic and Social Affairs, World Population Prospects: The 2015 Revision, 2015.

Fig. 6.5 Old dependency ratios, selected regions, 1950 to 2100 (Source: United Nations Population Division, Department of Economic and Social Affairs, World Population Prospects: The 2015 Revision, 2015)

Table 6.3 Old age dependency ratios: the world, major regions, and OECD countries, 1950–2100, and rates of change from 1950–2000, 2000–2050, and 2050–2100

	1950	2000	2015	2050	2100	1950 ~ 2000	2000 ~ 2050	2050 ~ 2100
WORLD	8.4	11.0	12.5	24.7	36.4	2.6	13.8	11.6
More developed regions	11.9	21.2	26.4	44.4	51.5	9.4	23.2	7.1
Less developed regions	6.6	8.2	9.6	21.9	34.5	1.7	13.6	12.6
Africa	5.7	6.1	6.2	9.5	21.8	0.4	3.3	12.4
Asia	6.8	9.1	11.0	27.0	44.4	2.3	17.9	17.4
Eastern Asia	7.3	11.5	15.3	41.8	52.0	4.2	30.4	10.1
China	7.3	10.2	13.1	39.0	49.8	2.9	28.8	10.8
Japan	8.3	25.2	43.6	71.8	70.2	16.9	46.6	−1.5
Republic of Korea	5.2	10.2	17.9	65.7	74.4	5.0	55.4	8.7
India	5.3	7.1	9.6	21.9	34.5	1.8	14.8	12.6
EUROPE	12.1	21.8	25.9	46.6	52.0	9.7	24.8	5.5
Eastern Europe	9.1	18.8	20.6	38.5	40.4	9.7	19.7	1.9
Russian Federation	7.4	17.9	18.8	32.8	35.3	10.5	14.9	2.5
Northern Europe	15.7	23.7	28.0	41.3	52.6	8.0	17.6	11.3
Sweden	15.3	26.8	31.8	38.5	50.3	11.5	11.7	11.8
United Kingdom	16.2	24.2	28.1	42.1	53.8	8.0	17.9	11.7
Southern Europe	11.6	24.3	29.4	61.1	62.2	12.8	36.8	1.1
Italy	12.4	27.1	33.8	62.3	62.4	14.7	35.2	0.1
Spain	10.9	24.7	27.6	66.9	63.0	13.8	42.2	−3.9
Western Europe	15.2	23.8	30.5	50.1	58.5	8.7	26.3	8.3
France	17.3	24.6	29.6	44.2	55.3	7.3	19.6	11.1
Germany	14.3	24.0	32.7	59.9	65.3	9.7	35.9	5.5
Latin America and the Caribbean	6.2	9.1	11.5	30.5	55.5	2.9	21.4	25.0
Northern America	12.7	18.6	22.4	36.2	47.8	5.9	17.5	11.7
Canada	12.2	18.4	23.7	42.0	53.4	6.1	23.6	11.4
United States of America	12.8	18.7	22.2	35.5	47.2	5.9	16.9	11.7
Oceania	11.7	15.3	18.4	29.0	44.3	3.6	13.7	15.3
Australia	12.5	18.5	22.7	36.7	54.5	6.0	18.2	17.8

Source: United Nations Population Division, Department of Economic and Social Affairs, World Population Prospects: The 2015 Revision, 2015

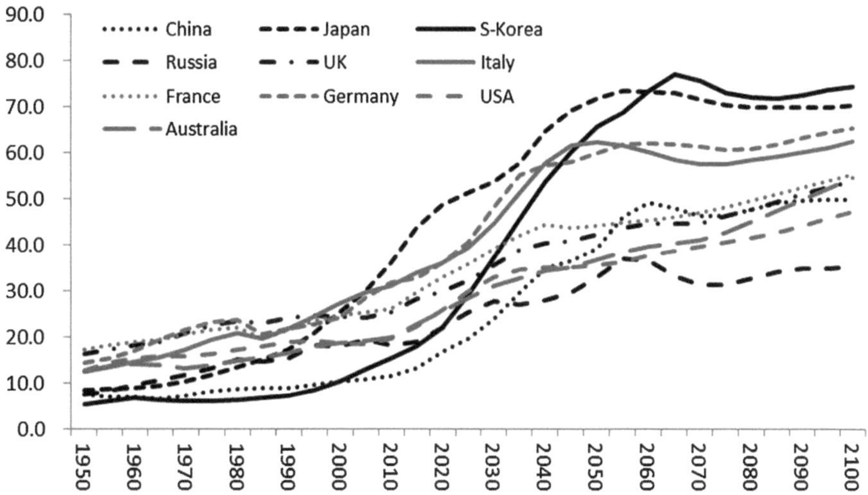

Source: United Nations Population Division, Department of Economic and Social Affairs, World Population Prospects: The 2015 Revision, 2015.

Fig. 6.6 Old dependency ratios, selected countries, 1950–2100 (Source: United Nations Population Division, Department of Economic and Social Affairs, World Population Prospects: The 2015 Revision, 2015)

Italy (62.4), France (55.3), Australia (54.5), the United Kingdom (53.8), Sweden (50.3), China (49.8), the USA (47.2), Russia (35.3), and India (34.5). In other words, in 2100 in Korea, there are projected to be almost 75 elders for every 100 persons in the producing ages of 15–64. This is a dramatic increase compared to the value of the ratio in the Republic of Korea in 1950 of 5.2 elders per 100 producers.

In the initial years when a population is starting to experience population aging, when both the youth dependency ratio and the old age dependency ratio are low, the numbers in the working ages are typically high. This bonus of persons in the working ages is known as the demographic dividend. During these years, there is an abundant working age population with few young and old dependents for them to support, resulting in rapid economic growth. However, with a continuation of low fertility, the dividend no longer remains, resulting in reduced economic growth.

It is thus of considerable interest to ascertain approximately when the total dependency ratio attains its absolute minimum value. Then, with the aging of the population, the ratio will begin to increase, and, accordingly, the burden on the working age population to provide for the young dependents and the old dependents will increase. We show in Table 6.4 for the World, for its major regions and for selected countries the year when the total dependency ratio was at its lowest value. We have also plotted in Fig. 6.7 the values of the total dependency ratio and the youth and aged dependency ratios for every 5 years from 1950 to 2100.

Table 6.4 The year when the total dependency ratio was at its lowest value: the world, major regions, and selected countries

	Year when total dependency ratio was at minimum value	Value then of total dependency ratio	Value then of Youth dependency ratio	Value then of Old dependency ratio
WORLD	2015	52.3	39.7	12.6
More developed regions	2005	47.5	25.0	22.6
Less developed regions	2015	52.5	42.8	9.7
China	2010	34.5	23.4	11.1
Japan	1990	43.4	26.3	17.1
Republic of Korea	2015	37.2	19.2	18.0
India	2040	47.1	31.4	15.8
Russian Federation	2010	38.8	20.7	18.2
Sweden	2005	53.1	26.7	26.5
United Kingdom	2010	51.2	26.8	24.5
Italy	1990	45.5	24.0	21.5
Spain	2005	44.8	20.7	24.1
France	1985	50.7	31.6	19.1
Germany	1985	43.8	22.9	20.8
Canada	1985	46.0	31.1	14.9
United States of America	2005	48.7	30.4	18.3
Australia	2010	48.2	28.2	20.0

Source: United Nations Population Division, Department of Economic and Social Affairs, World Population: The 2015 Revision, 2015

For the world as a whole, the year of the lowest value of the ratio was 2015. For the more developed countries, the year was 10 years earlier. With regard to specific countries, the year the ratio reached its lowest value was in around 1985 for France, Germany and Canada, and 1990 in Japan and Italy. UN (2015) projections indicate that the total dependency ratio will not reach its lowest value in India until 2040.

Impact of Aging on Economic Growth

Given the above trends, we inquire now about the impact of aging on economic growth. Since many of the developed countries in the world have already experienced percentages of elderly in their populations of greater than 20% (see our above discussion), the impact of population aging on economic growth has become a major issue of concern.

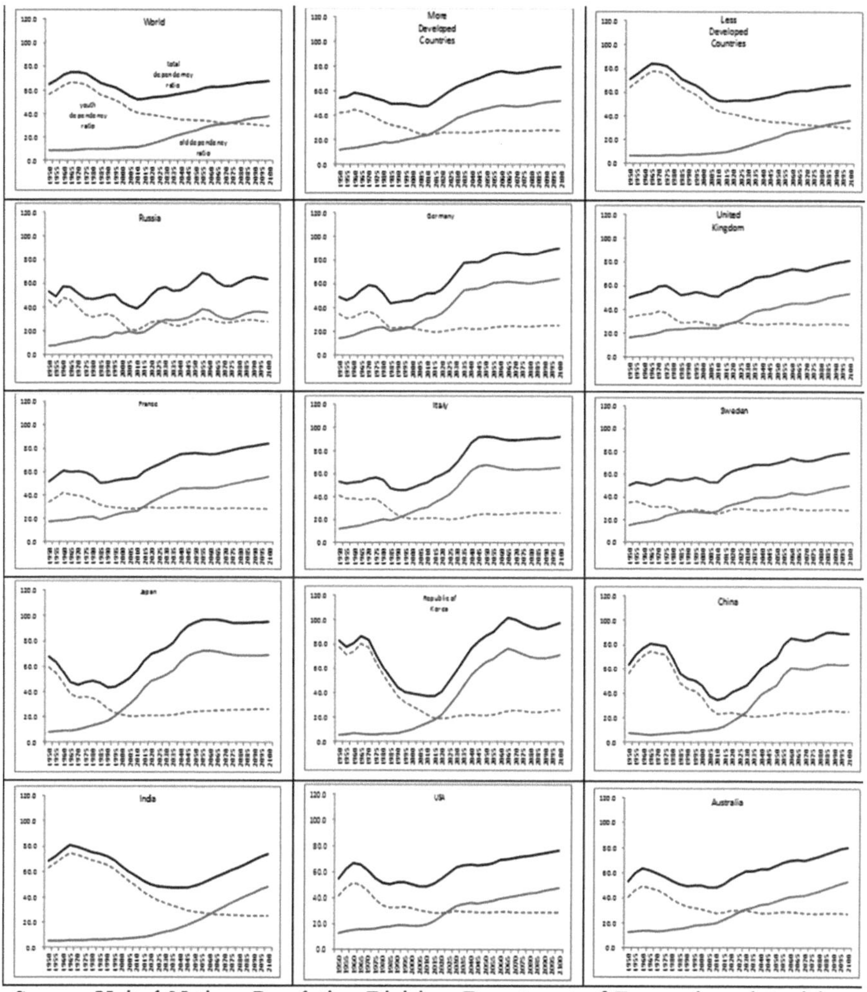

Source: United Nations Population Division, Department of Economic and Social Affairs, World Population Prospects: The 2015 Revision, 2015.

Fig. 6.7 Trends in dependency ratios for the world and selected countries, 1950–2100 (Source: United Nations Population Division, Department of Economic and Social Affairs, World Population Prospects: The 2015 Revision, 2015)

We have already noted that the continuation of low fertility in a society results in the aging of its population; the numbers of working-age population decrease, and the numbers of old dependents increase. The decreases in the working-age population lead to decreases in the labor force supply, which in turn result in the slowdown of economic growth. An increase in a country in the percentage of elderly dependents has direct and indirect negative effect on economic growth. It results in a decrease in the savings rate, thereby dropping the accumulation of capital.

Changes in the age structure also affect changes in economic performance owing to the heterogeneity of economic actions by age. According to the life-cycle income hypothesis, income and consumption vary by age. Investments for health and education are necessarily concentrated on the young people; the middle age people focus on labor supply and savings; the elders require health insurance and pension incomes. Increases in life expectancy thus affect not only the traditional labor supply factors such as family size, retirement, and female labor participation, but also investments in human capital realized via decision-making with respect to education. Hence, it is clear that population aging affects economic growth.

For example, research has documented a positive but weak relationship among OECD countries in the year of 1990 between the population growth rate and the economic growth rate (see Fig. 6.8). However, by 2012 the positive relationship between the two rates increased in magnitude, implying that the economic growth rate is affected more and more so by change in the rates of population growth.

For the OECD countries, however, the economic growth rates begin to decline with increases in population aging (see Fig. 6.9). And this negative relationship became more and more apparent with time. We have already noted that a continuation of low fertility results in a decrease in the supply of labor and an increase in population aging, resulting in a negative effect on the rate of economic growth.

Let us look specifically at the relationship between population aging and economic growth for the Republic of Korea. With a 2.0% growth rate in total factor productivity (TFP), the potential growth rate would decrease from 5.1% per annum during the 2003–2010 period to 1.38% per annum during the 2040–2050 period; during this period the percentage of elderly would increase from 8.3% in 2003 to 37.3% in 2050, assuming that the total fertility rate is maintained at 1.19 (Moon et al. 2004). However, the potential growth rate would decrease to 1.75% in 2050 if the total fertility rate increased to the replacement level of 2.1 by 2035 and was thereafter maintained at 2.1. Under these assumptions the percentage elderly would increase to 31.6% in 2050.

Another analysis of the Republic of Korea indicated that if the total fertility rate increased from 1.08 in 2005 to 1.28 in 2035 and was thereafter maintained at that level, the real growth rate in GDP would decrease from 4.8% per annum during the 2006–2010 period to 1.2% per annum during the 2041–2050 period (Han et al. 2007). However, it would decrease to 1.6% per annum during the 2041–2050 period, if the total fertility rate increased to 1.6 by 2015 and was maintained thereafter at that level. The researchers assumed that TFP growth rate per annum would decrease from 1.4% during the 2006–2010 period to 1.3% during the 2011–2020 period, and to 1.2% after 2021.

There are three main views on the relationship between changes in population structure and economic growth; these depend on whether it is assumed that they are determined endogenously or exogenously. First, based on the assumption that both population structure and economic growth are endogenously determined, it has been argued that population aging would result in a decrease in per capita income mainly because of decreases in the savings rate and labor supply. This argument has been supported empirically by research examining the life-cycle income hypothesis

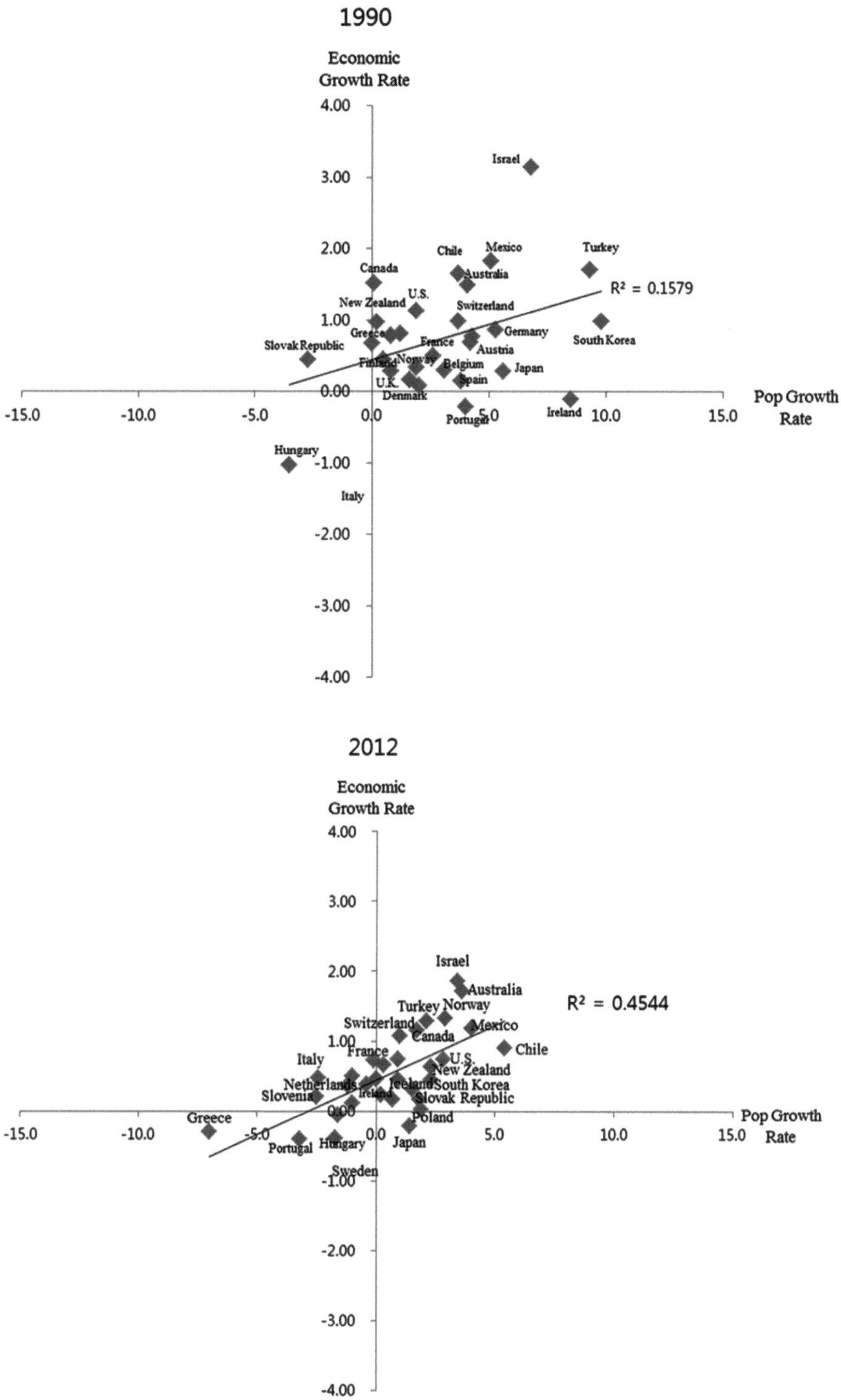

Fig. 6.8 Relationship between population growth rate and economic growth rate, 1990 and 2012. United Nations Population Division, *The 2015 Revision of World Population Prospects*

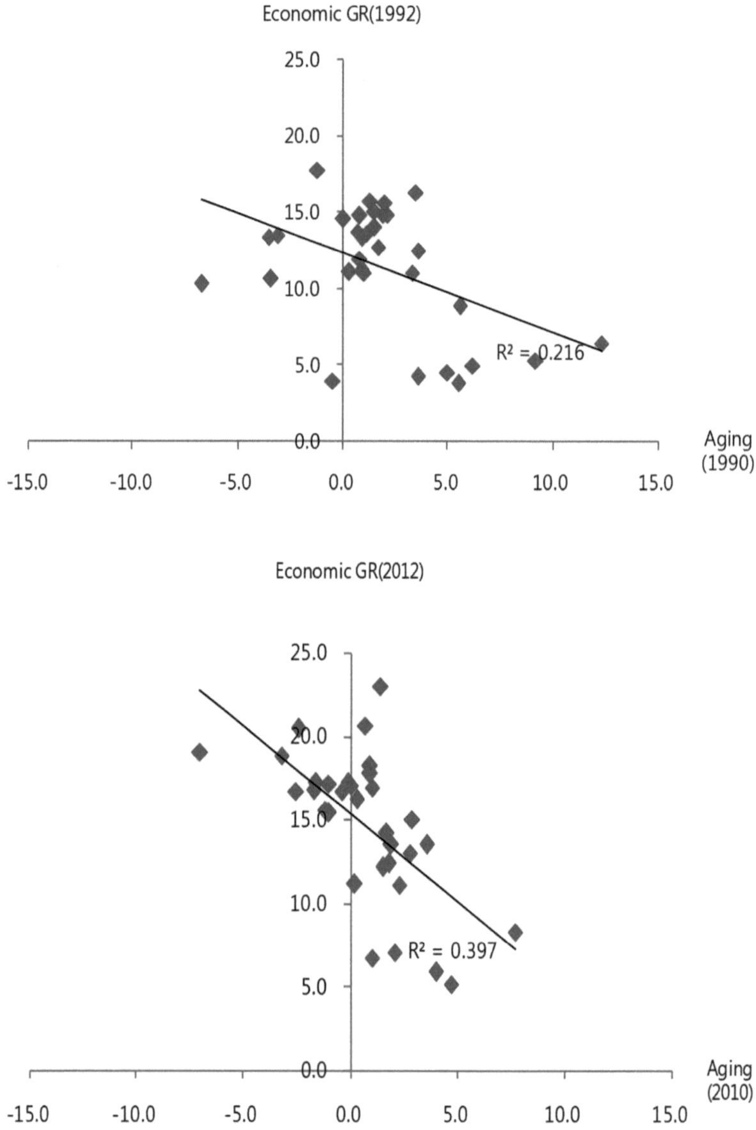

Source: The World Bank.http://www.worldbank.org

Fig. 6.9 Relationship between population aging and economic growth rate (Note: United Nations Population Division, The 2015 Revision of World Population Prospects. Source: The World Bank. http://www.worldbank.org)

positing a relationship between population structure and savings (Auerbach and Kotlikoff 1987).

Second, based on the assumption that population structure is exogenously determined and economic growth is endogenously determined, Fougere and Merette (1999) have shown that decreases in the population growth rate and increases in the old dependent ratio due to declining fertility will lead to decreases in savings. But there will be a reduction in the economic slowdown because of the improvement in labor quality, namely the accumulation of human capital and the improvement of total factor productivity (TFP).

Third, based on the assumption that population structure is endogenously determined and that economic growth is exogenously determined, Becker et al. (1990) have argued that there would be a high possibility of change in the economic environments resulting in an increasing earnings rate of investment in human capital under the condition of an exchange between the quantity and quality of the labor force; this would result in an increase in economic growth and a decrease in the growth of the population. Along similar lines, Lucas (2002) has shown that in countries with institutional factors such as protection of intellectual property and an open domestic market, a fertility decline and an expansion of investment on children's human capital would lead to changes in population structure and continuous economic growth.

Although the mechanisms through which low fertility and population aging affect economic growth are diversified and rather complex, we may further examine these associations by focusing in turn on supply, demand, and finance.

From the supply side, low fertility and population aging can play a role in the slowing or in the decline of economic growth by decreasing the rate of labor and capital input. Low fertility and population aging will decrease potential economic growth by reducing the size of the working-age population and decreasing the input of the labor force. With regard to the input of capital, low fertility and population aging will decrease the potential economic growth rate by increasing the numbers of old dependents, decreasing the saving rate, and slowing down the accumulation of capital. However, a decrease in the percentage of the young population will likely have a positive effect on the economic growth rate by decreasing expenditures in education, increasing the savings rate, and also the accumulation of capital.

From the demand side, low fertility and population aging will have a negative effect on economic growth by decreasing population size and increasing the dependency ratio, thus reducing consumption. The increase in the percentage of consumers, via the increase in the elderly may well have a positive effect on the population growth rate. However, a slower savings rate will likely occur because the reduced savings among the elders will decrease the demand for investment. Thus, with the aging of the population, there is an increase in the number of households heavily relying on their savings. This thus results in a decrease in the household saving rate and thereby the domestic saving rates, both of which have a negative effect on investment.

From the financial side, there is a possibility owing to the relationship between fertility declines and population aging that tax revenues will decrease with a decrease in the number of working-age population, and that the financial deficit will increase owing to increases in social security expenditures for the elderly. Population aging will tend to increase pension recipients, health insurance payments, and care for the elderly, thus deteriorating fiscal balance. It will likely threaten the stability of finance for social security, will increase the people's burden, will weaken overall competitiveness, and may have a negative effect on the potential growth. For instance, Atkinson (1995) has argued that population aging would likely increase the people's overall economic burden and possibly expand the government's distribution system for social expenditures. But if such a distribution system is ineffective, the efficiency of the economy could well be damaged owing to the slow economic growth.

Conclusion

We began this chapter with a brief discussion of the classic model of demographic transition, and then the model of the second demographic transition, so to provide a perspective for our presentation of the demographic issues of aging and age dependency. We discussed the dynamics of the transitions and illustrated their operations in selected countries. We reviewed the dynamics of fertility change and below replacement levels within the context of the first and second demographic transitions, and then considered the issue of population aging.

The main measure of population aging used by demographers is the percentage of persons in the population aged 65 years and older. We first showed that population aging is a consequence of fertility decline and the prolonging of human life, but that the former has the major influence. We then presented aging percentages for the World, its major regions, and selected countries for the years of 2015, 2050 and 2100. The percentage of elders in the World will likely increase from 17.5 in 2015 to 28.7 in 2100. By 2100, nearly one-third of the population of Southern Europe will be of age 65+, the highest percentage of any world region. By 2100 the Republic of Korea is projected to be the oldest country in the world with a percentage of elders of over 37%; Japan is projected to be in second place with as percentage of 35.7%.

We then turned to a discussion of age dependency, specifically the old age dependency ratio, that is, the number of persons in the population of age 65 or more per 100 persons in the producing ages of 15–64. The Republic of Korea is projected to be the country in the world in 2100 with the highest old age dependency ratio of 74.4; this means that in 2100 there will be almost 75 elders in the Korean population per 100 persons in the producing ages. This is a truly dramatic increase compared to the value of the ratio for Korea in 1950 of just over 5 elders per 100 producers. In the 150 years between 1950 and 2100, the number of elders per 100 producers in the Republic of Korea will have become 15 times larger.

We then addressed the impact of aging on economic growth. Since many of the developed countries in the world have already experienced percentages of elderly in their populations of greater than 20%, the impact of population aging on economic growth is a major issue of concern. We discussed the three main views on the relationship between changes in population age structure and economic growth; these views depend on whether it is assumed that age structure and economic growth are determined endogenously or exogenously. Our detailed discussion makes clear that the mechanisms through which low fertility and population aging affect economic growth are diversified and very complex.

The arguments and data presented in this chapter point to the major importance and relevance of population aging. As countries and populations pass through the classic demographic transition from high birth and death rates to low birth and death rates, and then move on to the second demographic transition, one of the most crucial structural consequences is the aging of the population. We have shown this to be especially the case with regard to the effects of aging on economic growth.

References

Atkinson, A. (1995). *Incomes and the welfare state*. Cambridge: Cambridge University.

Auerbach, A. J., & Kotlikoff, L. J. (1987). *Dynamic fiscal policy*. Cambridge: Cambridge University.

Becker, G. S., Murphy, K. M., & Tamura, R. (1990). Human capital, fertility, and economic growth. *Journal of Political Economy, 98*(5), S12–S37.

Caldwell, J. C. (1976). Toward a restatement of demographic transition theory. *Population and Development, 2*, 321–366.

Davis, K. (1963). The theory of change and response in modern demographic history. *Population Index, 29*, 345–366.

Easterlin, R. A. (1983). Modernization and fertility: a critical essay. In R. A. Bulatao & R. D. Lee (Eds.), *Determinants of fertility in developing countries: Vol. 2, Fertility regulation and institutional influences* (pp. 562–586). New York: Academic.

Easterlin, R. A. (1987). *Birth and fortune (2nd ed.)*. New York: Basic Books.

Fougere, M., & Merette, M. (1999). Population aging and economic growth in seven OECD countries. *Economic Modelling, 16*, 411–427.

Han, J. H., et al. (2007). *Long-term prospects of macro-economic variables in aged society: 2006–2080*. Seoul: Korean Development Institute.

Lee, S. S., Byun, Y. C., Kim, D. H., & Kim, H. S. (2004). *Population aging and population policy*. Seoul: Korean Institute for Health and Social Affairs.

Lucas, R. E. (2002). *Lectures on economic growth*. Cambridge: Harvard University.

Moon, H. P., Kim, D. I., Kim, D. S., Kim, S. Y., Kim, Y. H., Park, C. G., & Ahn, J. B. (2004). *Population aging and the macro-economy*. Seoul: Korean Development Institute.

Namboodiri, K. & Luying, W. (1997, October 11–17). *Fertility theories and their implications regarding how low can low fertility be*. Paper Presented at the 23rd general population conference of the International Union for the Scientific Study of Population, Beijing, China.

Preston, S. H. (1987). Changing values and falling birth rates. In K. Davis, M. S. Bernstam, & R. Ricardo-Campbell (Eds.), *Below replacement fertility in industrial societies* (pp. 176–195). New York: Cambridge University.

Reher, D. S. (2004). The demographic transition revisited as a global process. *Population Space and Place, 10*, 19–41.

United Nations, Department of Economic and Social Affairs, Population Division. (2015). *World population prospects: the 2015 revision*. New York: United Nations.

van de Kaa, D. J. (1987). Europe's second demographic transition. *Population Bulletin, 42*(1), 1–57.

Chapter 7
Good Mothering in China: Effects of Migration, Low Fertility, and Birth Constraints

Nancy E. Riley

Introduction

One might expect that with decreasing fertility, women's lives would change greatly. In many ways and in many cases, they do. Low fertility—replacement level or below-replacement level fertility—often occurs in a context in which other changes occur: more education, in general and for women; and, related to increases in education and to less time devoted to child-raising, an increase in labor force participation for women, patterns that include more years working or a greater likelihood of full time work, or both. With women released from spending a significant portion of their lives around having and raising many children, we might expect their family lives—their lives in general—to be much changed from earlier regimes of high fertility.

In this chapter, I argue that because of the intractability of gender inequalities, the new order resembles the old in many ways. In a declining fertility or low fertility scenario, while women might gain some traction toward gender equality, fertility change certainly does not automatically lead to gender equality. As I will explain, gender inequality takes on new forms. One of the underlying reasons is the way that individual and family but also, national and state goals, get mapped onto old systems of gender ideology. A key to understanding gender inequality is motherhood (Arendall 2000). The practice and the ideology of mothering are central to gender inequality. It is as mothers that women have a particularly difficult time.

The difficulties that women have, and the gender inequality those struggles reflect, happen across a broad range of societies. In societies with significant government intervention or even with little, in places with very low fertility or higher fertility, even where women's labor force participation is low, we see similar patterns, albeit to different degrees. The experiences of working mothers suggest there

N.E. Riley (✉)
Bowdoin College, Brunswick, ME, USA
e-mail: nriley@bowdoin.edu

D.L. Poston, Jr. (ed.), *Low Fertility Regimes and Demographic and Societal Change*, DOI 10.1007/978-3-319-64061-7_7

are continuing problems with gender equality. Thus, although in this chapter I focus on China, I also bring in comparative evidence from other societies, partly to show that China is not an unusual case, but just one version of a more general pattern, although state goals and the shape of the continuing gender inequality differs from one society to another. Furthermore, I argue that while these issues of motherhood indeed affect all working women, marginalized women are particularly vulnerable. The marginalized groups would include poorer women in the United States, and the group I look at more closely in this chapter, rural migrant mothers in China.

Women's Education and Labor Force Participation

The measures most commonly used—and sometimes the only ones used—to examine gender equality are women's education and labor force participation. I will now consider both.

In education, women are closing the gender gap, and in some places girls' education actually exceeds that of boys. Evidence for differentials between women's and men's access to education is easily available. For nearly all countries, data indicate changes in literacy, primary school and secondary school enrollment, and participation in higher education as well; girls have made progress in educational attainment across the world. Nearly everywhere, girls are closing the gap. When we look more closely at what is happening in higher education (Fig. 7.1), we see that women's education relative to men's varies somewhat across countries. In some places, such as in Latin America, girls' participation in tertiary education exceeds that of boys, while in others, such as Sub-Saharan Africa, girls still lag behind boys. Based on the trends over recent decades, we might expect that girls' education, at least through high school, will catch up to boys' across the world (see Knodel and Jones 1996).

Women's work, another measure commonly used to assess gender equality, allows us to see what women are able to do with their increased education, and how those changes are translating into other outcomes for women. When we examine women's labor force participation we see a different pattern from that of education. It is important to recognize that measures of work are more complicated than measures of schooling. We might measure changes in women's work over time; whether women are employed outside the home; what kind of work women are doing (horizontal segregation); what kind of status women have in their jobs (vertical segregation); and whether women and men are paid equal amounts. Nevertheless, across all of these measures, it is here that we begin to see important and continuing differences between women's and men's lives.

When we look at the numbers, we see that women's labor force participation has increased in many areas of the world, but not in all of them (Fig. 7.2). We also see differences between the kind of work women and men do in nearly all places as well, with women tending to be in work involving less heavy physical work and more likely to be in clerical and retail positions. Women are also much less often found in leadership positions, and not surprisingly, given these differences, in most

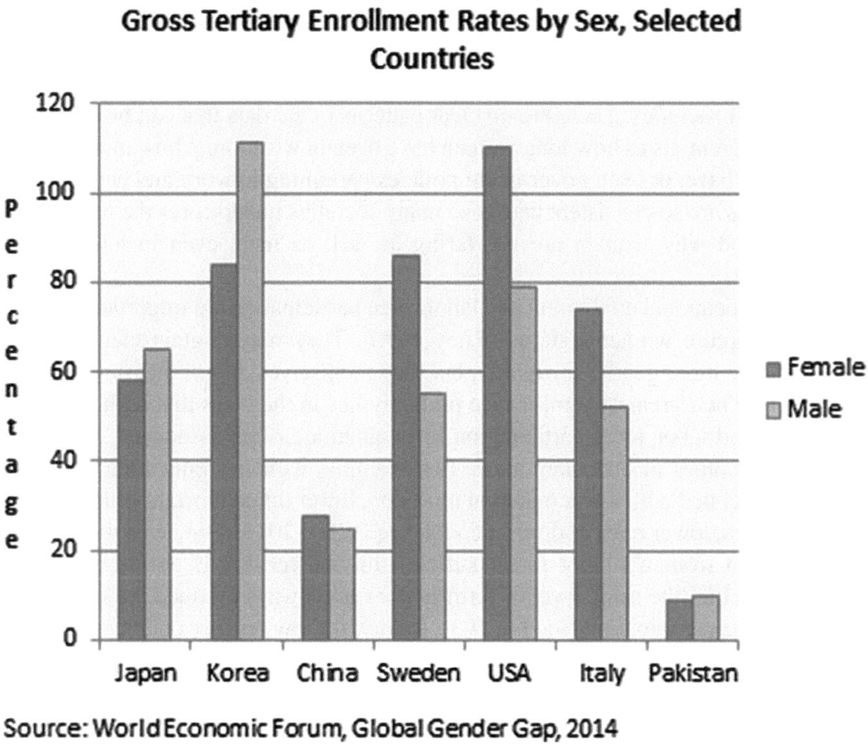

Fig. 7.1 Gross tertiary enrollment rates by sex, selected countries

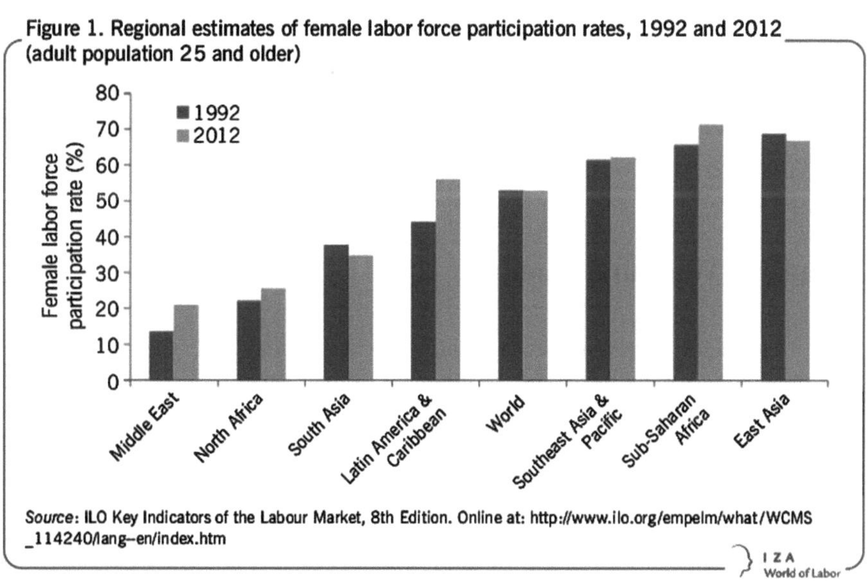

Fig. 7.2 Regional estimates of female labor force participation, 1992 and 2012

societies they receive lower wages than men. While there are quantitative and sometimes qualitative differences across societies—for example, how much more men earn than women, or how work is gendered —these patterns of gender difference are present in all societies. There are no clear patterns in the data that can be explained by such differentials as how long women have been in workforce, how much education women have, or even government policies pertaining to work and gender. That such patterns are so consistent across so many societies underscores the need for us to understand why women are not faring as well as men, even in low fertility environments.

While educational attainment and labor force participation are important, they do not fully capture women's status (Riley 1998). They may contain elements that might enable more gender inequality, but they themselves do not measure equality accurately. Their greatest significance probably lies in the ways that higher rates in education and labor force participation for women are often associated with other positive outcomes in other key areas. For example, women's education is almost always associated with lower maternal mortality, lower infant mortality, and, at least in some cases, lower rates of domestic violence (WHO 2013). But, even the connection between women's labor force participation and fertility is not all that clear. Across societies, the same level of fertility does not always produce the same level of labor force participation (see Fig. 7.3). Rather, for low fertility countries, there is a great deal of variation in women's labor force participation. We get an important clue about the influences on women's work lives when we look at the shape of women's labor force participation over the course of a lifetime and the ways it varies from one society to another. In some countries, women leave the labor force at young ages, especially around the time marriage; in other countries, women either stop working or reduce their hours with the birth of a child. These patterns may reflect continuing gender discrimination and questions about access into higher paying careers or jobs. But it is also possible, perhaps, that women have a different pathway into and through work than do men. All of these measures of work hint at the importance of motherhood as a key to understanding women's relationship to work.

Balancing Work and Family

One of the issues that is frequently discussed when women enter the work force is how they will go about balancing the demands of work and family. The struggles to balance work and family affect men as well, of course, but research shows that it is women who face the biggest struggles and adjustments (Stone 2008; Gerson and Jacobs 2004: Roos 2010). We know that women have always done most of the work at home, particularly with regard to taking care of children. What happens with some of these big societal changes such as more education for women and, particularly, lower fertility?

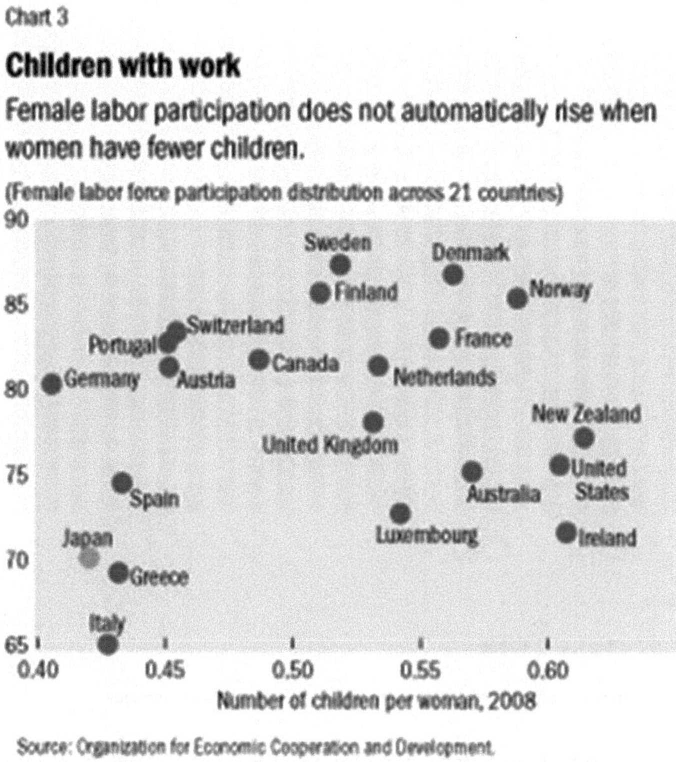

Fig. 7.3 Female labor force participation and number of children per woman, various countries

When we look at who does the unpaid labor (usually housework and childcare) in the family, we see that in virtually all societies across the globe most of it falls to women (Fig. 7.4). Women do most of the housework, and it makes little difference whether we measure that labor either relatively or by actual minutes spent by women and men (Fig. 7.5). The lack of balance between women and men is made even clearer when we look at data that show that even when women are working at or nearly at full time in the labor force, they are still doing most of the housework; in a study of seven European countries, Scott and Piagnol found that women do most of the unpaid household labor, whether or not they are full- or part-time in the labor force: as might be expected, women do 88% of unpaid household labor when only the husband employed, but still over 68% when both partners work full time in the labor force and over 57% of that labor when they are employed full time and their husbands are not working full time (Scott and Plagnol 2012:185). Clearly, while the tensions between work and family may affect all family members, it is women who are the ones who really struggle to balance the two. Important to note is that while there are differences among countries, the pattern persists everywhere. This is true

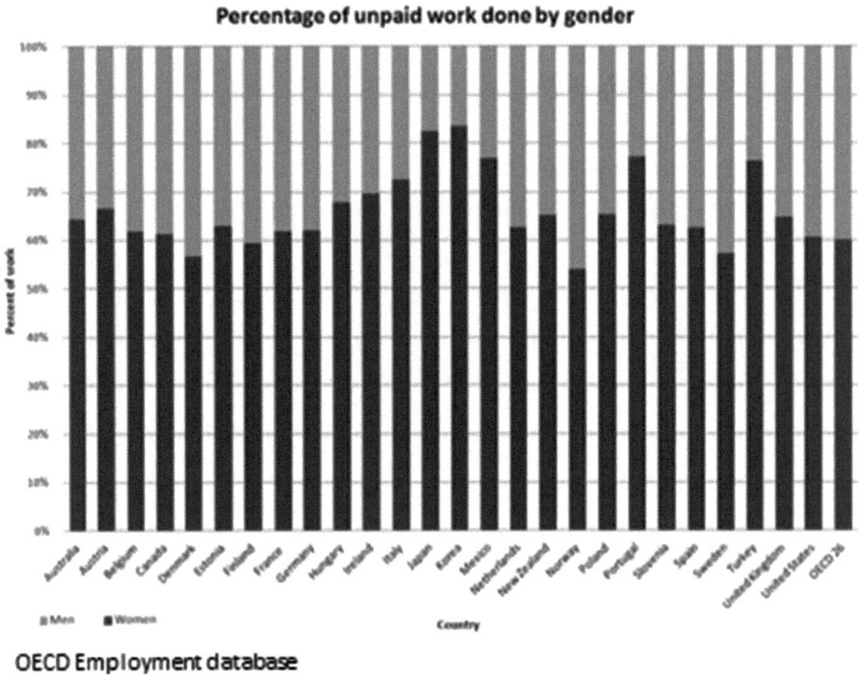

Fig. 7.4 Percentage of unpaid work done, by gender, for selected countries

in high and low fertility countries. We might see Sweden as important here; even in Sweden, where there is good government support for balancing work and family, support available to both women and men, and where men are reported to be contributing a larger share in unpaid labor, we still see major gender differences.

Explaining these continuing gender differences in the double burden facing women regarding work and family requires our looking at several factors. As I showed earlier, even though lower fertility suggests that there are more opportunities for women in work and in the public world, and higher levels of education—which suggests a means to achieve such opportunities—gender inequalities can and do persist. The data from various societies point to entrenched attitudes about gender and the ways that women's entry into the labor force does not necessarily bring with it changes in attitudes about gender. There are continuing concerns about the welfare of children, the need for mothers' care, and even whether women should be working outside the home. Attitudes about gender are particularly obvious when we focus not on women, but specifically on mothers. A 2007 Pew Research Poll found that in the U.S., 41% of adults stated it is bad for society when mothers of young children work. Only 22% said that mothers working is good (Pew 2007). These attitudes are similar to those found in a study conducted in Asia in 1994 (Bumpass and Choe 2004; Tsuya et al. 2000). A significant proportion of respondents surveyed in the United States, Korea, and Japan (among 30 to 39 year olds, 36%, 45% and 70% respectively) believe that maintaining separate spheres is better. Further,

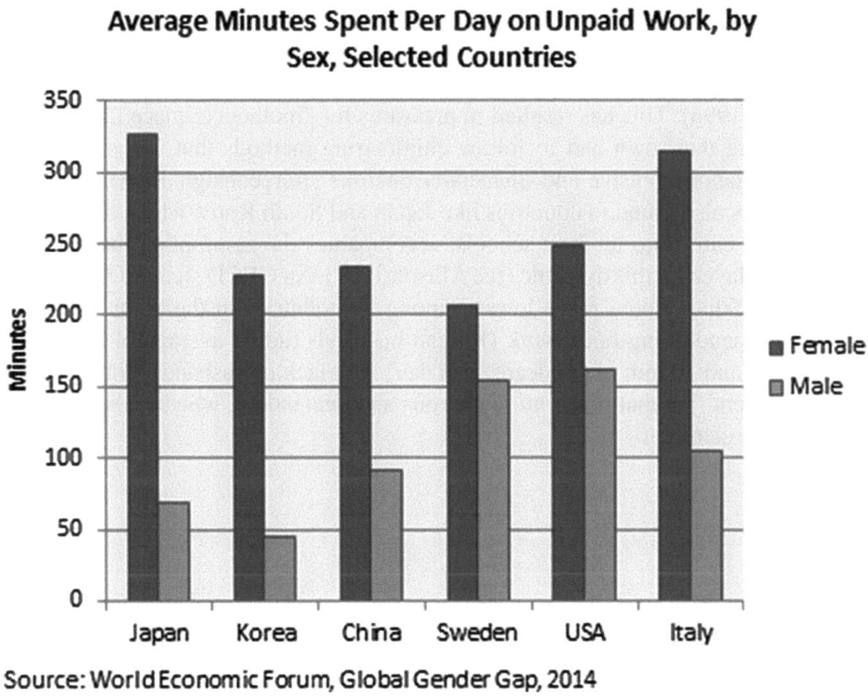

Fig. 7.5 Average minutes spent per day on unpaid work by sex, selected countries

the same study indicates that in all three countries, many believe that kids suffer if their mother is working. There are cohort differences, with lower percentages among younger than older age groups expressing concern; that may well reflect changing attitudes or those differences may reflect the fact that younger cohorts have not yet had the experience of older cohorts in trying to achieve a balance. In addition, we know from research around the world (Desai and Jain 1994; Stone 2008; Roos 2010) that inequalities at work are connected to inequalities at home; each influences the other, and affects the way that women experience the tensions.

Mothering

The data and trends that I have reviewed above suggest that it is when women become mothers that we really see how women's and men's lives diverge and that the ideology and pressures of mothering have a major impact on gender equality. With the arrival of children, women across the globe have to or, some argue, choose to turn toward home and family. But even as mothering comes to dominate the shape of women's lives and, I argue, gender inequality, there are nonetheless differences among societies. In many, the job of mothering has taken on a new intensity.

For example, in the United States, mothering has taken on an intensity because of the emphasis on individual achievement and competition, and also because at the same time there remains a continuing responsibility of mothers for their child's success (Hays 1996). This has resulted in pressures for "mothers to place their child's needs before their own and to follow childrearing methods that are emotionally absorbing, labor-intensive and financially onerous" (Greenhalgh 1998). Intensive mothering is also found in countries like Japan and South Korea where fierce competition for entry into the best schools, accompanies the assumption that mothers are major players in this dynamic (see Allison 1991). An OECD study of housework found that South Korea ranks lowest among 29 countries in the amount of time husbands spend doing housework (Korean husbands did an average of 21 min of housework and 10 min of childcare each day). The lack of husbands' contributions made mothers' job that much more onerous and demanding, whether they were in the labor force or not.

China

China is an interesting society to examine when we consider the relationship between gender equality and fertility. It has below-replacement fertility and a high rate of women's labor force participation, and both have been government mandated. In such a situation, we might expect the mother/worker role to be well accepted or at least well supported because the government pushed both changes as part of the modernization of the country (Greenhalgh 2010; Fong 2006).

Not long after the establishment of the People's Republic of China in 1949, government leaders began a program to move women into the labor force. They argued that this was an important mechanism for achieving gender equality. But because women represented such a huge workforce addition, it was also intended to move the economy forward (Davin 1979; Stacey 1983). Women were required to work outside the home, and with that directive came support for women's work and for the balancing act that was necessary between work and motherhood. Over the course of the next several decades, China instituted a nationwide system of public child care, declared women equal to men under the law, and put into place paid maternity leave; in some places at some times during those decades, there was further support given for household labor such as communal kitchens. In spite of any support from the government and for all the equal-gender rhetoric, by nearly all measures, women in China are still not equal to men (Yang 2011; Riley 2012; Evans 2008; Yang 1999). In addition to their work outside the home, they have been asked to take on a second shift within the home, including the responsibility of most of the childcare labor (Qi and Dong 2013).

The government also made fertility decline a key piece of its modernization goals, imposing smaller families on all Chinese citizens, and restricting at least urban residents to one child. Chinese leaders, trying to find a way to modernize China and to move China into the front of global politics and power, believed that planning had to include more than just the economy. Population needed to be planned in the same way (White 2009). Chinese leaders surmised that if the experience of other countries had shown that economic growth could lead to fertility decline, all China needed to do was to reverse the causal sequence: fertility decline could lead to economic growth. Thus a deliberate, government mandated reduction in fertility might lead to a more rapid modernization (Greenhalgh 2010; Wang et al. 2012). In their deliberations and explanations, government leaders argued that lower fertility was necessary for future generations and for the country. In addition, it would be the single children who would be the vanguard of the revolution (Fong 2006).

The burden of this modernization scheme would fall to families. One piece of China's modernization focused on developing a consumer market, economy and society. These changes have put increased pressure on parents, with parents needing to buy everything from the latest electronics to fancy snacks after school (Fong 2006; Chee 2000; Guo 2000). But even more pressure came from the place of education in this modernizing model. If children were the vanguard of the new China, it was the parents who were responsible for getting children to where they needed to go. In particular, education—always valued and sought after in China—became even more necessary for the country's modernizing projects and for individual children's success. Today, the goal of many families is to get their children into highly ranked schools, particularly at the university level. Parents put a lot of resources—time, money, energy and anxiety— into efforts to achieve this goal. Whether deliberately or explicitly, the government's modernizing goals have pushed an agenda promoting intensive mothering, and this has occurred in spite of the very low levels of fertility in China today. Many scholars have shown how urban parents—and particularly mothers—are working hard to move their children onto the pathway to success (Fong 2006). The goal of these parents may not be to further the country's modernization, but in the end, their own goals—to allow their children to achieve successes in this changing economy—dovetails nicely with the government's goals. The burden is particularly heavy on women. They have full time jobs outside the home and full time jobs inside the house. They are the conduit for children's, and the country's success; all of this means added expectations.

Thus, China is a society in which both low fertility and women's labor force participation are considered necessary for a strong future. Even here, where both were deliberate pieces of the state's modernizing goals, we see continuing gender inequality.

The Struggle of Marginalized Groups in Low Fertility Societies

A work/family balance is hard for most families, especially those in which both parents are working, and especially for women, who are most likely the ones struggling with these tensions. But the struggles to achieve this balance are particularly burdensome for those families, and those women, who are most vulnerable. In many societies, it is the economically disadvantaged who face very difficult days. For example, in the United States, we find that structures and attitudes about the tensions between work and family, and the expectations and attitudes about the role of mothers, permeate all sectors of society, including richer and poorer families, and families in different ethnic and racial groups. But it is poor families and other marginalized families that find it particularly difficult to meet those expectations. In Fig. 7.6, we see that tensions between work and family are particularly sharp in low income, low education families. For parents in these families with few resources, their time is not easily structured to give them a break from such challenges, such as hiring helpers to take care of their children, or being able to eat out in order to save some housework time.

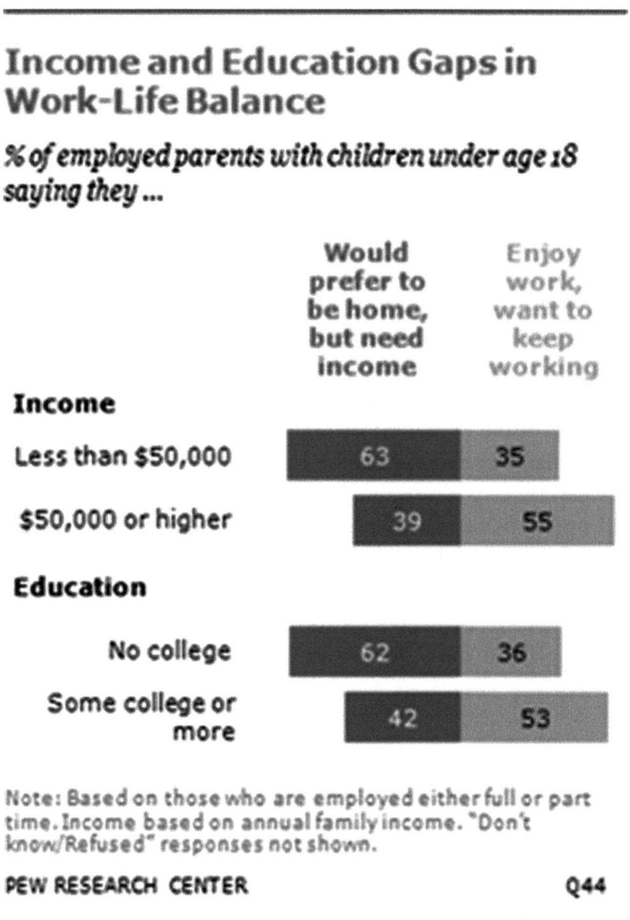

Fig. 7.6 Income and education gaps in work-life balance, U.S. (Source: Pew Research Center)

Mean Household Per capita Income, 2002 (in yuan)	
National	5,559
Urban	9,323
urban registered/hukou	9996
urban migrant	6,083
Rural	3,143
Ratio of urban migrant to registered	0.61
Ratio of migrant to rural	1.64
Ratio of urban to rural	2.97

Adapted from: Sicular, et al. 2005. (http://home.wlu.edu/~smitkam/274/pdfs/sicular%20urban-rural%20gap.pdf

Fig. 7.7 Mean household per capita income, China 2002

In China, one of the most vulnerable groups is rural migrants now living in cities. The divide between rural and urban China is one of the most significant in the country, regularly described as a class system of inequality based on residence (Potter 1983; Cheng and Seldon 1994; Solinger 1999). Because of the enormous inequality between rural and urban areas (see Fig. 7.7), rural peasants have been migrating into cities in huge numbers. Urban areas provide better opportunities in jobs and housing and also have better health care and, most importantly, schools. Perhaps as important as these resources is the pervasive ideology in China today that equates being successful with being urban; rural migrants move to the cities because they want the successes that they think only urban areas can give them. However, rural migrants who end up in urban areas continue to face severe disadvantages. Many of these disadvantages come from the government's continuing *hukou* (residence permit) system, which divides Chinese citizens into urban and rural residents and distributes services and resources unequally to each (Solinger 1999). In this hukou system, only those officially registered as urban residents are allowed regular access to the city's resources. Urban benefits such as many jobs, housing, and particularly education and health care are not available to rural residents who have moved to the city without formal government approval. It is estimated that about one-third of the urban population of China is undocumented (Barreda 2014b), and thus unable to access those resources. Consequently, rural migrants often have difficult challenges succeeding or even surviving in the city; these challenges are complicated by much lower their income is relative to official urban residents (see Fig. 7.7).

Migrant families—parents—are thus struggling to carve a path through these disadvantages they face as rural migrants living in cities; they are often especially determined to do so because they see the city as the only place for them and their children to achieve success. Education is one of the most important resources sought by rural migrants. Long seen as a ticket to a better life, education has taken on new expectations in China. It is now seen as the path--the best path--upward, thus making access to education key for rural migrants. While there are other reasons peasants move to the city, education is one of the most important because of the unavailability of good education in rural areas. Rural peasants see moving to the city as essentially the only way to get a taste of modern resources and to have a chance to move up the social ladder. But the inequalities rural migrants face in the cities includes poorer access to services and institutions, including schools. More than three-fourths of rural migrants in cities do not receive any social benefits such as health insurance or maternity leave (Barreda 2014a). A key to the role of migrant parents is that while all children of legal urban residents attend urban schools, only 40% of the children of rural migrants do (Barreda 2014b).

In this environment, therefore, the key goal of mothers and families to get their children a good education is especially challenging. Rural mothers have to strategizie and work in the midst of cross currents. They are part of a generation of rural women who have experienced low fertility (most have one child, and some have two) and new routes open through migration, but they also face continuing disadvantages for them and their children because they hold a rural hukou. In addition, they have to fulfill the expectations of good mothering in a society where being a mother encompasses everything, from an enormous responsibility in the household to long hours outside the household. And rural migrant women usually experience worse job conditions and lower pay than do legal urban residents. Like others in China, they believe that good mothering includes doing everything possible to get a child into a good school and on the way to being well educated. They see their role as forging a path for their children. They work in order to get their children into urban areas and onto a path of at least potential success. And once in the city, they strive to find a way to get their children enrolled in the best schools.

In my research (Riley 2012) with rural migrant mothers living in the Dalian Economic Zone (see Fig. 7.8), I found evidence of the intensive mothering in which rural migrants often participate.[1] In my sample, all of the women were responsible for the vast majority of both housework and childcare. They worked long hours outside the house and then came home to housework and childcare. And little of what they did strictly benefitted themselves, whether we measure that by what they purchase for the family or in how much leisure time they have relative to their husbands. They spend much of their energy and time in intensive mothering, but of a different sort than what we might see in the U.S. These women see mothers as central to their family's success, and particularly the success of their children. They acted and talked in ways indicating that they see themselves as living for their kids. In interview after interview, these mothers talked about the role they play in their families, how their families depended on them to find routes to success, particularly

[1] Here, I draw from my extensive fieldwork in the Dalian Economic Zone. I interviewed rural migrant mothers about their family lives. See Riley (2012) for more details and findings.

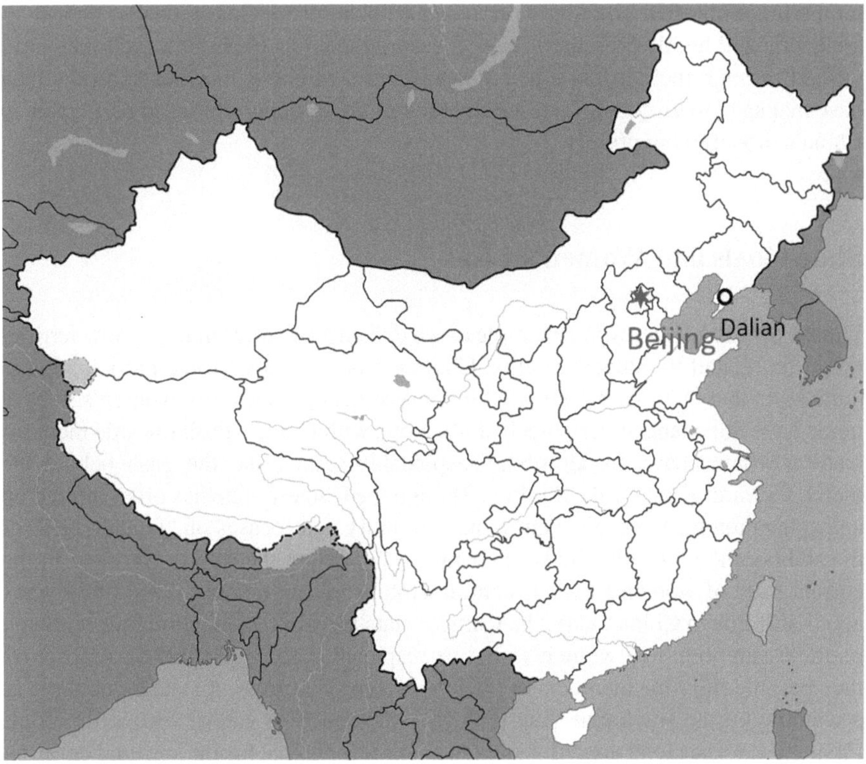

Fig. 7.8 China, showing Dalian

for the children. In fact, these women defined their own success in terms of how well they were able to help their children succeed in modern, urban China.

The main reason they gave about why they worked so hard at home and at work was that they believed that they were the main, and perhaps only, ticket to their child's success. Jiangli, a respondent in my study in Dalian, spoke in ways that echoed the attitudes and actions of many others around her. She argued that mothers have to do everything to get and keep children in school, no matter how difficult that was. She exclaimed, "I have only one child. I really want a lot for that one child. I want her to have a good job. She needs education!" But rural migrants have to pay high fees to enroll their children in urban schools, fees that are usually out of reach of many. Still, Jiangli argued "You have to find a way to pay the fees. That is just true, you have to do that…If you don't pay, think about the future! Forever your child will say, you did not pay for my schooling. Just think about the influence on the future. No, parents have to pay, they just have to."

In some places, such as among elite women in the United States (Stone 2008), intensive mothering defines women who are solely focused on being good mothers, having left the labor force. But for these Dalian mothers, they combine such intense mothering with often grueling work hours outside home. Consequently, their lives are hectic and highly pressured. They measure their success in how well they have pushed through the barriers erected against rural migrants in cities and how they have managed to give their families and their children opportunities to participate in China's modernizing project.

State Goals and Women's Lives

Thus, China is an interesting example as we consider the ways that very low fertility might be related to gender equality. Chinese women's labor force participation is quite high, and that rate is supported by government policies. But women's roles at home have not changed very much at all. Now, with China's push towards modernization, women have an additional responsibility: they are the push behind the march forward of their only children. Though the Chinese state has often offered up an explanation for women's continuing inequality that focuses on "feudal" ideas or the stubbornness of individuals to change, recognizing the role of the state in the current state of women's lives is central. Robinson's argument (1985) of 30 years ago is still true in China today: the Chinese state has built its modernizing economy on the assumption that women would be responsible for household work, even as they became full time members of the labor force. Two areas of state focus serve as a window on the ways that state policy is implicated in gender inequality today. First, the state has long argued that women are responsible for the spiritual development of their children's minds so that they become vital members of the society. The state has also underscored women's dual roles as worker and mother in its development of China's consumer economy. The state has supported a consumer-based economy as a way to both develop the economy and to increase the standard of living. Consumer durables of many types have increased, but the increase in goods for the household has been particularly notable, especially shortly after the economic reforms began in the early 1980s; between 1978 and 1982, the production of washing machines increased 753%, a steeper increase than for any other product. That kind of production was seen as a way to "liberat[e]…housewives from the bondage of household chores of many years, to participate in production" (Nanjing Xinhua Ribao, cited in Robinson 1985: 43). Robinson points to the irony of this model and how it contributed to women's unequal status. Women were encouraged to contribute to the country through paid labor and the development of a robust consumer economy, "yet the reward for that labour is an appliance, which though useful in the performance of private duties, nevertheless remains tied to women's roles in mothering, not in wage work" (Robinson 1985: 46).

Implications and Conclusions

What does all this evidence tell us about gender in low fertility societies? There may be many changes accompanying such low fertility, some of them very important for women's lives. But we can see that gender equality certainly does not automatically follow a decline to low and very low fertility. The evidence from across the world speaks to the intractability of gender and gender inequalities. When a society is reshaped around a low-fertility regime, it often does so around still-existing ideologies of gender. While women experience many benefits from lower fertility, including new educational and job opportunities, even those opportunities often have the shadow and influence of old ways.

Data from many low-income societies suggest that women remain unequal to men even after their fertility has reached very low levels. Such measures of women's inequality are clear. Women have less leisure and less power in the household as measured by their role in decision making or access to money (Blackwood 2000; Blumberg 1991; Blumstein and Schwartz 1991). In addition, housework and childcare responsibilities continue to be women's responsibilities, even as they take on fulltime roles in the labor force. That means that the pressures and difficulties of balancing work and family fall especially hard to women. Because of the way that home and work are interconnected, such responsibilities also serve to undermine their achieving gender equality outside the home.

We might expect that with women free from many births and the rearing of many children, they would spend less time at home and in their role as mothers. But in many societies, motherhood has taken on new pressures and women can end up spending as much time focused on one or two children as mothers in earlier generations did with many children. Such intensive mothering takes different forms in different societies. Ideologies of motherhood are shaped by, but also shape many issues, structures, and behaviors in any society— including government services that support women's roles, expectations within households or about households and families, attitudes about gender roles and equality, and hiring practices. Those will tend to differ from society to society. In a highly consumerist society like the U.S., where individual achievement is paramount and where most services are privatized, we expect intensive mothering to take the particular form it does. In China, where the government has promoted modernity through single child achievement, it makes sense that it takes the form we see today. The ways that China has constructed its goal of modernity, and built women's labor force participation, its birth planning policy and internal migration and residency policies to push its modernizing goals have been key contributors to the kinds of lives women in China lead.

As I have shown in this chapter, the social and economic changes that have occurred in many societies that have accompanied lower fertility do not necessarily benefit women. And it is when women become mothers that we see those continuing gender ideologies most clearly. We must ask, why do these persist? Who is gaining by these continuing structures? I argue that it is not women who do, and I believe that it is not necessarily children either. We might suspect that it is men who gain most, since they have someone providing services and childcare, freeing them up to focus on their jobs. But I would also argue that men too are straight-jacketed into their expected roles. They do have more power than women; generally, what one does outside the household gives one more power than what one does inside the household. But the bigger gains go to those beyond the family. With women providing labor and childcare, workers are able to produce for the market in many countries, including in the U.S. It is individuals—women—who are bearing the burdens of this intensive mothering, not businesses or the government. In China, women end up shouldering a great burden of the state's push for modernity and the ways that it built its goals on existing gender ideologies.

Looking at the United States and China, but recognizing that these same patterns exist across the world, we can thus see how state or market goals use existing assumptions and expectations about women and men's lives. And in that way, the social and economic changes that many societies witness do not seem to challenge existing gender inequalities, and may even entrench them even further.

Women themselves often struggle in the midst of these changes. Indeed the existing gender ideologies often discourage them from pursuing the career and job path that would most benefit themselves, and pushes them into a balancing act, between their responsibilities at home and those at work. And those most vulnerable—poor women in the U.S. or Japan, or migrant workers in China—particularly suffer from these ideologies, where their efforts are likely to end up short of their goals.

Thus, any assumptions about lower fertility benefitting women are not very well supported by the existing evidence. Lower fertility regimes often just become a new phase of a long-standing pattern of gender inequality. Indeed, the gender inequality found throughout the world is likely contributing to low fertility, as women struggle to combine motherhood and work. The intricate connections between low fertility and gender inequality are thus areas where interventions might prove beneficial to women, families, and societies concerned about a shrinking workforce of an aging population.

References

Allison, A. (1991). Japanese mothers and obentos: The lunch box as ideological state apparatus. *Anthropological Quarterly, 64*(4), 195–208.

Arendall, T. (2000). Conceiving and investigating motherhood: The decade's scholarship. *Journal of Marriage and the Family, 62*(4), 1192–1207.

Barreda, D. (2014a). *The 'nongmin' breakdown*. Chinafile.com. Accessed 12 Feb 2015.

Barreda, D. (2014b). *China's fake urbanization*. Chinafile.com. Accessed 12 Feb 2015.

Blackwood, E. (2000). *Webs of power: Women, kin, and community in a Sumatran village*. Lanham: Rowman and Littlefield.

Blumberg, R. L. (1991). Income under female versus male control: Hypotheses from a theory of gender stratification and data from the third world. In R. Blumberg (Ed.), *Gender, family, and economy: The triple overlap* (pp. 97–127). Newbury Park: Sage.

Blumstein, P., & Schwartz, P. (1991). Money and ideology: Their impact on power and the division of household labor. In R. Blumberg (Ed.), *Gender, family, and economy: The triple overlap* (pp. 261–188). Newbury Park: Sage.

Bumpass, L., & Choe, M. (2004). Attitudes related to marriage and family life. In N. Tsuya & L. Bumpass (Eds.), *Marriage, work, and family life in comparative perspective* (pp. 19–38). Honolulu: University of Hawaii.

Chee, B. (2000). Eating snacks and biting pressure: Only children in Beijing. In J. Jing (Ed.), *Feeding China's little emperors* (pp. 48–71). Stanford: Stanford University Press.

Cheng, T. J., & Seldon, M. (1994). The origins and social consequences of China's hukou system. *China Quarterly, 139*, 644–668.

Davin, D. (1979). *Woman-work: Women and the Party in Revolutionary China*. Oxford: Clarendon.

Desai, S., & Jain, D. (1994). Maternal employment and changes in family dynamics: The social context of women's work in rural South India. *Population and Development Review, 20*(1), 115–136.

Evans, H. (2008). *The subject of gender*. Lanham: Rowman and Littliefield.

Fong, V. (2006). *Only hope: Coming of age under China's one child policy*. Stanford: Stanford University Press.

Gerson, K., & Jacobs, J. (2004). The work-home crunch. *Contexts, 3*(4), 29–37.

Greenhalgh, S. (1998). Review: The cultural contradictions of motherhood. *Population and Development Review, 24*(1), 173–174.

Greenhalgh, S. (2010). *Cultivating global citizens: Population in the rise in China*. Cambridge: Harvard University.

Guo, Y. H. (2000). Family relations: The generation gap at the table. In J. Jing (Ed.), *Feeding China's little emperors* (pp. 94–113). Stanford: Stanford University Press.

Hays, S. (1996). *The cultural contradictions of motherhood*. New Haven: Yale University Press.

Knodel, J., & Jones, G. (1996). Post-Cairo population policy: Does promoting girls' schooling miss the mark? *Population and Development Review, 22*(4), 683–702.

Nanjing, X. R., (1960). Selections from China's Mainland Press, No. 2261 (19 May 1960). Cited in Robinson.

Pew Research Center. (2007). *Fewer mothers prefer fulltime work*. Available at: http://pewsocialtrends.org/files/2010/10/WomenWorking.pdf

Potter, S. (1983). The position of peasants in modern China's social order. *Modern China, 9*(4), 465–499.

Qi, L. S., & Dong, X. Y. (2013). *Housework burden, quality of market work time, and men's and women's earnings in China* (Working Paper 2013–01). University of Winnipeg Department of Economics. Downloaded at: http://ideas.repec.org/s/win/winwop.html

Riley, N. E. (1998). Research on gender in demography: Limitations and constraints. *Population Research and Policy Review, 17*, 521–538.

Riley, N. E. (2012). *Gender, work and family in a Chinese economic zone: Laboring in paradise*. Dordrecht: Springer.

Robinson, J. (1985). Of women and washing machines: Employment, housework and the reproduction of motherhood in socialist China. *The China Quarterly, 101*, 32–57.

Roos, P. (2010). Not so separate spheres. *Contexts, 9*(4), 58–60.

Scott, J., & Plagnol, A. (2012). Work-family conflict and well-being in Northern Europe. In J. Scott, S. Dex, & A. Plagnol (Eds.), *Gendered lives* (pp. 174–205). Edward Elgar.

Solinger, D. (1999). *Contesting citizenship in urban China: Peasant migrants, the state and the logic of the market*. Berkeley: University of California Press.

Stacey, J. (1983). *Patriarchy and socialist revolution in China*. Berkeley: University of California Press.

Stone, P. (2008). *Opting out? Why women really quit careers and head home*. Berkeley: University of California Press.

Tsuya, N., Bumpass, L., & Choe, M. K. (2000). Gender, employment and housework in Japan, South Korea, and the United States. *Journal of Population and Social Policy, 9*, 195–220.

Wang, F., Cai, Y., & Gu, B. C. (2012). Population, policy, and politics: How will history judge China's one-child policy? *Population and Development Review, 38*, 115–129.

White, T. (2009). *China's longest campaign: Birth planning in the People's Republic* (pp. 1949–2005). Ithaca: Cornell University Press.
WHO. (2013). *Global and regional estimates of violence against women*. Available at: http://www.who.int/reproductivehealth/publications/violence/9789241564625/en/.
Yang, M. (1999). From gender erasure to gender difference: State feminism, consumer sexuality, and women's public sphere in China. In M. F. Yang (Ed.), *Spaces of their own* (pp. 35–67). Minneapolis: University of Minnesota.
Yang, S. (2011). *Findings from the Third Survey on Chinese women's social status*. http://blogs.lse.ac.uk/gender/2011/11/03/findings-from-the-third-survey-on-chinese-womens-social-status/

Chapter 8
Couple Relationships in Low-Fertility Settings

Linda J. Waite and Juyeon Kim

Introduction

The family is "a social network, not necessarily localized, that is based on culturally recognized biological and marital relationships" (Thornton and Fricke (1989)). In most industrialized societies, the structure of the family looks quite different than it did a half-century ago. Fewer people live in *families* as traditionally defined. Fewer are married, and alternative family forms, such as single parenthood, cohabitation, and same-sex unions have increased. And changes in the family are part and parcel of the changing nature of sexual, romantic and legal partnerships and relationships in the dyad. Changes in family structures affect family members, especially dependent children and elderly relatives. The departure from traditional marital unions seems to also coincide with the decline in fertility rates, although fertility within marriage tends to fall at the same time. And lower fertility rates, in turn, alter family structures, reducing family size and the number of relatives—from siblings to cousins to aunts and uncles and grandchildren—that people have.

Low and very low fertility appear in many developed and some developing countries. To the extent that fertility falls within marriage, the roles of husbands and wives also change, with fewer years of adult life and often few years of marriage devoted to raising children. Thus, low and very low fertility both enables and follows from changes in couple relationships. In this chapter we examine changes in marriage and cohabitation in low fertility societies compared to others. We examine differences in sexuality in these two fertility regimes, and discuss couple relationships

L.J. Waite (✉)
University of Chicago, Chicago, IL 60637, USA
e-mail: l-waite@uchicago.edu

J. Kim
University of Seoul, Seoul, South Korea

D.L. Poston, Jr. (ed.), *Low Fertility Regimes and Demographic and Societal Change*, DOI 10.1007/978-3-319-64061-7_8

among older adults in the U.S. as an illustration of what a low fertility regime might mean across the life course.

Marriage

Permanence, joint production, co-residence, and the social recognition of a sexual and child rearing union are, perhaps, the most important characteristics of the institution of marriage. These characteristics change the behavior of spouses and thereby their well-being. The specialization, economies of scale, and insurance functions of marriage all increase the economic well-being of family members, and the increase is typically quite substantial. Generally, married people produce more of the goods and services consumed in the home and accumulate more assets than unmarried people (Lupton and Smith 2003). Married people also tend to have better physical and emotional health than single people, at least in part because they are married (Mirowsky and Ross 1989), Waite and Gallagher 2000). The social support provided by a spouse, combined with the economic resources produced by the marriage, facilitate both the production and maintenance of health.

As a result, married men and women tend to face lower risks of mortality, and report better physical and mental health and greater overall happiness than others who are like them but who are not married or partnered (Waite and Joyner 2001). However, the benefits of marriage depend on the quality of the relationship. Research in the United States suggests that lower-quality relationships generally are no more beneficial than being single (Umberson et al. 2006; Williams 2003). More recently, studies have begun to focus on multiple dimensions of marital or partnered relationships, incorporating positive and negative experiences (Umberson et al. 2006; Warner and Kelley-Moore 2012). Sexuality in couples is important as a shared activity, as a bond between partners, and sometimes as a source of tension or strain.

The nature of coupled relationships has changed, especially in many developed countries, as part of the Second Demographic Transition (Lesthaeghe 2010). Age at marriage has risen substantially, divorce rates are high and stable, and rates of remarriage have fallen, so that a larger proportion of adults are unmarried now than in the past. In 1970, unmarried people in the United States made up 28% of the adult population. In 2010, 44% of adults were unmarried. In fact, the shift away from marriage has been so dramatic for blacks that in 2000, only 39% of black men and 31% of black women were married, compared to 59% of white men and 56% of white women (Fields and Casper 2000). The decline of marriage has been the largest among women with little education and is almost nonexistent among college graduates, creating a divide in the family building experience along lines of class as well as race.

Though marriage rates have declined in the United States and other developed countries, the vast majority of adults do marry at some time in their lives. In the U.S., more than 95% of men and women marry by age 50. And 75% of women who divorce remarry within 10 years. In the United States cohabitation has become an increasingly common step in the courtship process, preceding the majority of marriages and remarriages. Although a number of European countries have experienced similar increases in cohabitation, some have much more and some much less (Kiernan 2004). Cohabitation is strikingly common in the Nordic countries of Denmark, Sweden, and Finland. France also shows fairly high levels, with over 30% of the women and men ages 25 to 34 in cohabiting unions. By contrast, a group of countries including the Netherlands, Great Britain, Germany, and Austria shows moderate levels of cohabitation, with 15–22% of women from ages 20 to 34 in this type of union. And in the Southern European countries of Italy, Greece and Portugal cohabitation is rare, with less than 10% cohabiting among women in this same age group (Kiernan 2004).

Sexuality

In most societies, marriage circumscribes a large majority of sexual relationships, with cohabitation making up much of the rest. Data from the United States show that almost all married men and women are sexually active, and almost all have only one sex partner—their spouse. Unmarried men and women who are not cohabiting have much lower levels of sexual activity than the married and cohabiting, in part because a substantial minority have no sex partner at all. Under a quarter of the unmarried men and a third of the unmarried women who were not cohabiting had no sex partner in the previous year. Men and women who are cohabiting are at least as sexually active as those who are married, but are less likely to be sexually exclusive (Laumann et al. 1994; Waite and Joyner 2001). Thus, the married couple remains the locus of the vast majority of sexual activity. At older ages, virtually all sexually active people were married or, less frequently cohabiting. The lack of a coresidential partner is equivalent, in practice, to the lack of a partnered sex life, at least at the older ages (Lindau et al. 2007; Galinsky et al. 2014).

Sexual attitudes and experiences change over the life course for men and women, and often in different ways. Patterns in the availability of a partner over the life course are gender differentiated, primarily due to women's greater longevity and the likelihood that they are married to men older than themselves. Men's likelihood of being in a marital or cohabiting relationship remains over 80% and is stable into their sixties. Among women, however, partnership prevalence drops sharply after their early fifties (Waite et al. 2009). Physical health and sexual function structure sex and partnership patterns as well, and both change with age, often diverging by gender. At the older ages, when chronic conditions become more common, the health of the male partner is strongly linked to the sexual activity of the dyad, but the sex of the female partner appears less important (Lindau et al. 2007; Karraker and DeLamater 2013).

Attitudes and expectations about sexuality appear to play an important role in sexual expression. These depend in large part on culture, religion, socialization and experience; they change with age, and they differ by gender (Waite and Charme 2015).

The Second Demographic Transition, Attitudes and Low Fertility

Some countries with low fertility have experienced a series of associated changes in the family, and some have not. The changing behaviors that comprise the "Second Demographic Transition" include increasing age at marriage, declines in shares of people married, increases in cohabitation and other informal relationships, high rates of relationship dissolution, and declines in fertility. Childbearing and childrearing are increasingly decoupled from marriage during this transition (Lesthaeghe 2010; Van De Kaa 1987). Lesthaeghe and van de Kaa and other researchers point to changes in attitudes, secularization, and individualization as the key drivers in this transition. With increased prosperity comes a shift in values from what Maslow called material needs, such as food and shelter, to higher-order needs such as autonomy and self-expression (Maslow 1954). This changed the terms under which couples contracted marriage, or substituted less formal agreements from a focus on production, childbearing and childrearing, and religious activity toward emotional gratification, sexuality, and companionship. Giddens (1992) argues that with these other changes comes the idea of the "pure relationship," entered into for its own sake, for what each person gets out of the relationship individually and which each can leave at any time that they feel they are not getting enough satisfactions to remain in the partnership. Such relationships may include children, but do not need to do so, and are by their very nature transient, with individuals contracting any number of such relationships over their lives.

Goldscheider et al. (2015) argue that gender plays a major role in the second demographic transition, with dramatic and important changes in relationships in married and cohabitational dyads. During the first part of the second demographic transition, women enter the labor force in large numbers, but men's role in the family changes very little, with accompanying tensions in family life and increases in both divorce and single childbearing. During the second half, Goldscheider and her colleagues (2015) argue, men increase their time in childrearing and their time in care for the home. Men's support of their wives' time in paid work also increases, as women's earnings become a necessity. These changes strengthen the family and increase its stability by fostering interdependence between partners, by engaging men more intimately with their children, and by reducing the workload of employed women.

Both perspectives on the second demographic transition point to an increasing emphasis on the emotional content of couple relationships, and, thus, a focus on shared sexual expression, shared leisure activities, and satisfaction with the relationship. The bearing and rearing children within marriage declines in both practice and in importance, as attitudes become more accepting of single parenthood, divorce when children are present, and alternative family forms (Lesthaeghe 2010). Thus shared parenthood becomes less central to the marriage bargain. In low- or very-low fertility countries, couple relationships may look quite different from those in countries with larger family sizes. But this may depend on how quickly and how far the country has moved in the second demographic transition.

Lesthaeghe (2010) assesses the movement of a set of countries through the changes that typify the second demographic transition. Fertility postponement appears to be almost universal among countries in Europe, with the countries that first started this pattern—the Nordic countries, Germany, France and the United Kingdom, also showing the values, such as secularism and individualism, thought to underlie the transition. Countries recently beginning to postpone fertility show few changes in values. Asian industrialized countries, including Japan, South Korea, Taiwan, Hong Kong and Singapore all have very low levels of fertility presently, the result of widespread postponement of parenthood with very little catching up at later ages. In these Asian countries marriage rates have also fallen, so that a sizeable share of women ages 30–34 has never married. Both cohabitation and unmarried childbearing are rare in these countries, although both cohabitation and births following closely on marriage may be rising (Lesthaeghe 2010). Although Lesthaeghe does not present country differences in the shift toward materialistic, individualist, and secular values, he finds that higher acceptance of these values predicts the postponement of parenthood in Japan, South Korea and Singapore.

Couple Relationships in Low-Fertility Countries

To the extent that low- and very-low fertility are accompanied by changes in attitudes away from communalism, religiosity, traditional gender roles, and conservative views of sexuality toward autonomy, individualism, secularism, and materialism, the issues people seek from marriage, cohabitation, romantic or casual relationships might differ quite substantially in low- and very-low fertility regimes from those with moderate or high fertility. Relationships based on emotion, shared activities and values, companionship and sexuality might be expected to include partnered sex more frequently and to produce more satisfaction with this shared behavior, since, presumably dissatisfaction with these exchanges would often lead to relationship dissolution. At the same time, couples in relationships formed with the understanding that they are intended to provide sexuality, emotional closeness and companionship may put more effort and more other resources into these parts of the relationship. And the small number of children born to the typical couple, with relatively few years spent raising young children and not so many years with children in the home at all, means more privacy for the couple and fewer claims from children with regard to their time and attention. Thus, we might expect men and women in low- and very-low fertility countries to be more sexually active, more satisfied with sex, and to perceive fewer sexual problems than those in moderate or high fertility regimes.

In fact, the evidence on this is mixed. Laumann and his colleagues (2006) use data from the Global Study of Sexual Attitudes and Behaviors, a survey of 27,500 men and women aged 40–80 years in 29 countries. They focus on subjective sexual well-being, as measured by reports of how physically pleasurable and how emotionally satisfying the persons found their relationship with their partners to be. The people who participated in this study were also asked about their satisfaction with their sexual function/sexual health, and about the importance of their overall life. Laumann and his coauthors identified three distinct clusters of countries as characterized by the answers given by men and women these questions. In what they called the "gender-equality sexual regime," about two-thirds of both men and women report high levels of physical and emotional satisfaction with their relationships (extremely/very satisfying), a large majority are very/somewhat satisfied with their sexual functioning, and about half of the men and a third of the women say that sex is an extremely/very important part of their life. The gender-equality sexual regime countries include all the study countries in Europe (Austria, Belgium, France, Spain, Sweden, Germany, United Kingdom) and the Anglophile countries of Australia, New Zealand and the U.S. Among these countries, Austria shows the highest level of subjective sexual well-being, and Sweden the lowest for men and South Africa the lowest for women. The other two types of countries comprise what the authors call "male-centered sexual regimes". One consists of Islamic and some Asian and European countries, characterized by middle levels of sexual satisfaction. The other type consists of East Asian countries, which are characterized by low levels of sexual satisfaction. The countries in the middle level of sexual satisfaction include Algeria, Brazil, Egypt, Israel, Italy, Korea, Malaysia, Morocco, Philippines, Singapore and Turkey. The countries that show low levels of sexual satisfaction are China, Indonesia, Japan, Taiwan, and Thailand.

The values espoused by those in the low- and very-low fertility countries would lead one to expect that these people would also report high levels of sexual satisfaction and high importance for sex. The results are more complicated. Of the 12 countries with high levels of sexual satisfaction, only three have total fertility rates under 1.7, i.e., they are below-replacement fertility countries. The other nine have fertility levels at about the replacement level.

Of the 11 countries with middle levels of sexual well-being, three have low fertility, three have replacement-level fertility, and five have high fertility. Of the five countries with low levels of sexual well-being, three have very-low fertility rates, one (Thailand) has replacement-level fertility, and one (Indonesia) has high fertility.

The research by Laumann and colleagues (2006) suggests that couple relationships in very low-fertility countries are sometimes rated as very satisfying (Canada, Spain and Germany), sometimes as middling (Italy, Korea, and Singapore), and sometimes as poor (China, Japan and Taiwan). This does not fit with the perspective that a focus on higher-level needs such as self-fulfillment drives the movement toward low fertility. In fact, many people in these societies rate their sexual needs as not very well fulfilling. And countries in which many people are very satisfied with their sexual relationship and health often have replacement-level fertility (Australia, Austria, Belgium, France, Mexico, New Zealand, Sweden, United Kingdom and the United States). Note that there are no high-fertility countries in the group characterized by high levels of sexual satisfaction *nor* in the group with low sexual well-being, with the exception of Indonesia in the latter group. All the high-fertility countries in the study conducted by Laumann and associates are in the group with middling levels of sexual well-being.

Clearly, low or very-low fertility does not ensure a focus on the couple relationship, at least not a successful focus. And freedom from (very many) children does not ensure that couples will spend their freed up resources in ways that lead to a satisfying sexual relationship. By the same token, high fertility does not necessarily consign a country to poor subjective sexual well-being.

Relationship Quality, Shared Activity, and Sexual Expression among Older Couples in a Low-Fertility Setting

While the association between high- or low-fertility and couple relationships is not straightforward, previous studies have shown that couple relationships in low-fertility countries tend to place more emphasis on the content of relationships including quality, shared activities, and shared sexual expression than on shared parenthood (Lesthaeghe 2010). Since the benefits of marriage or couple relationships depend on the quality of the relationship (Umberson et al. 2006), higher levels of sexual satisfaction and marital quality seem to lead to a decrease in marital instability over time (Yeh et al. 2006; Dzara 2010). The dimensions of relationship quality do not appear to operate independently; the research indicates that they simultaneously influence one another, ultimately promoting or detracting from overall relationship quality. Thus, it is important to understand the associations among relationships quality, shared activities, and sexual expression. In the remaining sections we will discuss recent research on couple relationships among older adults in the U.S.

Previous studies on marital quality have emphasized the importance of distinguishing two dimensions of relationships quality: a positive dimension, which captures features such as happiness with the relationship and emotional closeness, and a negative dimension, which includes conflict, criticism, and distance (Bookwala and Franks 2005; Fincham and Linfield 1997; Glenn 1990; Johnson et al. 1986). The theoretical and empirical importance of distinguishing positive and negative dimensions is well documented (Bradbury et al. 2000) because it allows us to identify ambivalent relationships, which characterize those who score high on both positive and negative dimensions, or indifferent relationships, in which individuals show low scores on both positive and negative dimensions. Furthermore, a recent study found that activities shared by couples is a distinct dimension of marital interaction, separating both conceptually and empirically from positive relationship quality and negative relationship quality (Kim and Waite 2014). In the next section we introduce these measures among older couples in a low-fertility setting, describe differences by gender, and characterize married and cohabiting relationships along the dimensions of positive and negative marital quality and share activities.

We first introduce scales on relationships quality and shared activity using multiple indicators from the second wave of the National Social Life, Health, and Aging Project (NSHAP). We assess relationship quality using eight indicators identified in prior research as generally corresponding to the positive and the negative aspects of relationship quality (Bookwala and Franks 2005; Fincham and Linfield 1997; Warner and Kelley-Moore 2012). Once positive and negative dimensions of relationship quality are identified, we further differentiate ambivalent (high positive and high negative) and indifferent (low positive and low negative) feelings toward the spouse or partner on the basis of scores on positive and negative relationship quality suggested by previous research (Fincham and Linfield 1997). We draw on five indicators of activities shared by the couples. Of the five, two indicators asked directly about sexual behavior. These items are shown in Table 8.1.

Table 8.1 shows that husbands generally rated their relationships as happier than did wives, and said they thought things were going well more often than did women. Men were more likely than women to say that they can rely on their spouse/partner when they have a problem. However, husbands and male partners also were more likely to report negative features of their relationships; men more often said that their spouse/partner makes too many demands on them and that their spouse criticizes them. Women more so than men reported that their partners get on their nerves. Note that only one of the measures of shared activities differs between husbands and wives in dyads: men reported more often that when their partner wanted to have sex, they agreed than did wives in the same situation, although both genders said they almost always agreed.

Scales of relationships quality and shared activity were constructed based on the internal consistency of the measure using Cronbach's alpha. Then each scale was constructed based by standardizing each items (mean = 0 and standard deviation = 1) and dividing the sum of standardized item scores by the total number of nonmissing items. The relationship quality scale has a 2-factor structure, including positive relationships quality (PRQ) and negative relationship quality (NRQ). The shared activity scale has a 1-factor structure (for the details on scale construction, see Kim and Waite 2014).

Table 8.2 shows that husbands scored higher than wives on both positive relationship quality and negative relationship quality. This suggests that a greater share of older men experience ambivalent feelings toward their spouse or partner than do women. Women showed significantly lower scores than men, on average, on both positive and negative relationship quality, which suggests that at least on the dimensions of the relationship measured here, more women than men have relationships of indifferent quality, with relatively low costs and relatively low benefits.

To examine the share of ambivalent and indifferent husbands and wives among U.S. older adults, the groups of ambivalent and indifferent spouses were formed on the basis of scores on the PRQ and NRQ measures. Groups for husbands and for wives were formed independently. Ambivalent groups were composed of those who scored above the gender-specific median on PRQ (scores of 0.275 or higher for husbands and scores of 0.135 or higher for wives) and above the gender-specific median on NRQ (scores of 0.013 or higher for husbands and scores of −0.098 or higher for wives). Indifferent groups comprised spouses who scored below the median on both dimensions.

Table 8.1 Summary Statistics for Indicators of Relationships Quality and Shared Activity in NSHAP

		All Partnered (n = 2487)									
					Husband (n = 1307)			Wife (n = 1180)			
		Mean	SD	n	Mean[a]	SD	n	Mean[a]		SD	n
Relationships quality											
1	How would you describe your (marriage/relationship) with [current/recent partner]?	6.33	1.29	2479	6.44	1.21	1302	6.24	***	1.36	1177
	(range from 1 = very unhappy to 7 = very happy)										
2	In general, how often do you think that things between you and your partner are going well?	5.01	0.89	2027	5.08	0.91	1056	4.94	***	0.98	971
	(range from 1 = never to 6 = all the time)										
3	How close do you feel is your relationships with [NAME]?	3.59	0.62	2484	3.60	0.04	1304	3.57		0.02	1180
	(1 = “not very close,” 2 = “somewhat close,” 3 = “very close,” 4 = “extremely close”)										
	How often can you…										
	(0 = “never,” 1 = “hardly ever or rarely,” 2 = “some of the time,” 4 = “often”)										
4	Open up to your spouse or partner?	2.68	0.62	2482	2.69	0.61	1302	2.67		0.62	1180
5	Rely on your spouse or partner?	2.82	0.52	2483	2.86	0.45	1304	2.77	***	0.58	1179
	How often does spouse or partner …										
	(0 = “never,” 1 = “hardly ever or rarely,” 2 = “some of the time,” 3 = “often”)										
6	Make too many demands on you?	1.15	0.97	2482	1.23	0.94	1304	1.05	***	0.99	1178
7	Criticize you?	1.25	0.91	2480	1.40	0.86	1301	1.08	***	0.93	1179
8	Get on your nerves?	1.42	0.76	2016	1.34	0.76	1049	1.52	***	0.79	967

(continued)

Table 8.1 (continued)

		All Partnered (n = 2487)									
		Husband (n = 1307)						Wife (n = 1180)			
		Mean	SD	n	Mean[a]	SD	n	Mean[a]		SD	n
Shared activity											
9	Some couples like to spend their free time doing things together, while others like to do different things in their free time. Do you like to spend free time doing things together, or doing things separately?	2.34	0.69	2480	2.37	0.66	1303	2.31		0.71	1177
	(1 = "different/separate things", 2 = "some together, some different," 3 = "together")										
10	How often have you and your partner shared caring touch, such as a hug, sitting or lying cuddled up, a neck rub or holding hands?	4.66	1.76	1995	4.64	1.67	1041	4.69		1.85	954
	(from 1 = "never" to 7 = "many times a day")										
11	In the last month, how often did you sleep in the same bed with your spouse or romantic partner?	4.09	1.53	1946	4.08	1.54	1020	4.11		1.52	926
	(from 1 = "never" to 6 = "all the time")										
12	During the last 12 month, about how often did you have sex with current spouse or partner?	2.29	1.29	2252	2.35	1.28	1176	2.22		1.31	1076
	(1 = "none at all," 2 = "once a month or less," 3 = "2–3 times a month," 4 = "once or twice a week," 5 = "3–6 times a week," 6 = "once a day or more.")										
13	When your partner wants to have sex with you, how often do you agree?	4.49	2.04	2316	4.67	2.05	1208	4.29	***	2.02	1108
	(from 1 = "never" to 5 = "always," 0 = "if volunteered: My partner has not wanted to have sex with me in the past 12 months")										

***$p < 0.001$; **$p < 0.01$; *$p < 0.05$ (Wald tests using design-based SE)

[a]Survey-adjusted and weighted to account for the probability of selection, with post-stratification adjustments for non-response

Table 8.2 Means and standard deviations for relationship quality and shared activity scale, by age groups and gender[a]

	Husband		Wife	
	M[b]	SD[c]	M[b]	SD[c]
Relationship quality				
Positive dimension (α = 0.72)	0.06	0.67	−0.07	0.81
Negative dimension (α = 0.66)	0.05	0.78	−0.12	0.86
Shared activity (α = 0.66)	0.08	0.64	−0.02	0.67

[a]Survey-adjusted and weighted to account for the probability of selection, with post-stratification adjustments for non-response
[b]126 women and 11 men are age 61 and under, and 4 men are age 91 and older. These cases were excluded in age group comparisons
[c]Significant difference between men and women (p < 0.01)

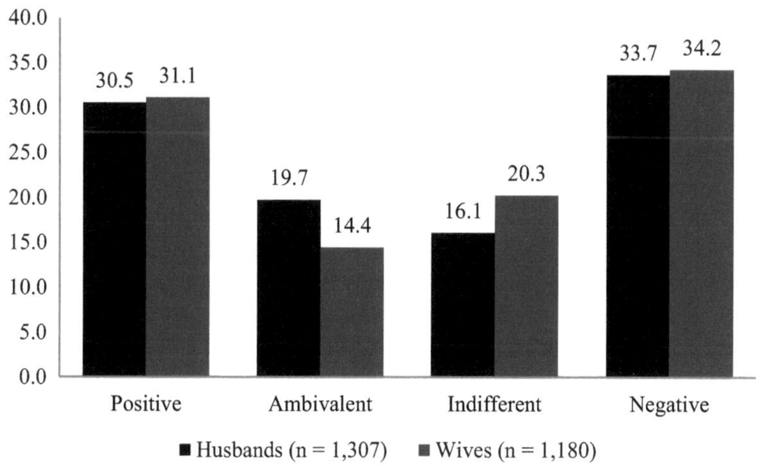

Fig. 8.1 Types of relationship quality by gender

Figure 8.1 shows that about 30% of men and women report high positive and low negative feelings toward their spouse or partner, and 34% have low positive and high negative feelings. The percentages are very similar for the two genders. However, men are more likely to have ambivalent feelings, with relatively high positive feelings and relatively high negative feelings, than are women, whereas women are more likely to have relatively low negative feelings combined with relatively low positive feelings. Thus, more men fall into the ambivalent group than fall into the indifferent group, whereas more women fall into the indifferent group than fall into the ambivalent group.

Relationship quality, both positive and negative, and shared activities, tend to go hand-in-hand. The positive dimension of quality was positively correlated with shared activity ($r = .39$, $p < .000$), whereas the negative dimension of quality was negatively correlated ($r = -.23$, $p < .000$). This suggests that couples who more often did things together were more likely to feel close, to be happy, to be able to open up to their spouse about their worries, to be able to rely on their spouse if they had a serious problem, and to evaluate their relationship as going well. Those who shared fewer activities were more likely to report that their spouse was demanding, got on their nerves, and/or criticized them, which was, perhaps, *why* they shared few activities. However, the evaluative dimensions of positive and negative relationship quality are empirically and conceptually distinct from the more objective shared activities scale.

How do the activities shared by couples and their partnered sexual expression differ among couples across the four types of relationship quality? Table 8.3 shows the distribution of the shared activity items and the scale by the types of relationships quality and gender. Indifferent and negative husbands and wives had significantly lower shared activity scale scores than positive husbands and wives had, respectively. However, some nuanced differences can be observed when we examine the specific items on shared activity that contribute to the difference across the types of marital quality for husbands and wives respectively. We see that both ambivalent and indifferent husbands shared caring touching less often than positive husbands. But ambivalent husbands had sex with their spouse or partner less often than positive husbands, while indifferent husbands reported spending less time with their spouse or partner than positive husbands. With respect to wives, there were no significant differences between positive and ambivalent wives in terms of the shared activities, but significant differences in the expected direction were found between positive and indifferent groups in spending time together and sharing caring touch. Thus, while couples' less frequent sex and caring touch appear among husbands with ambivalent feeling toward their spouse or coresident partner, sexual activity and caring touch are not related to wives' ambivalent feeling toward their spouse or partner. Our findings suggest different ways to protect marital quality among those with ambivalent, indifferent, or negative feeling toward their husbands and wives.

Discussion

Dramatic changes have taken place in the social institution of the family in many countries. These include some combination of the following: an increase in age at first marriage, increasing levels of relationship dissolution, increases in cohabitation (which is legally defined in some countries but not in others), increases in childbearing outside marriage, and declines in fertility. These changes do not appear in most countries; fertility remains fairly high in the United States, as do rates of divorce and unmarried childbearing. But long-term cohabitation remains rare. In the low-fertility countries of Japan, Korea and Singapore, unmarried childbearing is virtually absent, and cohabitation is rare, but age at marriage has risen dramatically. In fact, most low- or very-low fertility societies have reached that state through low rates of unmarried childbearing combined with low rates of marriage. Italy, Greece and Spain fall into this category.

Table 8.3 Summary statistics for indicators of shared activity by the types of relationships quality

		Husbands								Wives							
		Positive (reference)		Ambivalent		Indifferent		Negative		Positive (reference)		Ambivalent		Indifferent		Negative	
		M	SD	M	SD	M	SD	M	SD	M	SD	M	SD	M	SD	M	SD
Indicators of shared activity																	
9	Some couples like to spend their free time doing things together, while others like to do different things in their free time. Do you like to spend free time doing things together, or doing things separately?	2.51	0.60	2.50	0.60	2.26***	0.70	2.21***	0.70	2.53	0.56	2.47	0.64	2.26**	0.76	2.07***	0.76
	(1 = "different/separate things", 2 = "some together, some different," 3 = "together")																
10	How often have you and your partner shared caring touch, such as a hug, sitting or lying cuddled up, a neck rub or holding hands?	5.22	1.55	4.72*	1.54	4.62***	1.55	3.99***	1.71	5.45	1.39	5.21	1.46	4.71**	1.88	3.66***	1.92
	(from 1 = "never" to 7 = "many times a day")																
11	In the last month, how often did you sleep in the same bed with your spouse or romantic partner?	4.29	1.38	4.32	1.38	3.74	1.65	3.87**	1.67	4.40	1.32	4.33	1.34	4.08	1.53	3.70***	1.70
	(from 1 = "never" to 6 = "all the time")																

(continued)

Table 8.3 (continued)

		Husbands								Wives							
		Positive (reference)		Ambivalent		Indifferent		Negative		Positive (reference)		Ambivalent		Indifferent		Negative	
		M	SD	M	SD	M	SD	M	SD	M	SD	M	SD	M	SD	M	SD
12	During the last 12 month, about how often did you have sex with current spouse or partner?	2.69	1.34	2.30**	1.23	2.36	1.30	2.03***	1.12	2.44	1.26	2.40	1.28	2.20	1.45	1.94**	1.23
	(1 = "none at all," 2 = "once a month or less," 3 = "2–3 times a month," 4 = "once or twice a week," 5 = "3–6 times a week," 6 = "once a day or more.")																
13	When your partner wants to have sex with you, how often do you agree?	4.02	1.66	3.84	1.78	3.51	1.91	3.55**	1.90	3.69	1.62	3.71	1.48	3.29	1.95	2.99***	1.85
	(from 1 = "never" to 5 = "always," 0 = "if volunteered: My partner has not wanted to have sex with me in the past 12 months")																
Shared activity scale	0.29	0.60	0.19	0.57	0.01**	0.69	−0.12***	0.64	0.26	0.52	0.22	0.51	−0.03***	0.66	−0.32***	0.67	

Significantly different from the positive groups (*** at $p < 0.001$;** at $p < 0.01$; *at $p < 0.05$)

This chapter addressed the state of coupled relationships in the low fertility countries that have been affected by these changes in the family. Evidence on sexuality in these countries suggests that more child-free time due to small numbers of children does not always mean more focus on the quality of the relationship between marital or cohabiting partners. In some low- or very-low fertility countries, both men and women express low levels of satisfaction with sex.

Our research on marital and cohabiting couples in the U.S. shows that at older ages, many couples remain sexually active, and most are quite satisfied with their sexual relationship. At the same time, only about a third of the partners among older couples are entirely happy with the amount of support they get from their spouse and feel that their partners are not (very) critical or demanding. The other two thirds perceive some negatives in their relationship, either because they feel that their spouse is not supportive, or they feel that their spouse is critical or demanding or both. These couples do fewer things together, including having less sex. Given the importance of marital solidarity and marital quality to mental and physical health and disability in later life, the dissatisfaction among members of many older couples is a cause for concern. Attention to marital functioning could improve health, well-being and general happiness at older ages. This is especially important in low-fertility countries since many older adults have few close relatives other than their spouse.

Acknowledgments This work was supported by the National Institutes of Health, specifically, the National Institute on Aging, the Division of Behavioral and Social Sciences Research for the National Health, Social Life, and Aging Project (NSHAP) (R01 AG021487, R37 AG030481), and the NSHAP Wave 2 Partner Project (R01 AG033903).

References

Bookwala, J., & Franks, M. M. (2005). Moderating role of marital quality in older adults' depressed affect: Beyond the main-effects model. *Journal of Gerontology: Psychological Sciences, 60B*(6), 338–341.

Bradbury, T. N., et al. (2000). Research on the nature and determinants of marital satisfaction: A decade in review. *Journal of Marriage and Family, 62*(4), 964–980.

Dzara, K. (2010). Assessing the effect of marital sexuality on marital disruption. *Social Science Research, 39*(5), 715–724.

Fields, J., & Casper, L. M. (2000). America's families and living arrangements: March 2000. In *Current population reports*. U.S. Census Bureau: Washington, DC.

Fincham, F. D., & Linfield, K. J. (1997). A new look at marital quality: Can spouses feel positive and negative about their marriage? *Journal of Family Psychology, 11*(4), 489.

Galinsky, A. M., Mcclintock, M. K., & Waite, L. J. (2014). Sexuality and physical contact in the National Social Life, health, and aging project, wave 2. *The Journals of Gerontology Series B: Psychological Sciences and Social Sciences, 69*(Suppl 2), S83–S98.

Giddens, A. (1992). *The transformation of intimacy: Sexuality, love and eroticism in modern societies*. Stanford: Stanford University Press.

Glenn, N. D. (1990). Quantitative research in marital quality in the 1980s: A critical review. *Journal of Marriage and Family, 52*, 818–831.

Goldscheider, F., Bernhardt, E., & Lappegard, T. (2015). The gender revolution: A framework for understanding changing family and demographic behavior. *Population and Development Review, 41*(2), 207–239.
Johnson, D. R., White, L. K., Edwards, J. N., & Booth, A. (1986). Dimensions of marital quality toward methodological and conceptual refinement. *Journal of Family Issues, 7*(1), 31–49.
Karraker, A., & DeLamater, J. (2013). Past-year sexual inactivity among older married persons and their partners. *Journal of Marriage and Family, 75*(1), 142–163.
Kiernan, K. (2004). Redrawing the boundaries of marriage. *Journal of Marriage and Family, 66*(4), 980–987.
Kim, J., & Waite, L. J. (2014). Relationship quality and shared activity in marital and cohabiting dyads in the National Social Life, health, and aging project, wave 2. *The Journals of Gerontology Series B: Psychological Sciences and Social Sciences, 69*(Suppl 2), S64–S74.
Laumann, E. O., Gagnon, J. H., Michael, R. T., & Michaels, S. (1994). *The social organization of sexuality: Sexual practices in the United States*. Chicago: University of Chicago Press.
Laumann, E. O., Paik, A., Glasser, D. B., Kang, J.-H., Wang, T., Levinson, B., & Gingell, C. (2006). A cross-national study of subjective sexual well-being among older women and men: Findings from the global study of sexual attitudes and behaviors. *Archives of Sexual Behavior, 35*(2), 145–161.
Lesthaeghe, R. (2010). The unfolding story of the second demographic transition. *Population and Development Review, 36*(2), 211–251.
Lindau, S. T., Schumm, P., Laumann, E. O., Levinson, W., O'muircheartaigh, C. A., & Waite, L. J. (2007). A national study of sexuality and health among older adults in the U.S. *New England Journal of Medicine, 357*(8), 762–774.
Loe, M. (2008). The new view in action: College students discuss 21st-century sexuality. *Feminism and Psychology, 18*(4), 495–504.
Lupton, J., & Smith, J. P. (2003). Marriage, assets, and savings. In S. Grossbard-Shechtman (Ed.), *Marriage and the economy* (pp. 129–152). Cambridge: Cambridge University Press.
Maslow, A. H. (1954). *Motivation and personality*. New York: Harper.
Mirowsky, J., & Ross, C. E. (1989). *Social causes of psychological distress*. New York: Aldine de Gruyter.
Thornton, A., & Fricke, T. E. (1989). Social change and the family: Comparative perspectives from the West, China and South Asia. In J. M. Stycos (Ed.), *Demography as an interdiscipline* (pp. 128–161). Transaction: New Brunswick.
Umberson, D., Williams, K., Powers, D. A., Liu, H., & Needham, B. (2006). You make me sick: Marital quality and health over the life course. *Journal of Health and Social Behavior, 47*(1), 1–16.
Van De Kaa, D. J. (1987). Europe's second demographic transition. *Population Bulletin, 42*, 1–59.
Waite, L. J., & Charme, C. (2015). Sexuality over the lifecourse. In J. Wright (Ed.), *International encyclopedia for the behavioral and social sciences* (2nd ed., pp. 840–845). New York: Elsevier.
Waite, L. J., & Gallagher, M. (2000). *The case for marriage: Why married people are happier, healthier and better off financially*. New York: Doubleday.
Waite, L. J., & Joyner, K. (2001). Emotional satisfaction and physical pleasure in sexual unions: Time horizon, sexual behavior, and sexual exclusivity. *Journal of Marriage and Family, 63*(1), 247–264.
Waite, L. J., Laumann, E. O., Das, A., & Schumm, L. P. (2009). Sexuality: Measures of partnerships, practices, attitudes, and problems in the national social life health and aging study. *Journal of Gerontology: Social Sciences, 64B*(S1), i56–i66.
Warner, D. F., & Kelley-Moore, J. (2012). The social context of disablement among older adults: Does marital quality matter for loneliness? *Journal of Health and Social Behavior, 53*(1), 50–66.
Williams, K. (2003). Has the future of marriage arrived? A contemporary examination of gender, marriage, and psychological well-being. *Journal of Health and Social Behavior, 44*(4), 470–487.
Yeh, H. C., Lorenz, F. O., Wickrama, K. A. S., Conger, R. D., & Elder, G. H., Jr. (2006). Relationships among sexual satisfaction, marital quality, and marital instability at midlife. *Journal of Family Psychology, 20*(2), 339.

Chapter 9
What Is Driving Marriage and Cohabitation in Low Fertility Countries?

Gavin Jones

Introduction

The argument of William Goode (1963) many decades ago that family patterns in developing countries would converge in the process of their development towards those of Western countries has come under considerable criticism from scholars including McDonald (1992) and Cherlin (2012). Goode's argument was that the Western family pattern was best suited for advanced industrial societies, and therefore there was likely to be a convergence toward this model as countries underwent industrialization. There are a number of problems with convergence theory. The most fundamental problem is that the Western family pattern to which other societies are supposed to converge is itself changing in quite fundamental ways. Thus it is not clear what these other societies are supposed to be converging towards. The "male breadwinner" model has now been greatly modified in Western countries.

In terms of marriage, any idea of convergence is also challenged by the ongoing changes in partnering patterns in Western societies – a transition from companionate marriage to individualistic marriage, with emphasis on personal fulfilment, self-development and flexible roles, along the lines of the "second demographic transition" (van de Kaa 1987; Lesthaeghe 2010). As Cherlin (2012: 597) notes, the mid-twentieth century was actually the high point of uniformity in family patterns in Western countries – they were less uniform in the past, when informal marriage and extra-marital births had at some times and in some places been much more common (especially among the poor), and are less uniform today, with a spread of informal coupling and childbearing across the social hierarchy.

As will be discussed below, in terms of increasing singlehood, the low-fertility East Asian societies have not converged toward, but instead "overshot," Western societies. There is also increasing diversity in marriage trends in Asia. Over recent

G. Jones (✉)
Australian National University, Canberra, Australia
e-mail: gavinj881@gmail.com

D.L. Poston, Jr. (ed.), *Low Fertility Regimes and Demographic and Societal Change*, DOI 10.1007/978-3-319-64061-7_9

decades, age at marriage seemed to be increasing in all Asian societies, but over the recent past, age at marriage fell in Sri Lanka, Indonesia and Vietnam. South Asian marriage patterns seem very resistant to the kinds of changes that are supposed to accompany rising levels of education and economic development. This chapter will not deal with trends in the whole of Asia, however, but will focus on the low fertility countries of East Asia. The emphasis will be on the question: do East Asian – European comparisons support the idea of convergence of family patterns (in this case marriage patterns) toward the patterns supposedly representative of advanced industrial societies?

Which Are the Lowest Fertility Countries?

First, a comparison of fertility levels in the low fertility countries of Europe and East Asia is in order. East Asian countries have reached period fertility levels even lower than those in the lowest fertility countries of Europe (Frejka et al. 2010). This has been the case since the early 2000s when period fertility rates declined to very low levels in East Asia at the same time as the rates in many different European countries turned upward to some extent from the very low rates reached in the late 1990s and around the turn of the century (Myrskyla et al. 2009; Goldstein et al. 2009). Some recovery in fertility has also been observed in some East Asian countries, notably Japan, but it is less pronounced than in Europe. The most recent figures for period fertility are shown in Table 9.1 Clearly, fertility in the lowest-fertility East Asian countries is below that in almost all of the lowest-fertility countries in Europe.

Historical Trends in Singlehood

Current high levels of singlehood in parts of Europe and in East Asia are not historically unprecedented. In the early decades of the twentieth century 12 to 25% of women in Europe were never-married at the end of their reproductive period (Therborn 2004: Table 5.1). Age at marriage subsequently declined sharply, and marriage became near-universal in most Western countries in the third quarter of the century, before entering a period of gradual retreat from marriage which has continued up to the present (Therborn 2004, Chapter 5; Festy 2000).

Some years ago, I drew the distinction between singlehood in the formal sense of never having been married, and "effective singlehood," defined as never having been married or in a cohabiting relationship (see Jones 2007). A comparison of data from Europe and East and Southeast Asia showed that if the "flight from marriage" was measured simply by the increase in population which had not entered formal marriage at any given age, then Europe had outstripped East and Southeast Asia. However, such a comparison ignores the marriage-like aspect of many cohabiting relationships. When "currently cohabiting" couples were removed from the single

Table 9.1 Total fertility rates, lowest fertility countries of Europe and Asia, 2008 and 2011

	2008	2011
European countries		
Hungary	1.35	1.24
Poland	1.39	1.30
Spain	1.45	1.34
Portugal	1.40	1.35
Germany	1.38	1.36
Greece	1.51	1.39
Italy	1.41	1.39
Slovakia	1.32	1.45
Moldova	1.28	1.47
Romania	1.35	1.53
Asian countries		
Taiwan	1.05	1.06
Hong Kong	1.06	1.20
Singapore	1.28	1.20
S. Korea	1.19	1.24
Japan	1.37	1.39
China	1.5?	1.5?

Source: OECD, Family Database; World Bank, World Development Indicators

category in Europe, many Asian countries exceeded the figures for most European countries. And if "ever cohabited" persons were removed, then most of the main countries of East and Southeast Asia exceeded the proportions effectively single in northern and Western Europe. Only Italy and Spain matched the figures for most of the Asian countries studied.

In other words, "effective singlehood" in East Asia had run ahead of the West, if cohabitation was equated with marriage in the West.

A weakness of this comparison was that although there is little cohabitation in Asia, there is certainly some. I admitted (Jones 2007: 458–461) that the comparison of singles in East Asia with the "effectively single" in Europe was not ideal (for example, we know there is considerable cohabitation in Japan and the Philippines), but lack of data on cohabitation in Asia left no alternative.

A Decade On – Trends in Singlehood in Europe and East Asia

Europe

Now is a good time to update the comparison of singlehood in European and East Asian countries. First, the trends in Europe over the 2000–2012 period will be discussed. Table 9.2 shows that the proportion remaining single is very high in the age

Table 9.2 European countries around 2000 and 2012: Percentages single; single, not cohabiting; and single, never cohabited: Ages 25–34

	2000			2010		
Country	% Single	% Single, not currently cohabiting	% Single, never cohabited	% Single	% Single, not currently cohabiting	% Single, never cohabited
Sweden	72	33	13	70	36	20
Denmark	63	31	14	69	38	20
Norway				62	25	9
Finland	57	28	17	59	31	16
UK	43	32	16	60	42	23
France	61	30	15	60	36	16
Belgium	41	26	20	60	32	18
Netherlands	53	31	23	54	29	17
Germany	52	28	18	62	39	24
Austria	48	26	13			
Hungary				59	41	23
Poland				37	31	22
Russian Federation				38	29	14
Spain	56	45	41	69	48	32
Portugal	39	34	32	60	44	34
Greece	44	34	29			
Italy	66	59	55	69	59	44

Sources: Eurobarometer data from Kiernan (2004); Centre for Comparative Social Surveys (2012).

group 25–34 – above 60% in most countries, though much lower in Poland and the Russian Federation.[1] However, when the percentages currently cohabiting are removed from the "single" category, on the ground that cohabitation is a marriage-like relationship, the proportion effectively single falls sharply. For example, in the UK, France, Belgium and Portugal, all of which had 60% single in this age group, removal of those currently cohabiting from the "single" category lowers the proportion to 42, 36, 32 and 44%, respectively.

A further adjustment can be made to the proportion "effectively single" by removing from the single category all those who have ever been in a cohabiting relationship. This is equivalent to removing the ever-divorced from the numerator in measuring the "never married" in a conventional analysis of marital status. If we follow this strategy for 2000, much clearer patterns of regional difference are revealed (Jones 2007: 437). This continues to be the case with the 2012 data, which show that Italy, Portugal and Spain had much higher levels of effective singlehood according to this measure than did the other European countries. Effective

[1] The figures for Poland and the Russian Federation indicate a much lower mean age at marriage than in any of the other countries in the table. Unfortunately, data on these two countries are not available for 2000.

singlehood in Italy in 2012 was roughly twice or more than twice as high as in any of the Western and Central European countries shown in the table, and in Spain and Portugal twice as high as in Finland, France and the Russian Federation.

Did singlehood increase in Europe over the first decade of the twenty-first century? There are 11 countries in Table 9.2 with comparable data for both 2000 and 2010–12. Comparison of the figures on percentage single in the 2 years shows that the percentage rose in 8 countries, stayed roughly the same in 2 countries, and decreased in one country. The sharpest increases were in the UK, Spain and Portugal. When those currently cohabiting are removed from the "single" category, the trend in "percentage single, not currently cohabiting" is similar: it rose (in some countries quite sharply) in 9 countries, stayed roughly the same in one country (Italy) and decreased slightly in one country (the Netherlands). The UK, Germany and Portugal showed the sharpest increases.

However, the clear trend toward higher proportions effectively single according to these two measures is somewhat modified when those who had ever cohabited are removed from the single category. Those who are "effectively single" according to this more rigorous definition increased in 5 countries, stayed roughly the same in 2, and decreased in 4 countries. No clear trend is apparent for Europe according to this measure. It would appear, then, that for Europe as a whole (at least as represented by these 11 countries drawn from different parts of Europe) singlehood is increasing if singlehood is defined as not married or living with a partner. However, there is no clear trend in the proportion who have **never** lived with a partner. The tendency for "effective singlehood" to rise if measured by the proportion not married or currently living with a partner but to show inconclusive results if measured by the proportion never having lived with a partner appears to support the conclusion of Noack et al. (2014: 28-29) that the declining frequency of living together as a couple is usually due to more frequent relationship break-ups than to fewer people entering a co-residential union.

In general, then, according to this not fully representative sample of European countries, levels of singlehood seem to have increased over the period. In terms of regional differences, while these patterns remain quite strong in 2010, they are less marked than in 2000. The key difference is that "% single, never cohabited" in Italy and Spain has fallen sharply, suggesting that cohabitation has increased considerably in those 2 countries. The evidence of Table 9.1 suggests that the trend toward cohabitation has gone further in Spain than in Italy. This is confirmed by other evidence (Pereiro et al. 2014). Even so, Italy and Spain still have much higher proportions effectively single than do Scandinavia or Western Europe.

East Asia

While effective singlehood is still generally on the increase in European countries, it appears to be increasing more sharply in some of the countries of East Asia, thus tending if anything to widen the gap between the higher levels of effective singlehood in East Asian countries than in Europe. As Fig. 9.1 shows, all the countries of East Asia that have reached ultra-low fertility levels had remarkable increases in proportions single for women aged 30–34 between 1970 and 2010.[2] There was no slowing of this increase between 2000 and 2010, except in Singapore; in Japan, South Korea and Taiwan, the percentage single for women aged 30–34 rose from 27 to 33, 11 to 29, and 21 to 37 respectively.[3] The trends in marriage and fertility were, of course, not unrelated.

The rise in singlehood over the 1970–2010 period in East Asian countries has occurred in a period of remarkably rapid economic and social development. For example, average educational attainment of younger cohorts in Japan, South Korea, Taiwan and Singapore has reached levels higher than in most of Europe. For females, singlehood rates are substantially higher for the better educated. This leads to the question of whether the continuing rise in singlehood in recent times is purely compositional, that is, arising from the higher proportions in the better educated categories. The answer to this question in the 2000–2005 period is that in Japan, South Korea and Taiwan, the change was not just compositional, but was "across the board," with rising singlehood evident for all educational groups. However, in Singapore, it was purely compositional (Jones and Gubhaju 2009). Although detailed data on marital status by educational level in the subsequent 5-year period (2005–2010) have not yet been analysed, we can infer from the continuing rapid rise in singlehood in that period in Japan, South Korea and Taiwan that it continues to be a trend across all educational groups.

The East Asia – Europe Comparison

The most recent data for East Asian and European countries are presented in Table 9.3. As was the case a decade earlier (see Jones 2007, Table 9.2), the European countries tend to have higher proportions single than even the latest-marrying East Asian countries. Among East Asian countries, only Hong Kong reaches the 50% figure for proportion single at ages 25–39, whereas in Europe, many countries in western and southern Europe exceed 50%.

However, when current cohabiters are removed from the "single" category in Europe, only Italy can match the proportions single in East Asian countries (except China), and Thailand and Myanmar also exceed many of the European countries. When "ever cohabited" persons are also removed from the single category in

[2] As an aside, it might be noted that Fig. 9.1 shows that, although all the highly developed East Asian countries have experienced remarkable increases in singlehood, singlehood has not increased nearly as dramatically for Asia as a whole, because the three largest Asian countries (China, India and Indonesia) have had only modest increases from very low rates of singlehood.

[3] Aside from Singapore, the one exception to sharp increases in proportions single is China, where fertility has reached low levels (probably a TFR of 1.5, if not lower), though not as low as those of most other East Asian countries. It is likely that the lower level of socio-economic development in China than in other East Asian countries is the main reason (Jones and Yeung 2014).

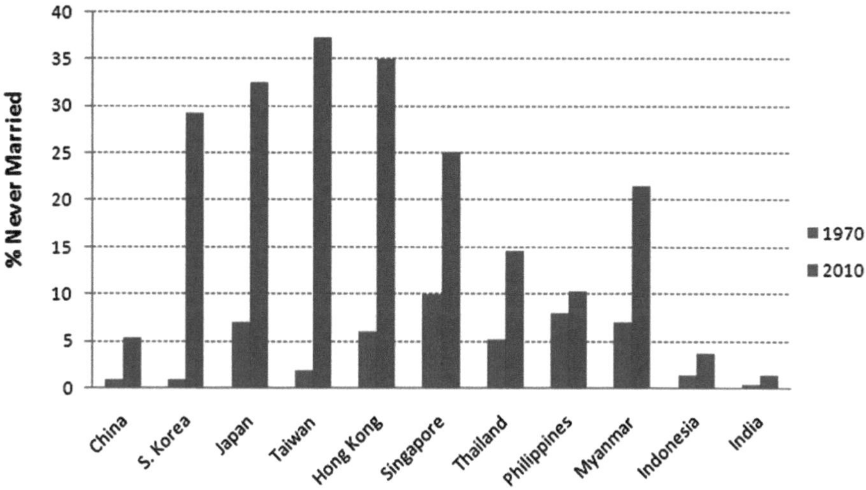

Fig. 9.1 Percent never married, females aged 30–34, selected Asian countries, 1970 and 2010

Table 9.3 Comparison of the percentage of single, never-cohabited (European countries) and the percentage of single, never married (Pacific Asian countries) men and women combined aged 25–39, 2010–2012

Pacific Asia		Europe			
	% Single		% Single	% Single, not currently cohabiting	% Single, never cohabited
Japan	42.8	Belgium	48.8	26.8	14.0
South Korea	45.5	Denmark	54	28.8	14.7
Taiwan	49.4	Finland	51.3	27.4	12.3
Singapore	38.1	France	51.6	30.0	13.4
Malaysia	27.6	Germany	52.6	32.1	18.1
Hong Kong SAR	50.6	Hungary	50.1	36.4	19.2
China	14.0	Italy	56.1	48.0	34.8
Thailand	31.8	Netherlands	49.6	28.5	15.4
Philippines	22.4	Norway	51.2	21.5	7.4
Indonesia	13.0	Poland	30.8	25.5	17.7
Myanmar	30.8	Portugal	49	36.3	26.0
		Russian Federation	30.6	22.3	10.3
		Spain	57.8	39.4	23.7
		Sweden	60.3	29.3	14.5
		United Kingdom	51.2	34.3	18.4

Sources: European data from Centre for Comparative Social Surveys 2012.
Pacific Asian data calculation from population censuses, 2010

Europe, singlehood rates in many European countries are less than a third as high as those in Japan, South Korea, Taiwan and Hong Kong. Only China and Indonesia have lower levels of "effective singlehood" than all but a few countries of Europe.

The highly developed, very low fertility East Asian countries, then, still seem to have much higher proportions "effectively single" than all but a few countries of Europe. In thinking ahead about likely trends, it is important to understand where cohabitation fits into the picture of family change in both regions.

What Are the Meanings of Cohabitation Across Europe?

A considerable literature has grown up around the issues of cohabitation in European countries. A rather detailed listing can be found in Kasearu and Kutsar (2010). From this literature, it is hard to generalize about reasons for the sharp rise in singlehood and more gradual rise in "effective singlehood" in European countries, the wide differentials between different European countries, and the different meanings attached to cohabiting relationships in these countries. On cohabitation, Heuveline and Timberlake (2004) argue that it can be seen as an alternative to marriage in some societies (e.g. France and Sweden), but as a precursor to marriage in others (e.g. Austria and Finland). This is consistent with another study's conclusion that "cohabiting couples form a rather heterogeneous group and the meaning and practical functions of this kind of living arrangement differ across national contexts" (Noack et al. 2014: 27). Unmarried cohabitation is clearly a very widely differentiated pattern across Europe (Sobotka and Toulemon 2008; Perelli-Harris et al. 2009), showing even greater diversity in the eastern than the western part of Europe (Fokkema and Liefbroner 2008).

Hiekel et al. (2011) argue that most cohabiters view their union as a prelude or as an alternative to marriage, rather than as an alternative to singlehood. They argue (p. 23) that "cohabiters are more likely to view cohabitation as a stage in the marriage process than as an alternative to it." To some extent, though, there is variation across regions of Europe. Noack et al. (2014) drew the tentative conclusion that based on data on marriage intentions, cohabitation is viewed mostly as a prelude to marriage in the low-frequency countries of Eastern Europe, whereas in high-frequency countries such as Norway and France, a majority of cohabitees had no concrete marriage plans. Another feature of cohabitation found in most countries is as a poor man's marriage – a feature harking back to the role of cohabitation in Europe a century ago.

Why is cohabitation relatively infrequent in Italy and Spain? One interesting comparison between Italy and Germany stresses that cohabitation is not an attractive choice in Italy. The rental market is expensive, so "the best choice for young people would often be between staying with their parents or buying a house. But buying a house not only requires a huge financial investment, it is also a long-term binding decision. For this reason marital and cohabitational decisions would implicitly have very similar consequences for the life course of young Italians" (Nazio and

Blossfeld 2003: 77). Employment uncertainties and weak social security systems also make an extended stay in the parental home more attractive than cohabitation or living as a single person. In contrast, in West Germany, rental accommodation is relatively affordable, and the welfare state and parents provide support for the unemployed, so cohabitation or living as a single person may be more attractive options versus staying with parents (Nazio and Blossfeld 2003: 78).

Dominguez-Folgueras and Castro-Martin (2013), however, take a somewhat different perspective on prospects for Spain, a country often considered to share many social features with Italy. They argue that the observable trend towards cohabitation could go further, as a result of a favorable attitudinal context, and the powerful role of social networks and diffusion processes; moreover, the very high unemployment will tend to favor cohabitation rather than marriage, because of its less demanding prerequisites in terms of home ownership, savings and job stability. Increased cohabitation has been accompanied by a dramatic rise in the non-marital fertility ratio, from 11.1% in 1995 to 35.5% in 2010, suggesting that "cohabitation might be becoming an increasingly accepted context for childbearing and possibly childrearing" (Dominguez-Folgueras and Castro-Martin 2013: 433). It appears that Spain has gone further than Italy along the path towards acceptance of cohabitation, with a higher share of first unions that started as cohabitations after the 1990s and a more pronounced crossover from marriage to cohabitation among younger cohorts (Pereiro et al. 2014: 65).

There is a good deal of evidence supporting the argument that cohabitation is diffusing across Europe, and that reflects a convergence in patterns of cohabitation. But "cultural traditions, religion, policy and socio-economic situations determine the speed and extent of this movement" (Kasearu and Kutsar 2010: 320). The issue of a "standard development pathway," whereby other countries will converge towards the Scandinavian pattern, remains unresolved. Hiekel et al. (2011) claim they found no evidence of such a pathway. The recent trends in Italy and Spain might suggest a convergence, but the authors note that in these two countries the pattern remains considerably different from that in Western Europe. Path dependency – the individual historical trajectory of societies – will contribute to the specific evolution of cohabitation in each society (Reher 1998: 221).

How Much Cohabitation in Asia?

Given the extended periods of singlehood after adolescence experienced by the younger cohorts in East Asian countries, it is probably unrealistic to assume that most young people are abstaining from sexual relationships during this period. While the issue of an increase in sexual relations among the never-married in the region is of considerable interest (Jones 2007: 461–2; Xenos et al. 2006), it is not the focus of this paper. Marriage and marriage-like partnering arrangements are the concern here, and the key issue is whether it is still realistic to assume that cohabitation is rare in East Asian countries.

Another issue is whether "living apart together" (LAT) relationships can be categorized as relationships resembling cohabitation. In most East Asian countries, the LAT category is likely to be more prevalent than full cohabitation. This is due in part to the cost and unavailability of housing, and to the strong cultural emphasis on the need to continue living with parents until married. In many respects, however, it is not appropriate to conflate LAT and cohabiting relationships. A cohabiting couple shares the day-to-day intimacies, irritations and issues of such proximity in a way that those in a LAT relationship do not.

For one East Asian country – Japan – we have fairly good information on cohabitation (Raymo et al. 2009). Cohabitation in Japan is more prevalent among those with less education and more liberal family attitudes. There have been substantial increases in the prevalence of cohabitation, and indeed in 2004, 20% of 25–34 year old females reported that they had lived in a cohabiting union at some time. Though this is a sharp increase, the proportion of women who have ever cohabited at this age in Japan remains much lower than in most European countries or the USA. On the heroic assumption that the same proportion of **single** women in this age group in Japan had ever cohabited, the proportion of single women who had never cohabited falls to 34%, a figure that is still higher than in any of the European countries except Italy.

In South Korea, there appears to be relatively little cohabitation, but there is very limited evidence. The context is a situation of dramatic social and economic change, in which behavioral change of various kinds could also be expected to develop quite rapidly. One evidence of this is the sharp increase in divorce rates in the late 1990s. Chang Kyung-Sup (2010) applies a "compressed modernity theory" to the Korean situation. The essence of this theory is that major economic, political, social and cultural changes occur in an extremely condensed time, and the dynamic coexistence of disparate historical and social elements leads to continuing modifications – some of them mutually contradictory – of a highly complex and fluid social system. Does this result in a discrepancy between values, attitudes and behaviours?

Though there is a dearth of information on cohabitation in Korea, Korean family scholars seem to agree that Korea has not gone as far as Japan in the practice of cohabitation. Nevertheless, there is evidence of more liberal attitudes towards cohabitation among younger than older generations. For example, in a 2010 survey, 53% of those aged 15–24 agreed with the statement "men and women can live together even if they are not married." In another survey, 60% said yes to the question "is it good to cohabit before getting married?"

Out of wedlock births in Korea have risen from 0.6% in 1997 to 2.1% in 2011 – a considerable rise, but still a very low figure. It is also argued that the practice of marrying but delaying the registration of marriage is increasing. But this does not indicate anything about trends in cohabitation because these people are already married in their own eyes and those of the community, so delayed registration is in no way equivalent to cohabitation.

In Singapore, it can be speculated that the incidence of cohabitation lies somewhere between that in Japan and Korea, although solid data to back up this speculation do not exist. As Jones et al. (2012) note, community attitudes toward cohabitation remain conservative, and there are also practical obstacles to cohabitation, but there appears to be a trend toward the greater acceptance of cohabitation among the young, and probably some increase in its practice. For China, too, there is some emerging evidence that cohabitation is increasing, especially in the cities.

Why Are Singlehood Rates Rising in East Asia?

As argued by Jones and Yeung (2014), the Asian evidence indicates that singlehood trends are very much influenced by levels of socio-economic development; however, the relationship is less clear-cut if we confine attention to countries that have not reached high levels of socio-economic development – e.g. Myanmar has much higher singlehood than we would expect.

One way to categorize factors influencing singlehood is to refer to singlehood by chance or singlehood by choice, though it must be recognized that path dependency is crucial, and chance may well turn into choice or vice versa. The factors relating to the "chance" category include imbalances in numbers of marriageable males and females, including "specialized imbalances" resulting from educational trends in the face of strongly entrenched attitudes of hypergamy. Remarkable advances in female education throughout East Asia have sharply altered the male/female ratio facing well educated females; the growth in number of males considered appropriate matches for such females has not kept pace, while cultural attitudes mean that such males have a wider range of women to choose from. Correspondingly, poorly educated males face a difficult task in finding brides, and this has contributed to the strong increases in foreign brides for males in Japan, Korea, Taiwan and Singapore observed in the early 2000s (Jones 2012b).

As for singlehood by choice, this is related to the changing roles and opportunities for women. Educational advances have opened up many opportunities for women in the labor market, thus weakening the reliance of women on men for financial support, which was a feature of traditional family patterns in East Asia. It also required a longer period of time to take advantage of the economic opportunities, through extended education, and then a period of finding suitable employment and consolidating their position in the workforce. This could be done while living at home with minimal expenses. By the time all this was done, not only would the opportunity cost of marriage start to look high, but also the supply of suitable potential marriage partners (not only sharing a similar educational and social background but also sharing more liberal attitudes to gender relations in the family) was seen to be very limited. The contribution by men to housework in Japan remains minimal, even when the wife is working full-time (Tsuya et al. 2013). Women face a "marriage package" which includes looking after the housework and child raising activities, perhaps also looking after the husband's elderly parents, and increasingly, working full time as well. Not surprisingly, women in Japan showed considerable ambivalence about marriage (Bumpass et al. 2008: 11).

There may well be additional factors. A lack of desire for children (for various reasons), or at least an ambivalence, is evident in data from Japanese surveys. The evidence of substantial increases in divorce rates in East Asian countries, in all of which divorce continues to be stigmatized, no doubt contributes to caution about marrying.

Is Rising Singlehood by Choice in East Asia and Some European Countries Evidence of the Second Demographic Transition?

There is a great similarity in some aspects of family patterns between Southern European countries and East Asian countries. And both the Southern European and the East Asia examples raise some issues about both economic and second demographic transition explanations of marriage change and low fertility (Kertzer et al. 2006). The Southern European patterns have been commented on elsewhere, notably by Livi Bacci (2001) and Dalla Zuanna and Micheli (2004). Livi Bacci turns SDT theory on its head by arguing that it is "too much family" that leads Italians to have so few children. "Familism" is the feature of the Southern European family system stressed by Dalla Zuana, who notes that "in a familistic oriented society, throughout their life most people seek their own happiness and at the same time that of their nuclear family and – if possible – their relatives" (p. 109). Familism can persist even where traditional family life declines. Some authors have contested the familistic interpretation, considering familism not as a cause, but rather an effect of poverty and underdevelopment and (more recently) of aspects of the incapacity of the state. Also, differences between north and south, town and country, and social class need to be considered. But these reservations do not seem to greatly undermine the salience of familistic interpretations according to most observers. Dalla Zuanna and Micheli (2004) note that Italian familism is characterized by a much higher trust in kin than in others. It is also characterized by a marked delay in leaving the parental home, both for practical reasons (greater comfort in living on with parents) and because of strong affective bonds between parents and children. Familism has contributed to the shortage of rental housing, though such a shortage is only a partial contributor to the tendency for young people to remain in the parental home.

What is the effect of familism on Italian fertility? Dalla Zuanna and Micheli (2004) contend that late home leaving notwithstanding, the problem is not the late beginning of childbearing but rather the low probability of having a second or third and – for the youngest cohorts – a first child. Familism tends to lower fertility through a number of processes. One is that the social security system is oriented towards an interdependence of the generations but not towards the effective encouragement of women's involvement in the workforce as well as raising children; young men continuing to live in the family home do not learn to do housework, and thus when they marry or cohabit, their partner faces the "double shift" in rather extreme form; and young people able to stay on in the parental home become "risk averse," resulting in delays in having children, and perhaps in the end a decision not to have them at all.

East Asian family systems are in many respects very different from those of Italy, the underlying rationale being Confucianism. But some key elements are held in common, in particular an overriding concern for the family rather than for the individual member, and a strong cultural emphasis on co-residence of a child with parents until the child marries. Not only in Italy but also in East Asia, unmarried 29-year olds living in the same city as their parents would need to have a strong justification for leaving the family home if they wished to avoid bringing unhappiness and almost a sense of "betrayal" to their parents. In East Asia, as well as in Italy, a shortage of affordable rental housing is a further, and not unrelated, consideration. In Singapore, one element of government policy to encourage marriage is the unavailability of government-provided housing to singles unless they are aged over 35 (Jones 2012a).

How does all this relate to Second Demographic Transition (SDT) theory? Lesthaeghe (2010) has discussed the various features of the SDT in East Asian countries, in particular Japan. There is no doubt that Japan is exhibiting some of these (though not a willingness to have children in cohabiting relationships). But it may be a little myopic to equate East Asian trends with Western individualism. It is not at all clear that we should interpret women's reluctance to marry in many East Asian countries, along with the ultra-low fertility rates in these countries, as evidence of growing individualism and desire for self-actualization. Indeed an alternative hypothesis would suggest a revolt against aspects of the patriarchal family and employment structures in which they are placed. Of course, both interpretations may be partly correct. There is evidence that women in Japan are more likely to have negative attitudes towards marriage than men (Bumpass et al. 2008; Tsuya 2015). This is hardly surprising, given the elements of the "marriage package" already discussed. To equate such reluctance to marry by increasingly educated women in the face of the persistence of traditional patterns with the individualism and increasing secularism of the SDT would be a distortion of the SDT arguments. Thus while the factors stressed by the SDT may be playing a part in the retreat from marriage and childbearing in Japan and other East Asian countries, the particular circumstances in which this retreat is playing out need to be recognized if the retreat is to be properly understood.

It might be noted that the reluctance of some researchers (e.g., Suzuki 2008) to attribute East Asian patterns to Second Demographic Transition arguments is mirrored by a similar reluctance of some scholars to attribute the low fertility in Italy to a move from familism to individualism (Kertzer et al. 2006).[4] On the other hand, for many Latin American countries, Esteve et al. (2012) conclude that although the rise

---

[4] Kertzer et al. (2006) claim that the argument low fertility in Italy has to do with factors such as the reluctance of the Italian state to provide public daycare for very young children overlooks the strong cultural bias in Italy against the practice of sending very young children to daycare centers. ***

in cohabitation among population groups where it was not common (that is, groups with higher education and social class) may have been partly a response to the turbulent economic conditions of the 1980s and early 1990s, it seems to have been more closely related to 2nd demographic transition aspects (growing individual autonomy and greater overall tolerance).

Some Implications of Increasing Singlehood in East Asia

Fertility Trends

It is notable that in Europe, fertility tends to be higher in the countries with higher levels of cohabitation. Figure 9.2 shows the cross-sectional relationship measured at a particular point in time (2010). The positive relationship is clear, though the amount of explained variance (R^2) is not very high (0.33). The difference between

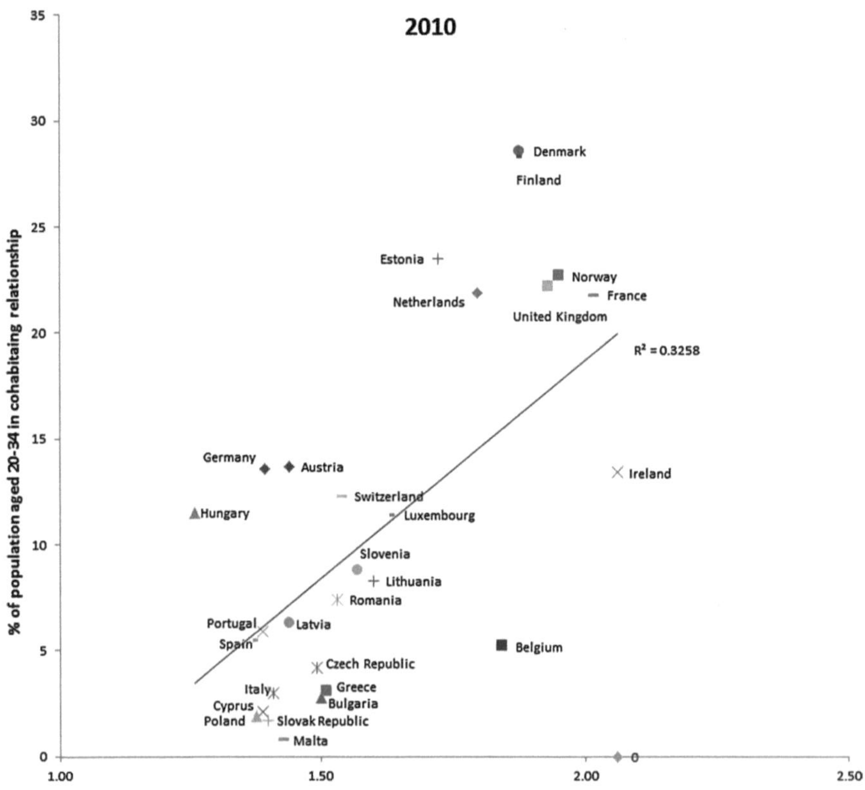

Fig. 9.2 Relationship between TFR & Cohabitation in European Countries

European countries and Japan is that, although cohabitation is increasing in Japan, having children in cohabiting relationships is not. With singlehood still rising in East Asia, it is hard to imagine much of an increase from ultra-low fertility levels unless cohabitation increases and childbearing in cohabiting relationships becomes acceptable. The number of births to unmarried mothers is extremely low in East Asia – less than 2% of all births in Japan, Korea and Singapore, and about 3% in Taiwan. Marriage delay is an important cause of fertility decline in these countries; in Japan, marriage delay and non-marriage were responsible for most of the decline in fertility since the mid-1970s (Tsuya et al. 2013; Bumpass et al. 2008). But while only 2% of Japanese births are registered to unmarried mothers, one in four first marriages is preceded by pregnancy. Cohabitation may tend to hasten marriage by making pregnancy more likely, and thus affect fertility.

Social and Family Structures – Alternative Adult Lifestyles

In East Asia, young adults are spending an increasing proportion of their adult lives outside marriage. Half of the Japanese population between the ages of 20 and 45 is unmarried, as is over 48% of the Taiwanese population at these ages. Given the drawbacks of the "marriage package" already described, it is reasonable to expect that as more people live without the costs and obligations of this package, the role of the package in the society may well come to be redefined. "The prevalence and visibility of alternative adult lifestyles are expressed in the marketing of goods and services, the content of popular media, and contact with those living this life style" (Bumpass et al. 2008: 25). As the state of being single in one's 30s shifts from being seen as deviant to representing a norm of sorts, many aspects of society will change to accommodate the new reality.

There has been an awkwardness in the region in dealing with the place of unmarried adults in family gatherings, weddings, annual get-togethers, and so forth. In Singapore, many adult singles find Chinese New Year annoying at best, because they face intrusive questions about why they have not yet married and whether they are too choosy (Jones et al. 2012). In time, as society gradually comes to realize that it is not at all unusual to remain unmarried, attitudes will no doubt change and the roles of the unmarried in the wider family network will settle into a "new normal."

Ageing Issues

Will unmarried women take on the same roles with regard to their elderly relatives as married women did in the past? It is claimed that in Japan, young women avoid marrying eldest sons because of the tradition of the eldest son's wife caring for his parents as they age. The problem with this avoidance is that in the low-fertility context, there are relatively few second or third sons for them to choose from. But the more general issue is that with low fertility and higher proportions of women working, the traditional family-based care system tends to break down.

Another aspect of ageing issues arising from changes in marriage patterns is that with the ageing of the cohorts with increased proportions remaining unmarried, there will be an increasing proportion of single childless elderly, and more generally, of elderly without any close family. The traditional reliance on the family to care for its dependent members will therefore come under serious challenge, and governments and community organizations will inevitably have to step in.

Conclusion

Economically advanced societies have low fertility and relatively late patterns of marriage. In this sense, economic determinism can be said to rule. However, within this broad parameter of low fertility and late marriage, there is considerable variation. In the modern, globalized world, the transition to adulthood is extended by longer periods of education and uncertain job markets, but the adjustments to these trends differ widely according to the historical and cultural circumstances in the different countries. It has been noted that in the USA, aggregate fertility rates have remained fairly constant for more than three decades at near-replacement levels, yet there has been a "transformation of childbearing patterns: childbearing has become increasingly delayed, teenage childbearing rates have declined while those of older women have risen, non-marital childbearing has become commonplace, and the labor force participation of women and mothers has increased substantially" (Johnson-Hanks et al. 2011: 73). In East Asian countries, fertility has remained at ultra-low levels for more than a decade, with little sign of a significant increase. During that period, age at marriage, extending into non-marriage for many, has continued to increase. Some analyses of tempo effects on fertility assume that the delay of marriage will eventually stop and fertility will increase because the late marriers will still want to have the children they have delayed having. East Asia will provide a serious test of this assumption if the proportion of women who are excluded from the childbearing cohort by non-marriage continues to increase.

Acknowledgments The author thanks Wajihah Hamid and Divya Ramchand for research assistance in the preparation of this chapter.

References

Bumpass, L., Rindfuss, R., Choe, M. K., & Tsuya, N. (2008, November 12–14). *The institutional context of low fertility: The case of Japan*. Paper presented at the International Conference on Low Fertility and Reproductive Health in East and Southeast Asia, Tokyo, Japan.

Centre for Comparative Social Surveys. (2012). *European Social Survey (ESS), Round 6 (2012)*. London: City University London, Centre for Comparative Social Surveys.

Chang, K.-S. (2010). *South Korea under compressed modernity: Familial political economy in transition*. London: Routledge.
Cherlin, A. (2012). Goode's world revolution and family patterns: A reconsideration at fifty years. *Population and Development Review, 38*(4), 577–607.
Dalla Zuanna, G., & Micheli, G. A. (2004). *Strong family and low fertility: A paradox? New Perspectives in interpreting contemporary family and reproductive behaviour*. Dordrecht: Kluwer.
Dominguez-Folgueras, M., & Castro-Martin, T. (2013). Cohabitation in Spain: No longer a marginal path to family formation. *Journal of Marriage and Family, 75*, 422–437.
Esteve, A., Lesthaeghe, R., & Lopez-Gay, A. (2012). The Latin American cohabitation boom, 1970–2007. *Population and Development Review, 38*(1), 55–81.
Festy, P. (2000, October 16–18). *Looking for European demography, desperately?* Paper presented at the Expert Group Meeting on Population Responses to Population Ageing and Population Decline, United Nations, New York.
Fokkema, T., & Liefbroner, A. C. (2008). Trends in living arrangements in Europe: Convergence or divergence? *Demographic Research, 19*, 1351–1418.
Frejka, T., Jones, G., & Sardon, J.-P. (2010). East Asian childbearing patterns and policy developments. *Population and Development Review, 36*(3), 579–606.
Goldstein, J. R., Sobotka, T., & Jasilionene, A. (2009). The end of "lowest-low" fertility? *Population and Development Review, 35*(4), 663–699.
Goode, W. (1963). *World revolution and family patterns*. New York: The Free Press.
Heuveline, P., & Timberlake, J. (2004). The role of cohabitation in family formation: The United States in comparative perspective. *Journal of Marriage and Family, 66*(5), 1214–1230.
Hiekel, N., Liefbroer, A. C., & Poortman, A.-R. (2011). *The meaning of cohabitation across Europe*, Netherlands interdisciplinary Demographic Institute. http://epc2012.princeton.edu/papers/120762
Johnson-Hanks, J. A., Bachrach, C. A., Philip Morgan, S., & Kohler, H.-P. (2011). *Understanding family change and variation: Toward a theory of conjunctural action*. Dordrecht: Springer.
Jones, G. W. (2007). Delayed marriage and very low fertility in Pacific Asia. *Population and Development Review, 33*(3), 453–478.
Jones, G. W. (2012a). Population policy in a prosperous city-state: Dilemmas for Singapore. *Population and Development Review, 38*(2), 311–336.
Jones, G. W. (2012b). International marriage in Asia: What do we know, and what do we need to know? In D.-S. Kim (Ed.), *Cross-border marriage: Global trends and diversity*. Seoul: Korea Institute of Health and Social Affairs (KIHASA).
Jones, G. W., & Gubhaju, B. (2009). Factors influencing changes in mean age at first marriage and proportions never marrying in the low-fertility countries of East and Southeast Asia. *Asian Population Studies, 5*(3), 237–265.
Jones, G. W., & Yeung, W.-J. J. (2014). Marriage in Asia. *Journal of Family Issues, 35*(12), 1567–1583.
Jones, G. W., Yanxia, Z., & Zhi, P. C. P. (2012). Understanding high levels of singlehood in Singapore. *Journal of Comparative Family Studies, 43*(5), 731–750.
Kasearu, K., & Kutsar, D. (2010). Patterns behind unmarried cohabitation trends in Europe. *European Societies, 13*(2), 307–325.
Kertzer, D. I., White, M. J., Bernardi, L. & Gabrielli, G. (2006, April). *Toward a better theory of very low fertility: Lessons from Italy*, Paper presented at the annual meeting of the Population Association of America, Los Angeles, CA.
Kiernan, K. (2004). Unmarried cohabitation and parenthood in Britain and Europe. *Law and Policy, 26*(1), 33–55.
Lesthaeghe, R. (2010). The unfolding story of the second demographic transition. *Population and Development Review, 36*(2), 211–251.
Livi Bacci, M. (2001). Too few children, too much family. *Daedalus, 130*(3), 139–156.

McDonald, P. (1992). Convergence or compromise in historical family change? In E. Berquo & P. Xenos (Eds.), *Family systems and cultural change* (pp. 15–30). Oxford: Clarendon Press.

Myrskyla, M., Kohler, H.-P., & Billari, F. C. (2009). Advances in development reverse fertility declines. *Nature, 460*, 741–743.

Nazio, T., & Blossfeld, H.-P. (2003). The diffusion of cohabitation among young women in West Germany, East Germany and Italy. *European Journal of Population, 19*, 47–82.

Noack, T., Bernhardt, E., & Wiik, K. A. (2014). Cohabitation or marriage? Contemporary living arrangements in the West. In A. Abela & J. Walker (Eds.), *Contemporary issues in family studies: Global perspectives on partnership, parenting and support in a changing world* (pp. 16–30). Chichester: Wiley.

Pereiro, T. G., Pace, R., & Didonna, M. G. (2014). Entering first union: The choice between cohabitation and marriage among women in Italy and Spain. *Journal of Population Research, 31*, 51–70.

Perelli-Harris, B., Sigle-Rushton, W., Lappegard, T., Jasilioniene, A., Di Giulio, P., Keizer, R., Koeppen, K., Berghammer, C., & Kreyenfeld, M. (2009). *Examining nonmarital childbearing in Europe: How does union context differ across countries?* (MPIDR Working Paper WP 2009-021) Rostock: Max Plank Institute for Demographic Research.

Raymo, J., Iwasawa, M., & Bumpass, L. (2009). Cohabitation and family formation in Japan. *Demography, 46*(4), 785–803.

Reher, D. S. (1998). Family ties in Western Europe: Persistent contrasts. *Population and Development Review, 24*(2), 203–234.

Sobotka, T., & Toulemon, L. (2008). Changing family and partnership behaviour: Common trends and persistent diversity across Europe. *Demographic Research, 19*, 85–138.

Suzuki, T. (2008). Korea's strong familism and lowest-low fertility. *International Journal of Japanese Sociology, 17*, 30–41.

Therborn, G. (2004). *Between sex and power: Family in the world, 1900–2000*. London: Routledge.

Tsuya, N. O. (2015). Below-replacement fertility in Japan: Patterns, factors and policy implications. In R. R. Rindfuss & M. K. Choe (Eds.), *Low and lower fertility: Variations across developed countries*. Dordrecht: Springer.

Tsuya, N. O., Bumpass, L. L., Choe, M. K., & Rindfuss, R. R. (2013). Employment and household tasks of Japanese couples, 1994–2009. *Demographic Research, 27*, 705–718.

van de Kaa, D. (1987). Europe's second demographic transition. *Population Bulletin, 42*, 1–59.

Xenos, P., Achmad, S., Lin, H. S., Luis, P. K., Podhisita, C., Raymundo, C., & Thapa, S. (2006). Delayed Asian transitions to adulthood: A perspective from national youth surveys. *Asian Population Studies, 2*(2), 149–185.

Part III
Institutional Change

Chapter 10
Children at Risk: Diversity, Inequality, and the Third Demographic Transition

Daniel T. Lichter and Zhenchao Qian

Introduction

The so-called second demographic transition refers to shifting patterns in family structure, namely, delayed marriage, growing shares of single parents, rising non-marital fertility, increasing cohabitation, and family instability (Lesthaeghe 2010). Throughout much of the developed world, including the United States and Europe, family change has been accompanied by the diverging experiences of children. On the one hand there are affluent or middle class children living in stable two-parent families, while on the other there are children left behind in single parent families (Heuveline and Weinshenker 2008; McLanahan 2004). Less often appreciated is that declining fertility and shifting family life in most rich countries also have become increasingly differentiated by race and ethnicity and by nativity (Coleman 2006; Lichter 2013). Indeed, in developed countries with rapidly aging populations, growing ethnic minority and immigrant populations have left an out-sized demographic imprint on ethnic composition and diversity in the wake of slow growth and native depopulation. Moreover, most demographic and economic impacts are often experienced first by children.

The United States is an illustrative case. U.S. Census Bureau projections suggest that the U.S. will become a majority-minority society as early as 2043 if current rates of fertility, mortality, and immigration continue (U.S. Census Bureau2012). Increasing racial and ethnic diversity starts from the "bottom up" – with children (Frey 2014; Lichter 2013). The majority of all births today are racial and ethnic minorities (i.e., populations other than non-Hispanic white) and a recently-released

D.T. Lichter (✉)
Cornell University, Ithaca, NY 14853, USA
e-mail: dtl28@cornell.edu

Z. Qian
Brown University, Providence, RI 02912, USA

D.L. Poston, Jr. (ed.), *Low Fertility Regimes and Demographic and Societal Change*, DOI 10.1007/978-3-319-64061-7_10

report indicates that children of all ages will be a majority minority population by 2020 if current immigration and fertility trends continue (U.S. Census Bureau 2015). What makes the new demography of race especially troubling is that large shares of today's minority and immigrant children experience chronic poverty as they make their way to adulthood (Brown et al. 2015). Many are "born poor" (Lichter et al. 2015). They begin life's race behind at the "starting line" and never seem to catch up.

Indeed, poverty and inequality are often reproduced and perpetuated from parental to filial generations (Tach 2015). Intergenerational poverty is a persistent and pernicious characteristic of America's historically disadvantaged minority populations. It is a legacy of slavery, conquest, and, in the case of Native American Indians, genocide. For today's children, class boundaries have crystalized and upward socioeconomic mobility and social integration have been compromised by unprecedented family instability, declining school quality and re-segregation, unauthorized immigration, and mass incarceration. The implication is clear: the United States and other high-income countries, especially those with below replacement fertility, require a new public and private commitment to invest in minority and immigrant children – and to invest now. Perhaps as never before, minority children are threatened by growing income inequality and stagnant family incomes in a global economy (Smeeding 2015).

In this chapter, we draw on a variety of current data sources to examine racial change and diversity, the changing living arrangements of U.S. children, and the shifting patterns of poverty and economic inequality. McLanahan (2004) has linked the second demographic transition to the "diverging destinies" of America's children. Here, we argue that inequality is being amplified as the second demographic transition gives way to a newly-emerging third demographic transition, one characterized by unprecedented growth of racial and ethnic minority populations in the developed world (Coleman 2006; Lichter 2013). Inequality and poverty among America's children are reinforced by a new and growing intergenerational divide, one marked by an aging white population and a rapidly growing population of minority children. We conclude our chapter by exploring the options available to U.S. policymakers and identifying lessons from other low-fertility and aging countries in the developed world that face similar demographic challenges.

An Emerging Third Demographic Transition?

The second demographic transition has captivated the attention of demographers worldwide (Esping-Andersen and Billari 2015; Lesthaeghe 2014; Zaidi and Morgan 2017). It has followed directly from the first demographic transition, which was marked by shifts from high to low fertility in response to declining mortality. For most Western societies today, the second demographic transition has brought rapid family change and below-replacement fertility, which are both the cause and the consequence of delayed marriage and non-marriage, rising cohabitation, increasing union instability, and growing shares of single-parent families. In much of Eastern and Southern Europe, for example, total fertility rates (TFR) are at historic lows of 1.5 and less, and well below replacement levels (Billari and Kohler 2004; Goldstein et al. 2009; Kohler et al. 2002). In Italy, the TFR was 1.4 in 2005–2010, declining from 2.5 in the late 1960s (United Nations 2015). Indeed, lowest-low fertility is now characteristic of much of Europe (Morgan2003), but it is also widely observed in East Asia (mostly reflecting low marriage rates and low marital fertility rates). In South Korea, for example, the TFR is one of the lowest on record (1.2). In Japan, the TFR has been at roughly 1.3 or lower since at least 2000 (United Nations 2015). Lowest-low fertility has gone hand-in-hand with rapid population aging, natural decrease – an excess of deaths over births – and depopulation across many subregions of the United States, Europe, and East Asia (Reher 2015; Johnson 2011).

Low and declining fertility has fueled rapid population aging throughout the developed world. Incipient native depopulation and natural decrease, in turn, have created labor shortages and new demands for immigrant workers. Transnational migration has accelerated globally. In the European Union, for example, we have seen an unprecedented South to North movement of workers, and the rapid growth of new immigrant groups from former colonies. France (especially in the Paris region) is now home to immigrants from outside of Europe, often from ex-colonies in North Africa, West Africa, and Indochina (Afulani and Asunka 2015; Kaplan 2015). Since the late 1990s, net immigration in England also has spiked upward, with large influxes of low-skill workers from Eastern Europe (e.g., Bulgaria and Romania), but also of non-citizens from outside the EU. Government projections suggest that more than one-half of population growth by 2027 will be directly (through new immigration) or indirectly (through the fertility of the immigrants) traced to immigration. In Sweden, 1.33 million people or 14.3% of the resident population in 2010 was foreign-born, mostly from outside the EU. Some of the largest immigrant groups are refugees seeking asylum, originating from Iraq, Iran, and Syria. Many are Muslim, with high rates of fertility, often far higher than the fertility of the natives. In the United States, roughly one million new immigrants are added to a rapidly aging native white population every year. Minorities accounted for over 90% of U.S. population growth during the first decade of the new century (Frey 2014). Immigration in the United States and elsewhere is directly linked to globalization and the growing demand for cheap labor in the face of population aging, low fertility, and incipient population decline in the so-called "Global North."

In the developed world, this societal transformation from a low-fertility, native-born majority population to a high-fertility, racial and ethnic immigrant population is sometimes called the third demographic transition. Coined by David Coleman (2006), this population transition is general (at least across today's developed world, but especially in Europe) and is irreversible (Coleman 2009). In the United States, our focus in this chapter, the 2010 U.S. decennial census revealed that the percentage of non-Hispanic whites decreased from 69.1% to 63.7% between 2000 and 2010 (Humes, Jones, and Ramirez 2011). Newly-released U.S. Census Bureau projections (based on the 2010 Census) indicate that the non-Hispanic white population is expected to *decline* from roughly 197 million in 2010 to slightly more than 186 million in 2050, as white natural decrease takes a demographic grip on America's

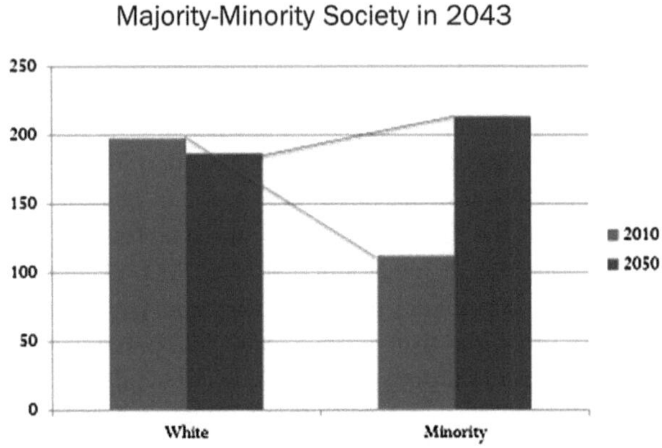

Fig. 10.1 Population of non-Hispanic whites and minorities, U.S., 2010–2050

future (U.S. Census Bureau 2012a). As shown in Fig. 10.1, America's minority populations, in contrast, will nearly double in size over the next 40 years, increasing from 112 million to 213 million persons if recent patterns of immigration, fertility, and mortality continue (U.S. Census Bureau 2012b). All of the projected U.S. population increase is expected to come from groups other than non-Hispanic whites. The U.S. is moving inexorably toward becoming a majority-minority society. In fact, only 46.6% of the U.S. population will be classified as white in 2050 if current demographic trends continue. The racial cross-over is projected to occur in 2043.

Of course, we do not have to wait until 2043 to observe America's transition from a majority white to a majority minority society. It has already occurred among America's children. We show in Fig. 10.2 that the share of all U.S. births to minorities (groups other than non-Hispanic whites) has increased rapidly over the past decade, from 42.4% in 2000 to 50.4% in 2011. The diversity is occurring from the "bottom up" and mostly reflects the high fertility of immigrant minority populations, especially Hispanics (Johnson and Lichter 2010; Lichter et al. 2012). High minority fertility represents a large second-order effect of past and current immigration (Johnson and Lichter 2008, 2010). Significantly, America's transition to a majority-minority society – beginning with children – has been exacerbated by below replacement fertility among the native white population. In 2013, the TFR of non-Hispanic whites was 1.75, the lowest on record (Martin et al. 2015). At the same time, America has experienced, for the first time, absolute declines in the population of white women of reproductive ages (Johnson and Lichter 2010). Below-replacement fertility rates of non-Hispanic white women, applied to a declining population base, have greatly accelerated shifts in racial composition at the bottom of the age distribution. Over the next few decades, members of the post-World War II baby boom cohort will be replaced by a burgeoning minority population of younger people, born of recent immigration and high fertility (Bratter 2015; Lichter 2013).

This third demographic transition is also well underway in Europe (Coleman 2006). As shown in Fig. 10.3, many parts of Europe are experiencing natural

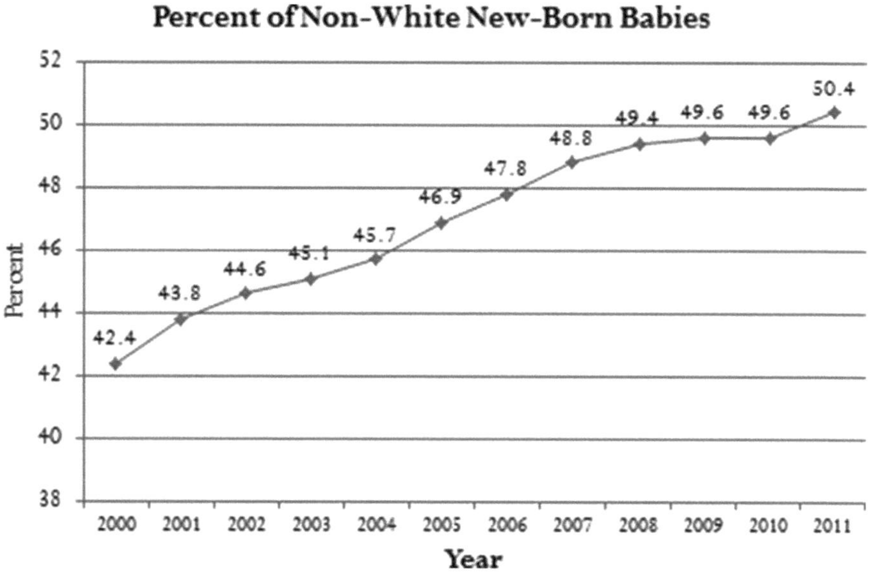

Fig. 10.2 Percentage of minority births to all births, U.S., 2000–2011

decrease. Although most European countries do not collect data on race and ethnicity, natural decrease undoubtedly reflects population aging and the below-replacement fertility of native born populations (mostly whites) rather than non-natives. Indeed, fertility is especially high among new immigrants, which, like in the U.S., has hastened the pace of racial and ethnic change at the bottom of the age distribution in Europe. And, like the United States, immigrants are comprised disproportionately of historically disadvantaged minorities who are seeking work and who face new anti-immigrant political opposition, job discrimination, and social exclusion and segregation. The growing electoral strength of anti-immigration political parties in many European countries (e.g., England, Sweden, and the Netherlands) suggests that the road to social integration and full political participation will be rocky for today's minority children (Alba and Foner 2015). All of this has become more uncertain with the fraying of public and political support for the EU, which has reduced the barriers to intra-European labor mobility and hastened the pace of growing ethnic diversity.

Poverty Among U.S. Children: Minorities on the Front Line

What does all of this mean for U.S. children today? What are their prospects for social and economic inclusion? In her 2003 presidential address to the Population Association of America, Sara McLanahan (2004:607) argued that many of the trends associated with the second demographic transition, such as nonmarital

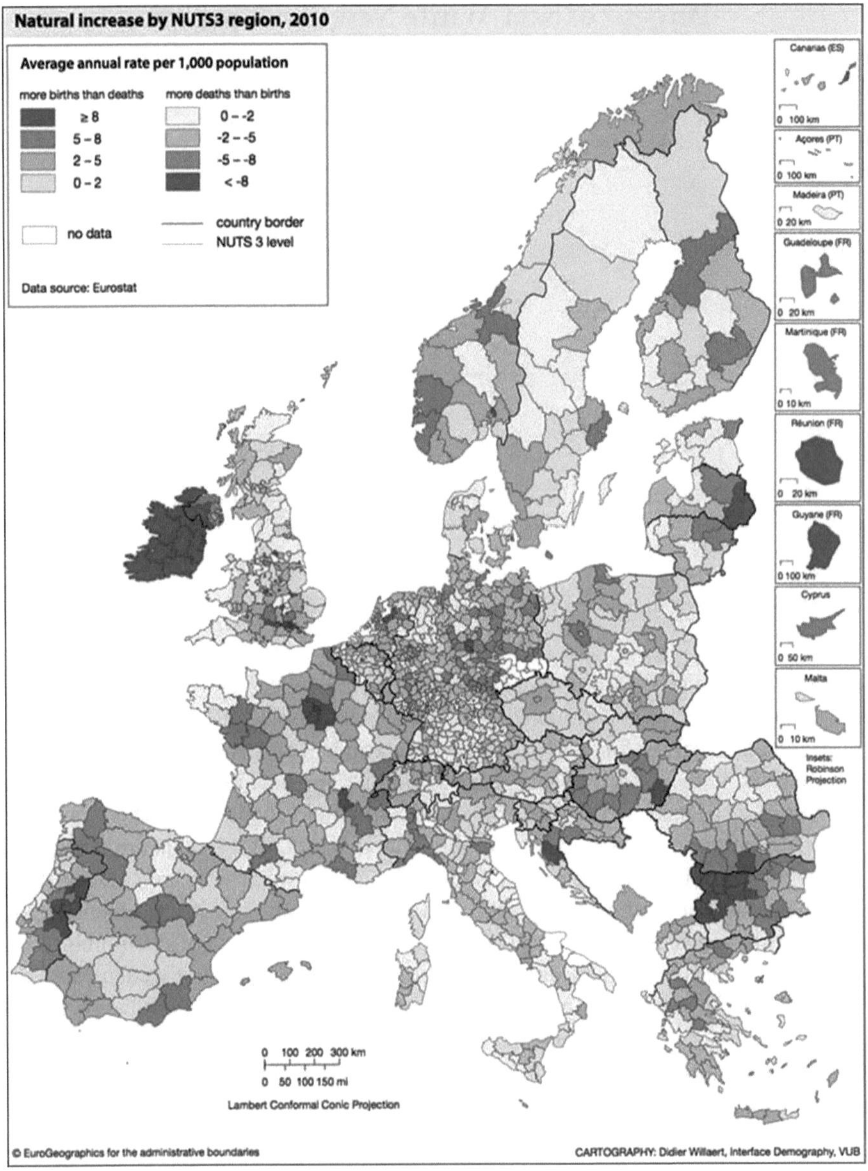

Fig. 10.3 Natural decrease areas in Europe, 2010

fertility, divorce, and cohabitation, have negatively impacted the resources available to America's children. Significantly, societal shifts in family structure and processes have disproportionately affected children at the bottom of the income distribution, reinforcing growing disparities between affluent and poor families and children. In a global economy, growing poverty and inequality among children represent threats to America's competitive future. McLanahan (2004) argued that government has a role to play in addressing the growing inequalities among America's children. Specifically, "how can we get women from disadvantaged backgrounds to delay childbearing, invest in education and training, and form stable partnerships? Similarly, how can we get men from disadvantaged backgrounds to remain committed to their children?" (McLanahan 2004:622).

Interestingly, McLanahan (2004) did not discuss race or ethnicity, perhaps not wanting to conflate policy concerns about children's wellbeing in unstable families with the more general issues of persistent racial inequality. Yet, from a strictly demographic standpoint, the experiences of all U.S. children today cannot be easily divorced from those of minority children, especially Hispanics and Blacks. Minority children are on the frontline of family and economic change. It is their experiences that are largely responsible for "diverging destinies" in as much as they disproportionately face firsthand the economic and developmental consequences of being born to never-married single or cohabiting mothers, or of having parents who divorce (Brown et al. 2015). Minority children represent the American future. What we do or do not do today to insure their long term economic success and integration into American society will be revealed later in growing poverty and inequality and in fraught racial and ethnic relations. Some social commentators raise the specter that America will rapidly become a white oligarchy, as minorities and those at the bottom of the income distribution fall farther and farther behind those at the top of the income distribution (i.e., the so-called 1%).

To be sure, in the absence of declines in racial inequality, the "browning of America" –the third demographic transition – means that growing shares of children face the prospect of poverty as they age into adulthood. Child poverty rates spiked during the Great Recession and its aftermath, even as poverty rates among the elderly declined (Fig. 10.4). Roughly one in five American children today are poor, compared with less than one in ten elderly. The gap in poverty between the young and old has never been greater.

Much of this difference in poverty can be linked directly to racial composition. In fact, as shown in Fig. 10.5, 72% of all poor children were racial and ethnic minorities in 2013, a figure well above the figure for the population overall (58.5%). As the racial composition of America's population changes, the poor have become increasingly comprised of minorities, a demographic fact that has its own implications for public and political support for government programs that support poor people. Today, pundits on the political left sometime refer to the "War on the Poor," which has supposedly been launched by older, mostly white, anti-tax conservatives (i.e., the tea party) who complain about government handouts and the 47% who make up the so-called "takers." The new "minority threat" can be linked directly both to growing intergenerational differences in ethno-racial composition and the emergence of a "majority minority" electorate (Lichter 2013).

From a demographic standpoint, the increasing share of poor children who are minorities (from less than 60% in 1990 to 72% in 2013) reflects patterns of immigration and differentials in fertility (Lichter et al. 2012). But it is also located in the lack of progress in closing the racial gap in poverty among American children over

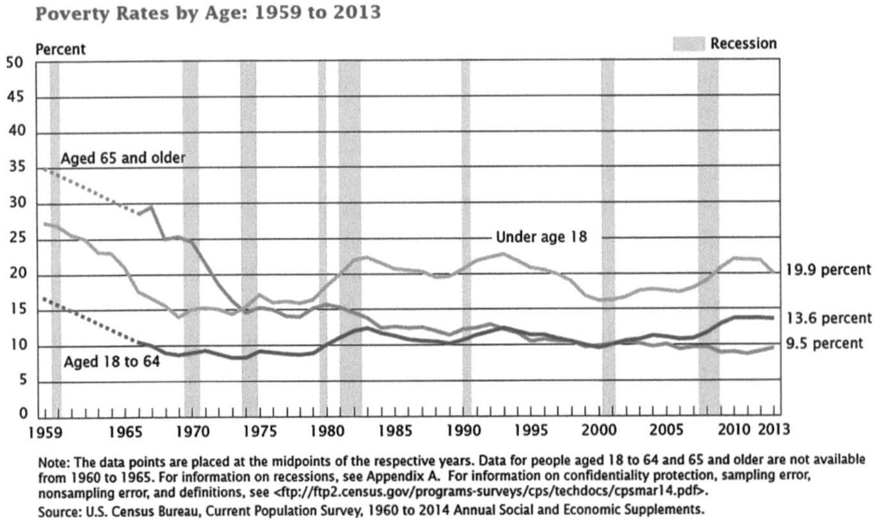

Fig. 10.4 Poverty rates by age, U.S., 1959–2013

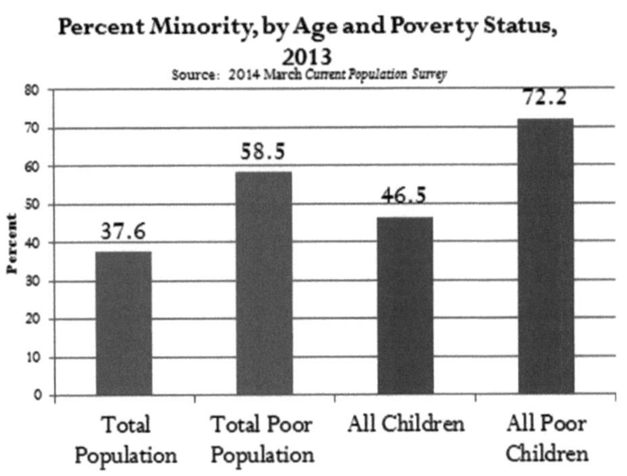

Fig. 10.5 Percent minority by age and poverty status, U.S., 2013

the past decade or so (see Fig. 10.6). For Hispanics, who now account for roughly 25% of all U.S. births, the poverty rate among children in the late 1990s was little different from the child poverty rate today (i.e., roughly 35%). Progress toward reducing or eliminating the poverty gaps among children has been slow. One of the reasons for such slow progress undoubtedly is located in recent immigration patterns; the massive influx of low-skilled immigrant families (many unauthorized) and their children. But this is not the only explanation. Poverty rates among African American children over the same period (the last 15 years) also have been "stuck,"

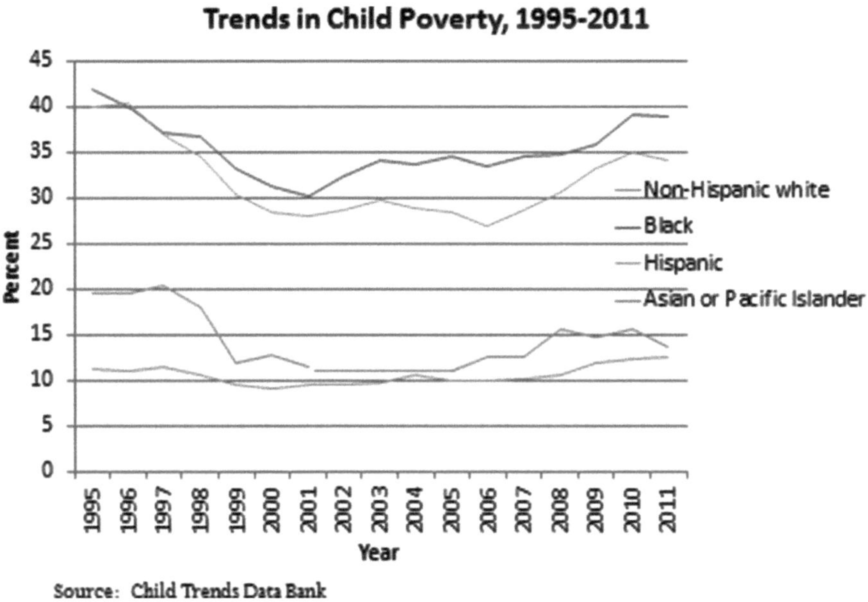

Fig. 10.6 Trends in child poverty, by race and ethnicity, U.S., 1955–2011

at nearly 40%. The inability to close the poverty gap cannot be blamed on new immigration; the foreign-born population does not constitute a large share of the U.S. black population. Moreover, African-born and Afro-Caribbean immigrants to the United States tend to have higher levels of education than native-born African Americans (Kent 2007).

To sum up, diversity is occurring from the "bottom up." And, as we have already noted, economic disparities also occur prominently among children, at the bottom of the age distribution, where the United States has witnessed the largest increases in the absolute and relative size of minority populations. This fact alone behooves us to consider the many current "threats" to upward socioeconomic mobility now facing historically disadvantaged minority children and the children of immigrants. We will start first with families, highlighting the changing living arrangements of American children and the implications for racial inequality and America's long-term future in a globalizing economy.

Children's Living Arrangements and Poverty

With whom the children live matters – and this is especially true in the United States vis-à-vis other European countries. In 2013, almost 20% of U.S. children were classified as poor by the federal government, compared with 14.5% for the population overall. Children make up almost one-quarter of the U.S. population, but account

Table 10.1 Shares of poor children and child poverty rates, by headship status, 2013

	Husband-wife	Male-headed	Female-headed	Total
Total	67.2	7.1	25.7	100.0
Poor	32.2	8.3	59.5	100.0
Non-poor	75.9	6.8	17.3	100.0
Total	100.0	100.0	100.0	100.0
Poor	9.5	23.3	46.1	19.9
Non-poor	90.5	76.7	53.9	80.1

for nearly one-third of the nation's poor population (DeNavas-Walt and Proctor 2014). Table 10.1 shows the poverty rates of children in 2013, disaggregated by living arrangements (or type of family). Here we distinguish among children living in husband-wife families, male-headed families, and female-headed families. These data reveal extraordinarily high poverty rates among children living with single mothers. Over 46% of children living with a single mother (or a female caretaker) are poor, which is nearly four times greater than the poverty rate among children living with married parents. Over 8.7 million children – nearly 60% of all poor children – live with a single mother (data not shown). These data clearly reinforce the central point of McLanahan (2004), i.e., that family change associated with the second demographic transition has placed a large share of children "at risk" of poverty. From the perspective of children today, it also suggests that public policy that addresses family change – either slowing such change or addressing its economic consequences – is fundamental for improving the lives of children and to insuring American prosperity in the years ahead.

This challenge, as we have argued, is complicated by an emerging third demographic transition that is now picking up steam. Disproportionately large shares of minority children, especially blacks and Hispanics, live with single parents and, based on the past, face the specter of chronic poverty as they age into adulthood and hopefully productive adult roles. For example, 55.1% of non-Hispanic black children live with single mothers (or female caretakers), a figure well above the national percentage in 2013 of 25.7%. For Hispanic children, the percentage is 30.7% (data not shown). More than one-half of these children are poor (i.e., 52.4%). Among black children living with female householders, 54.6% are poor. Clearly, racial and ethnic differences in family structure are contributing to racial disparities in economic wellbeing (Bloome 2014; Bratter and Damaske 2013). This demographic fact alone suggests one obvious target for policy intervention – the family.

A simple accounting exercise easily highlights the statistical link between ethnoracial differences in children's living arrangements and poverty status. We ask: What would be the poverty rate of minority children if they had the same living arrangements as white children? Previous work (Eggebeen and Lichter 1991; Lichter et al. 2005) has demonstrated the large economic role of family structure. Our analyses here, using methods of standardization, show that 24.1% of black children (rather than 39.1%) would be poor if black children had shares living in married-couple, single father, and single mother families that were the same as white children. This means that the poverty rate among black children would be almost two-thirds lower than the observed rate if blacks were distributed across married-couple, male headed, and female-headed families in the same percentages as white children. The black-white poverty gap in 2013 would be reduced from 28.4 to 13.6 percentage points. More than one-half of the black-white poverty rate among children is due to black-white differences in family structure. For Hispanics, our analyses revealed that the poverty rate among Hispanic children would be 25.7% rather than the observed rate of 30.4%. This represents a reduction in Hispanic child poverty of only 4.7 percentage points or 18.3%. Of the observed Hispanic-white poverty gap of 19.7 percentage points, Hispanic-white differences in family structure account for only 4.7/19.7 or about 23.8% of the gap. Of course, this crude approach has its limitations, especially if poverty itself is responsible for current family patterns (e.g., economically-distressed married couples divorce and separate into two poor households).

At a time of increasing racial and ethnic diversity at the bottom of the age distribution, it seems clear that poverty – now and in the future – is linked inexorably to family structure (either as cause or consequence). Indeed, over 40% of all babies today are born outside of marriage (Martin et al. 2015). This percentage is even higher among African Americans (over 70%) and Hispanics (over 50%). This has occurred even as pregnancy and birth rates among minority (and all) teenagers have plummeted over the past two decades. DeLeone et al. (2009) showed, for example, that nearly half of the black-white difference in the nonmarital fertility ratio was due to black-white differences in marriage. Marital births are comparatively low because shares of married persons are especially low among African American women (and men). Among Hispanics, we see a different pattern. All of the difference from whites in nonmarital fertility ratios (i.e., the share of all births to unmarried women) was due to the much higher rates of nonmarital fertility. Hispanic marriage rates (and early marriage rates) are high, but so are rates of childbearing among unmarried women. Of course, some of this difference in nonmarital fertility is due to higher rates of fertility among cohabiting Hispanic couples in marriage-like living arrangements (Lichter et al. 2014).

Compared with other developed countries, poverty in the United States is exceptional in showing an especially strong statistical link between family structure and child poverty (Brady and Burroway 2012; Caminada et al. 2012). That is, poverty rates among children are lower in most other Western industrialized societies, and children living with single parents are less likely to suffer from low family income, in part because family social policies do a better job supporting children. In the United States, as in Europe, most children born to unmarried parents are born to co-residential cohabiting couples. In Norway, for example, 54% of all first births in 1995–2004 were to cohabiting couples; only 5% were born to single (non-cohabiting) mothers (Perelli-Harris et al. 2012). The share of first births to cohabiting couples also exceeds those to single mothers in Austria, Bulgaria, France, Germany, Hungary, Italy, Netherlands, Romania, and the UK. Still, child poverty in Norway and in most other European countries is comparatively low (Gornick and Jäntti 2012), and these couples are much more stable than similar couples in the United

States. In the United States, nearly 60% of children born outside of marriage are born to cohabiting couples (Lichter et al. 2014). But many if not most of these couples have high rates of dissolution. If the parents marry, these children face higher rates of parental divorce than other children who were born to married couples or to their European counterparts. The obvious question is the following: What can America learn from the Europeans?

Other Threats to Children's Economic Wellbeing

Living with single parents is clearly linked to elevated rates of poverty among children, especially minority children, who, as we have argued here, represent America's future as the third demographic transition unfolds over the foreseeable future. The *proximate* demographic processes underlying growing shares of children (including minority children) in at-risk single-parent families are well known: rising nonmarital fertility (as a share of all births), declining marriage rates and increasing cohabitation, and union instability (Cherlin2010; Smock and Greenland 2010). But these proximate demographic processes are also tied indirectly to other *distal* factors that undermine family stability and exacerbate chronic or long-term poverty among today's children. These distal factors also represent possible targets for new policy intervention.

To start the discussion, we will begin with family income and the government safety net, the two institutional pillars of financial support for children. At the risk of some over-simplification, previous studies have shown that fertility rates, including nonmarital fertility rates, are inversely associated with income and education (Raley and Sweeney 2009; Sweeney and Raley 2014), while marriage rates have diverged by socioeconomic status and income (Sweeney 2002). High rates of fertility place upward demographic pressures on child poverty rates (Lichter et al. 2015). The implication is clear: poverty and family formation are self-reinforcing. That is, poverty among poor minority children begets more poverty later, often by exposing growing children to unhealthy school and neighborhood environments and by triggering maladaptive responses in the form of early unintended childbearing and unstable unions. Under these circumstances, it is hardly surprisingly that intergenerational poverty – from parental to filial generation – is connected through disruptive family processes (e.g., out-of-wedlock childbearing and low marriage rates and instability). The problem today is that U.S. wage growth has stagnated, especially for those at the bottom of the income distribution, and that the average family incomes at the 20th and 50th percentiles have dropped farther and farther behind incomes at the top of the distribution. For the minority population, in particular, family change has thwarted upward mobility as class boundaries have become more rigid, while reinforcing income and wealth inequality in America.

Since the mid-1990s overhaul of America's cash assistance welfare program, from AFDC to TANF, the welfare poor have been increasingly replaced by the working poor (Thiede et al. 2015). Indeed, Moffitt (2015) has recently documented the fact that income support and government assistance have shifted over time from the poorest poor to other low- and middle-income families (e.g., the growth of EITC). He claims that 57% of single-mother families in deep poverty in 1983 received cash support from AFDC, but that this percentage declined to 20% in 2004 under TANF. Over the same period, the receipt of food stamps declined from 73% to 54%. This is a troublesome development at a time when children, especially minority and immigrant children, are increasingly living with single parents and often require a helping hand.

Growing inequality and the rise in child poverty have gone hand-in-hand with other societal shifts that have placed poor children in harm's way. For example, after declining during the decades of the 1990s, spatially-concentrated poverty has increased over the past decade or so (Kneebone et al. 2011; Lichter et al. 2012). The number of high-poverty neighborhoods and the share of poor people living in them increased during the first decade of the new century. The deleterious consequences of living in poor and often racially segregated neighborhoods are potentially large (Ludwig et al. 2012; Sharkey and Faber 2014). Concentrated poverty matters for growing children and youth. Living in poor neighborhoods has been linked to subjective well-being, physical and mental health (e.g., obesity and depression), greater exposure to crime and violence, access to jobs, school outcomes (e.g., test scores and graduation rates), and early and unintended fertility. Poor children living in poor neighborhoods are doubly disadvantaged. Reardon et al. (2015: 85) recently reported that black and Hispanic minorities tend to live in much poorer neighborhoods (as indicated by median incomes of neighborhood), even when they have the same family incomes as their white and Asian counterparts. Their conclusion was the following: "neighborhood median income for poor black and Hispanic households is roughly two-thirds that of equally poor white and Asian households." Stated differently, poor blacks and Hispanics were more likely to live in the poorest neighborhoods.

Funding for local school districts often depends heavily on local property taxes. For poor and minority children attending public schools, the potential long-term effects of concentrated poverty on access to good schools and, hence, on school outcomes are large. Despite *Brown vs. Board of Education*, public schools in the United States remain highly segregated (Logan et al. 2008; Reardon et al. 2012). In their recent review, Reardon and Owens (2014) concluded that declines in black-white school segregation have come to a standstill or, worse, have increased (depending on the segregation measure used). They also suggested that students today have become more segregated by income across schools and districts since 1990. The gap between highly-resourced and poorly-resourced schools apparently has grown. Does this matter? Logan et al. (2014) recently showed that black, Hispanic, and Native American Indian students, on average, attended schools that scored between the 35th and 40th percentile on performance in comparison with other schools in the state. They concluded that "separate means unequal."

The social ecology underlying persistent racial and ethnic inequality in America cannot be underestimated (Massey and Brodmann 2014). Mass incarceration has upended family formation and stability among minority populations, especially

African Americans living in poor neighborhoods. This is a uniquely American phenomenon and a comparatively recent one that has coincided with the explosion of prison construction, beginning in the 1990s, along with strict mandatory sentencing guidelines, three strike rules, and punitive policing practices, such as racial profiling or targeting of minority men (i.e., "driving while black"). Wildeman (2009) recently showed that one in four black children born in 1990 had a parent imprisoned by the time they reached age 14. For black children whose parents were high school dropouts (and presumably heading poor or low-income families), the figure increased to over 50%. The "missing men" in many poor minority neighborhoods have also contributed to neighborhood and community instability, reduced marriage opportunities for the women left behind, added to the rise in out-of-wedlock children and single-parent families, and reduced the job opportunities for men returning to the community with a prison record. The effects on children's academic and psychosocial development have also been revealed in compromised trajectories into adulthood (for reviews, see Wildeman and Muller 2012; and Wakefield and Wildeman 2013). Mass incarceration has slowed or even reversed progress toward racial equality in America, and this has been felt most keenly by minority children, who have seen their own families and communities torn apart by unprecedented rates of imprisonment, even as violent crime has declined across the country over the past decade or so.

The racial and ethnic composition of children in America is changing rapidly – and so are the threats to their personal dreams and lifetime success as they make their way to adulthood and productive adult roles (i.e., partners, parents, employees, and citizens). The threats to children are uniquely American. Whether measured by comparative rates of poverty, access of public assistance, exposure to unstable families, incarcerated parents or family members, and poorly functioning schools or bad neighborhoods, U.S. children fare worse than their counterparts in other Western developed countries. All of these threats come down hardest on minority children.

What to Do?

> A nation that does not stand for its children does not stand for anything and will not stand tall in the 21st century world or before God. (Marian Wright Edelman – *Children's Defense Fund*)

Concerns about current threats to minority children reflect economic worries about America's place in an increasingly competitive global economy. They also reveal the ascendency of moral or religious values about doing more to be inclusive, to redress the problem of the poor. There are few disagreements about the problem, or its growing magnitude. Rather, the debate centers instead on alternative political ideologies or prescriptions in an era of neo-liberalism and anti-government sentiment. Is government the problem or the solution to eradicating poverty, to lifting up minority and immigrant children and preparing them for productive futures? We cannot adjudicate this debate here, even if it was feasible. Instead, we will start with the assumption that government has a role to play in addressing current inequalities, including confronting the racial divides that have grown intergenerationally as the third demographic transition has picked up speed. We are not the first to state that addressing poverty and inequality starts with the "political will" to do something about the problem. This does not mean "throwing money at the problem," but to identifying evidence-based solutions that reflect our common values. And it means more than just conducting narrowly gauged experiments (e.g., Moving to Opportunity or Healthy Marriage Initiatives) that have little real hope in today's acrimonious political climate of being ratcheted up to the national level or sustained on a grand scale.

From a public policy perspective, we will focus our attention here on immigration policy, the shredding of the family safety net, and housing policies (that affect neighborhood and school segregation). We will make three specific recommendations that work to insure the future of today's children – today's minority children – as they make their way to adulthood. These are (1) finding a pathway to legal status and citizenship for unauthorized children (i.e., the so-called "dreamers") and their parents, (2) developing a multifaceted effort to support – for the sake of children – strong, healthy, and stable families; and (3) creating new tax incentives and school funding formulas that break down neighborhood and school segregation, and that create the conditions for mutual understanding and respect in today's multi-racial, multi-cultural society.

Ethno-racial diversity in America is being driven by new immigration from Latin America and Asia, and by the large second-order effects of high fertility, which heighten diversity at the bottom of the age distribution (Johnson and Lichter 2010; Lichter 2013). Diversity has taken on demographic momentum that will not be reversed in the short-term by restrictive new immigration. Indeed, the large majority of children of immigrants (over 90%) are U.S. citizens by birth, even if their parents are not here legally (i.e., mixed status families). Yet, 1 million unauthorized U.S. immigrants in 2010 were under age 18. Another 4.5 million were born in the United States to parents who were unauthorized (Passel and D'Vera Cohn 2011). Like the children who accompanied their parents here without authorization, these U.S.-born children – American citizens – are "at risk" of compromised futures by virtue of the economic and social challenges faced by their parents. These children and their parents often live in the shadows of society, i.e., in segregated and poor neighborhoods, and the opportunities for economic integration and upward mobility are limited at best (see Donato and Armenta 2011; Zhou 1997).

The so-called "Dream Act" provided immediate relief for potentially 2.1 million children in the United States without authorization, i.e., DACA (Batalova et al.2014). President Obama's executive order to provide additional relief for over 4 million unauthorized parents of children who are lawful permanent residents, i.e., DAPA (National Immigration Law Center 2014) was stalled and later in 2016 not supported by the U.S. Supreme Court. To insure America's future, our recommendation is straightforward: We need to provide a humane pathway to the social and economic integration of today's immigrant children, and moving ahead with immigration reform and fully implementing President Obama's executive orders are but a first step (i.e. Deferred Action for Childhood Arrivals [DACA] and Deferred Action for Parental Accountability [DAPA]). Poverty among racial and ethnic minority children cannot be fully addressed without confronting immigration policy. These programs provide a stepping stone to a comprehensive immigration reform bill that benefits some of America's most vulnerable children.

Throughout this chapter, we have emphasized the role of changing living arrangements among American children, and the link to poverty, inequality, and intergenerational mobility. Cherlin and Seltzer (2014:231–232) have claimed that the growing complexity of American families is "fraying the family safety net that protects vulnerable children." Part of the problem is definitional: there is little agreement about "who is in the family and who is not." And, we would argue here, this seems much more likely to apply to historically disadvantaged minority and immigrant families, where children are disproportionately likely to live with single-parents; with cohabiting couples (where one or both may be biological parents); with extended family members (i.e., "doubling up"); with step-parents, step-siblings, and half-siblings in blended families; with foster or adoptive parents; or with grandparents or other caretakers, who may or may not be relatives. For immigrant children, they may also be part of a much larger transnational kin network, with divided national loyalties and sometimes ambiguous legal statuses. Family law and social policy have lagged the reality of growing family complexity (Cherlin and Seltzer 2014; Huntington 2015), and many children are falling through the safety net.

To help children, we can start with appropriate legal definitions that underlay the provisions of government support and the state and federal laws that provide the guidelines or rules for social welfare provisions. But there is no silver bullet or panacea. Our general recommendation is not new – to support strong and economically stable families. Strong families, however they are defined, are a public good. The Healthy Marriage Initiative, beginning under the Bush administration, was designed to promote marriage as a solution to the problems children face growing up in single-parent, and often poor, families. Estimates suggest that the federal government will have spent roughly $800 million to support a range of education and responsible fatherhood programs designed to encourage couples to marry – if that is their desire – or to have better relationships – for the sake of children. Despite large infusions of time and money, the results of this social experiment have been modest, and the retreat from marriage over the past decade or so has continued unabated. Our own work suggests another possible pathway: Support public and private efforts to reduce out-of-wedlock childbearing. Nonmarital childbearing reduces the likelihood of marrying, staying married, or marrying well, i.e., to a spouse making a living income (Lichter et al. 2003; Qian et al. 2005). Children – over 40% of whom today are born outside marriage – pay a huge price from their parents' behaviors. Lacking evidence of recent declines in poverty rates among female-headed families with children (due, for instance, to male-female wage gaps and lack of child support), then efforts to reduce out-of-wedlock childbearing is a key to insuring the future of American children. And this means directly addressing the question of broader access to reproductive health services at a time when many state legislatures are working to limit access to contraceptive and abortion services (Gold and Nash 2012).

Finally, government cannot be indifferent to where minorities and poor people live. After all, some scholars have outlined the large role that government – at all levels – has played, albeit often indirectly or unwittingly, in segregating America's racial and ethnic minorities from the mainstream, e.g., home mortgage programs, zoning ordinances, and annexation laws. Spatial integration is often viewed as a necessary condition for social and economic integration (Alba et al.2014). Spatial access to good schools, jobs that pay a living wage, and mainstream culture, e.g., the arts, museums, or institutions of higher learning, will all go a long way toward eliminating economic despair, widespread alienation from society, and the formation of a so-called "oppositional culture." As we have argued here in this chapter, for children living in racially segregated, poor, and neighborhoods prone to violence with poorly-funded schools, the current situation is hardly a recipe for insuring the economic future of today's minority children. If we are guided by traditional American values of inclusion and equal opportunity for all, then we can and must do better as a society.

In the social sciences, an emergent literature now emphasizes the growth of mixed-income housing development, which contrasts vividly with the days when poor people – disproportionately minority – were warehoused in high-rise public housing complexes, often set off from stable middle or working class communities and neighborhoods. Presumably the availability of mixed-income housing will help reduce minority segregation in impoverished and declining neighborhoods, i.e., to disperse concentrated poverty and provide greater access to middle-class social networks and to better schools (Brophy and Smith 1997). Mixed-income developments usually provide various housing options, including apartments and single-family homes that accommodate families of all income levels. The goals are to "to provide social diversity, help low-income people get access to higher-quality goods and services, and achieve social and economic integration" (Tach et al. 2014). Whether they are actually successful in promoting spatial inclusion and reducing segregation, while fostering positive interactions among neighbors, is far from clear (Bridge et al. 2012; Chaskin 2013; Tach 2009). President Obama has made a bid to increase diversity in wealthy neighborhoods by implementing new regulations on how monies are dispersed to municipalities. The new regulations would use HUD grant monies to incentivize communities, including affluent communities, to provide more affordable housing for low- and middle-income populations, which are disproportionately minority (Devaney 2015). Unless we can find a way to reduce segregation and concentrated poverty through fair housing legislation and school funding formulas, our racially-segregated public schools will continue to reproduce poverty and racial inequality from generation to generation. Reducing segregation by promoting mixed-income housing may be one way to break the cycle (Sharkey 2013).

Discussion and Conclusion

How can the United States contribute to the material success of today's children who are often starting life's race well behind the starting line, poor and economically disadvantaged? This question has become more important than ever as America and other developed countries move from the second to the third demographic transition as a result of unprecedented transnational migration, high immigrant fertility, and below-replacement fertility and depopulation among the native born (Coleman 2006; Lichter 2013). The title of Robert Putnam's (2015) book – *Our Kids: The American Dream in Crisis* – speaks volumes about the deteriorating circumstances of American children in an era of growing income inequality and dysfunction in our political system. Going forward, America will be challenged as never before to become racially more inclusive as the racial and ethnic composition changes – from the bottom up – and to reduce or remove the legacy of slavery, conquest, and racism.

In this chapter, we have placed the spotlight squarely on demographic and economic change among America's historically disadvantaged minority children, who disproportionately face the challenges of economic globalization and unprecedented family change first hand. U.S. fertility rates today are at record low levels among the native-born white population (the TFR is under 1.8). As America moves toward a minority-majority society, as early as 2043, it will be important to find appropriate and effective government and market solutions that work to reduce child poverty and racial inequality. Here we have emphasized children's changing living arrangements which reflect and reinforce poverty and racial inequality. But distal factors also matter and challenge us to do better as a society.

As we have argued in this chapter, minority and immigrant children are threatened by a fraying safety net, mass incarceration, racial segregation and concentrated poverty, poorly-funded public schools, and a polarized political system that makes solving our most pressing domestic problems difficult if not impossible. Without real immigration reform, for example, the children of immigrants – whether they are born in the United States or elsewhere – face an uncertain future. It is not at all likely that they will catch up with their native-born peers of native-born parents. This is why we included immigration reform and provided a pathway to legal status as an important goal, along with rethinking family social policy (e.g., Healthy Marriage Initiative) by placing the emphasis instead on reducing the out-of-wedlock birth rate. And, last but not least, we have argued that racial and economic segregation represents a persistent barrier to positive development among children. With growing diversity, we need to rethink government housing policies so as to insure today's children's access to safe neighborhoods, critical institutional resources, and positive social networks that can insure children's long-term success.

The United States is the single largest destination for new immigrants, with a foreign-born population of roughly 40 million in 2010. America has added about 1 million new legal permanent immigrants to the U.S. population every year since the late 1990s. No other rich country comes close to these numbers. The experience of massive immigration and unprecedented racial and ethnic diversity in the United

States provide some important lessons for Europe and East Asia. At a time of growing opposition to immigration in many European countries, one lesson from America is that diversity and immigration are important sources of long-term population and economic growth, industrial innovation, and creativity. How can European countries today absorb minorities and immigrants without losing their national identities or fracturing the existing social and political order? This is the question virtually all rich nations face as they grapple with lowest-low fertility and international labor mobility.

Shrinking the social safety net or restricting immigration may reduce immigration or discourage immigrants from staying. This has been a route increasingly taken in the United States (e.g., since the overhaul of welfare in 1996 placed limitations on helping immigrants). Indeed, for rich countries everywhere, taxes and transfers have had the effect of reducing child poverty, but have contributed to only small reductions in the United States compared with Nordic and Western European countries (Gornick and Jäntti 2012). The differences are due less to country-to-country differences in demography (i.e., race and family structure) than to institutional factors, including labor market structure and policy instruments (Smeeding and Rainwater 2003). In an age of neoliberalism, it is unclear whether rich countries will keep their borders open or continue to provide the same level of family social support that they have in the past, especially for new arrivals.

Finally, we have emphasized here an inexorable process of racial and ethnic change that will transform the United States over the foreseeable future. We have placed the spotlight on children because they are in the vanguard as the third demographic transition unfolds in the United States and around the globe. In a period of below-replacement native (white) fertility, policy efforts to encourage more childbearing have been mostly unsuccessful. Immigrants and minorities will fill the labor vacuum for the foreseeable future. It is hard to identify or imagine a demographic scenario that suggests otherwise. As a society, we need to act, and to act now.

Acknowledgements Support for this research was provided by grants from the National Institute of Child Health and Human Development to the Cornell Population Center of Cornell University and to the Population Studies and Training Center of Brown University (P2C HD041020).

References

Afulani, P. A., & Asunka, J. (2015). Socialization, adaptation, transnationalism, and the reproductive behavior of Sub-Saharan African migrants in France. *Population Research and Policy Review, 34*, 1–32.

Alba, R., Deane, G., Denton, N., Disha, I., McKenzie, B., & Napierala, J. (2014). The role of immigrant enclaves for Latino residential inequalities. *Journal of Ethnic and Migration Studies, 40*(1), 1–20.

Alba, R., & Foner, N. (2015). *Strangers no more: The challenges of integration in North America and Western Europe*. Princeton: Princeton University Press.

Batalova, J., Hooker, S., Capps, R., & Bachmeier, J. D. (2014). *DACA at the two-year mark: A national and state profile of youth eligible and applying for deferred action*. Washington, DC: Migration Policy Institute.
Billari, F., & Kohler, H. P. (2004). Patterns of low and lowest-low fertility in Europe. *Population Studies, 58*(2), 161–176.
Bloome, D. (2014). Racial inequality trends and the intergenerational persistence of income and family structure. *American Sociological Review, 79*(6), 1196–1225.
Brady, D., & Burroway, R. (2012). Targeting, universalism, and single-mother poverty: A multi-level analysis across 18 affluent democracies. *Demography, 49*(2), 719–746.
Bratter, J. L. (2015). The demography of race and ethnicity in the United States. In R. Saenz, N. Rodriguez, & D. Embrick (Eds.), *The international handbook of the demography of race and ethnicity* (pp. 47–69). New York: Springer.
Bratter, J. L., & Damaske, S. (2013). Poverty at a racial crossroads: Poverty among multiracial children of single mothers. *Journal of Marriage and Family, 75*(2), 486–502.
Bridge, G., Butler, T., & Lees, L. (2012). *Mixed communities: Gentrification by stealth?* Bristol: Policy Press.
Brophy, P. C., & Smith, R. N. (1997). Mixed-income housing: Factors for success. In *Cityscape* (pp. 3–31).
Brown, S. L., Manning, W. D., & Stykes, J. B. (2015). Family structure and child well-being: Integrating family complexity. *Journal of Marriage and Family, 77*(1), 177–190.
Caminada, K., Goudswaard, K., & Koster, F. (2012). Social income transfers and poverty: A cross-country analysis for OECD countries. *International Journal of Social Welfare, 21*(2), 115–126.
Chaskin, R. J. (2013). Integration and exclusion urban poverty, public housing reform, and the dynamics of neighborhood restructuring. *The Annals of the American Academy of Political and Social Science, 647*(1), 237–267.
Cherlin, A. J. (2010). Demographic trends in the United States: A review of research in the 2000s. *Journal of Marriage and Family, 72*(3), 403–419.
Cherlin, A. J., & Seltzer, J. A. (2014). Family complexity, the family safety net, and public policy. *The Annals of the American Academy of Political and Social Science, 654*(1), 231–239.
Coleman, D. (2006). Immigration and ethnic change in low-fertility countries: A third demographic transition. *Population and Development Review, 32*, 401–446.
Coleman, D. (2009). Divergent patterns in the ethnic transformation of societies. *Population and Development Review, 35*, 449–478.
DeLeone, F. Y., Lichter, D. T., & Strawderman, R. L. (2009). Decomposing trends in nonmarital fertility among Latinas. *Perspectives on Sexual and Reproductive Health, 41*(3), 166–172.
DeNavas-Walt, C., & Proctor, B. D. (2014). *Income and Poverty in the United States: 2013, Current population reports* (pp. 60–249). Washington, DC: U.S. Census Bureau.
Devaney, T.. (2015, June). Obama making bid to diversify wealthy communities. *The Hill*, p. 15.
Donato, K. M., & Armenta, A. (2011). Annual review of sociology. In G. J. Duncan & R. J. Murnane (Eds.), *Whither opportunity?: Rising inequality, schools, and children's life chances* (Vol. 37, pp. 529–543). New York: Russell Sage Foundation.
Eggebeen, D. J., & Lichter, D. T. (1991). Race, family structure, and changing poverty among American children. *American Sociological Review, 56*, 801–817.
Esping-Andersen, G., & Billari, F. C. (2015). Re-theorizing family demographics. *Population and Development Review, 41*(1), 1–31.
Frey, W. H. (2014). *Diversity explosion: How new racial demographics are remaking America*. Washington, DC: Brookings Institution Press.
Gold, R. B., & Nash, E. (2012). Troubling trend: More states hostile to abortion rights as middle ground shrinks. *Guttmacher Policy Review, 15*(1), 14–19.
Goldstein, J. R., Sobotka, T., & Jasilioniene, A. (2009). The end of "lowest-low" fertility? *Population and Development Review, 35*(4), 663–699.
Gornick, J. C., & Jäntti, M. (2012). Child poverty in cross-national perspective: Lessons from the Luxembourg income study. *Children and Youth Services Review, 34*(3), 558–568.

Heuveline, P., & Weinshenker, M. (2008). The international child poverty gap: Does demography matter? *Demography, 45*(1), 173–191.

Hume, K. R., Jones, N. A., & Ramirez, R. R. (2011). *Overview of race and Hispanic origin: 2010*. 2010 Census Briefs. Washington, DC: U.S. Census Bureau.

Huntington, C. (2015). Postmarital family law: A legal structure for nonmarital families. *Stan. L. Rev., 67*, 167.

Johnson, K. M. (2011). The continuing incidence of natural decrease in American counties. *Rural Sociology, 76*(1), 74–100.

Johnson, K. M., & Lichter, D. T. (2008). Natural increase: A new source of population growth in emerging Hispanic destinations in the United States. *Population and Development Review, 34*(2), 327–346.

Johnson, K. M., & Lichter, D. T. (2010). Growing diversity among America's children and youth: Spatial and temporal dimensions. *Population and Development Review, 36*(1), 151–176.

Kaplan, D. H. (2015). Immigration and the making of place in Paris. *Journal of Cultural Geography, 32*(1), 23–39.

Kent, M. M. (2007). *Immigration and America's black population (Vol. 62, no. 4)*. Washington, DC: Population Reference Bureau.

Kneebone, E., Nadeau, C., & Berube, A. (2011). *The re-emergence of concentrated poverty*. The brookings institution metropolitan opportunity series. Washington, DC: Brookings Institution.

Kohler, H. P., Billari, F. C., & Ortega, J. A. (2002). The emergence of lowest-low fertility in Europe during the 1990s. *Population and Development Review, 28*(4), 641–680.

Lesthaeghe, R. (2010). The unfolding story of the second demographic transition. *Population and Development Review, 36*, 211–251.

Lesthaeghe, R. (2014). The second demographic transition: A concise overview of its development. *Proceedings of the National Academy of Sciences, 111*(51), 18112–18115.

Lichter, D. T. (2013). Integration or fragmentation? Racial diversity and the American future. *Demography, 50*(2), 359–391.

Lichter, D. T., Graefe, D. R., & Brown, J. B. (2003). Is marriage a panacea? Union formation among economically disadvantaged unwed mothers. *Social Problems, 50*(1), 60–86.

Lichter, D. T., Qian, Z., & Crowley, M. L. (2005). Child poverty among racial minorities and immigrants: Explaining trends and differentials. *Social Science Quarterly, 86*(s1), 1037–1059.

Lichter, D. T., Parisi, D., & Taquino, M. C. (2012). The geography of exclusion: Race, segregation, and concentrated poverty. *Social Problems, 59*(3), 364–388.

Lichter, D. T., Sassler, S., & Turner, R. N. (2014). Cohabitation, post-conception unions, and the rise in nonmarital fertility. *Social Science Research, 47*, 134–147.

Lichter, D. T., Sanders, S. R., & Johnson, K. M. (2015). Hispanics at the starting line: Poverty among newborn infants in established gateways and new destinations. *Social Forces, 94*(1), 209–235.

Logan, J. R., Oakley, D., & Stowell, J. (2008). School segregation in metropolitan regions, 1970–2000: The impacts of policy choices on public education. *American Journal of Sociology, 113*(May), 1611–1644.

Logan, J. R., Minca, E., & Adar, S. (2014). *The geography of inequality*. Schools and Society: A Sociological Approach to Education, p. 245.

Ludwig, J., Duncan, G. J., Gennetian, L. A., Katz, L. F., Kessler, R. C., Kling, J. R., & Sanbonmatsu, L. (2012). Neighborhood effects on the long-term well-being of low-income adults. *Science, 337*(6101), 1505–1510.

Martin, J. C., Hamilton, B. E., Osterman, M. J. K., Curtin, S. C., & Mathews, T. J. (2015). Births: Final data for 2013. *National Vital Statistics Reports, 64*(1), 1–65.

Massey, D. S., & Brodmann, S. (2014). *Spheres of influence: The social ecology of racial and class inequality*. New York: Russell Sage Foundation.

McLanahan, S. (2004). Diverging destinies: How children are faring under the second demographic transition. *Demography, 41*(4), 607–627.

Moffitt, R. A. (2015). The deserving poor, the family, and the U.S. welfare system. *Demography, 52*(3), 729–449.
Morgan, S. P. (2003). Is low fertility a twenty-first-century demographic crisis? *Demography, 40*(4), 589–603.
National Immigration Law Center. (2014). President Obama's immigration announcement. http://www.nilc.org/execactionsummary.html. Accessed on June 18 2015.
Passel, J. S., & D'Vera Cohn, S. W. (2011). *Unauthorized immigrant population: National and state trends, 2010*. Washington, DC: Pew Hispanic Center.
Perelli-Harris, B., Kreyenfeld, M., Sigle-Rushton, W., Keizer, R., Lappegård, T., Jasilioniene, A., Berghammer, C., & Di Giulio, P. (2012). Changes in union status during the transition to parenthood in eleven European countries, 1970s to early 2000s. *Population Studies, 66*(2), 167–182.
Putnam, R. D. (2015). *Our kids: The American dream in crisis*. New York: Simon and Schuster.
Qian, Z., Lichter, D. T., & Mellott, L. M. (2005). Out-of-wedlock childbearing, marital prospects and mate selection. *Social Forces, 84*(1), 473–491.
Raley, R. K., & Sweeney, M. M. (2009). Explaining race and ethnic variation in marriage: Directions for future research. *Race and Social Problems, 1*(3), 132–142.
Reardon, S. F., & Owens, A. (2014). 60 years after Brown: Trends and consequences of school segregation. *Annual Review of Sociology, 40*, 199–218.
Reardon, S. F., Grewal, E. T., Kalogrides, D., & Greenberg, E. (2012). Brown fades: The end of court-ordered school desegregation and the Resegregation of American public schools. *Journal of Policy Analysis and Management, 31*(4), 876–904.
Reardon, S. F., Fox, L., & Townsend, J. (2015). Neighborhood income composition by race and income, 1990–2009. *The Annals of the American Academy of Political and Social Science, 660*(1), 78–97.
Reher, D. S. (2015). Baby booms, busts, and population ageing in the developed world. *Population studies, 69*(Suppl 1), 57–68.
Sharkey, P. (2013). *Stuck in place: Urban neighborhoods and the end of progress toward racial equality*. Chicago: University of Chicago.
Sharkey, P., & Faber, J. W. (2014). Where, when, why, and for whom do residential contexts matter? Moving away from the dichotomous understanding of neighborhood effects. *Annual Review of Sociology, 40*, 559–579.
Smeeding, T. M. (2015). Diverging destinies revisited: The threat to child development and social mobility. In *Families in an era of increasing inequality* (pp. 51–60). Cham: Springer.
Smeeding, T. M., & Rainwater, L. (2003). *Poor kids in a rich country: America's children in comparative perspective*. New York: Russell Sage Foundation.
Smock, P. J., & Greenland, F. R. (2010). Diversity in pathways to parenthood: Patterns, implications, and emerging research directions. *Journal of Marriage and Family, 72*(3), 576–593.
Sweeney, M. M. (2002). Two decades of family change: The shifting economic foundations of marriage. *American Sociological Review, 67*(1), 132–147.
Sweeney, M. M., & Raley, R. K. (2014). Race, ethnicity, and the changing context of childbearing in the United States. *Annual Review of Sociology, 40*, 539–558.
Tach, L. M. (2009). More than bricks and mortar: Neighborhood frames, social processes, and the mixed-income redevelopment of a public housing project. *City and Community, 8*(3), 269–299.
Tach, L. (2015). Social mobility in an era of family instability and complexity. *The Annals of the American Academy of Political and Social Science, 657*(1), 83–96.
Tach, L., Pendall, R., & Derian, A. (2014). *Income mixing across scales: Rationale, trends, policies, practice, and research for more inclusive neighborhoods and metropolitan areas*. Washington, DC: Urban Institute.
Thiede, B. C., Lichter, D. T., and Sanders, S. R. (2015). *America's working poor conceptualization, measurement, and new estimates*. Work and Occupations. 0730888415573635.
United Nations. (2015) World population prospects: The 2012 Revision. http://esa.un.org/unpd/wpp/Excel-Data/fertility.htm. Accessed 5 June 2015.

U.S. Census Bureau. (2012). *2012 national population projections*. Retrieved from https://www.census.gov/newsroom/releases/archives/population/cb12-243.html.
U.S. Census Bureau. (2015). *Projections of the size and composition of the U.S. population: 2014 to 2060*. https://www.census.gov/newsroom/press-releases/2015/cb15-tps16.html.
Wakefield, S., & Wildeman, C. (2013). *Children of the prison boom: Mass incarceration and the future of American inequality*. Oxford: Oxford University.
Wildeman, C. (2009). Parental imprisonment, the prison boom, and the concentration of childhood disadvantage. *Demography, 46*(2), 265–280.
Wildeman, C., & Muller, C. (2012). Mass imprisonment and inequality in health and family life. *Annual Review of Law and Social Science, 8*, 11–30.
Zhou, M. (1997). Growing up American: The challenge confronting immigrant children and children of immigrants. *Annual Review of Sociology, 23*, 63–95.
Zaidi, B., & Morgan, S. P. (2017, Forthcoming). The second demographic transition: A review and appraisal. *Annual Review of Sociology, 43*.

Chapter 11
Political Effects – Real and Imagined – In Low Fertility Societies

Michael S. Teitelbaum

The political effects, both real and imagined, of low fertility rates warrant thoughtful attention, especially in countries such as South Korea that are classified among those with the "lowest-low" fertility. This term is usually applied to countries in which the total fertility rate (TFR) has fallen to 1.3 or lower (Billari 2008; Kohler et al. 2002; Billari and Kohler 2004). Lists of such countries vary by source and over time, but often include Singapore, Macao and Hong Kong (China), Taiwan, South Korea, Bosnia and Herzegovina, Lithuania, Ukraine, and sometimes Spain, Portugal, Italy, and Greece. As may be seen, most countries in this category are located in East and Southeast Asia and in South and East Europe.

The demographic dynamics of such countries mean that while in some cases their populations may still be increasing, if such "lowest-low" fertility rates were to continue for many years all would eventually experience declines in population size – unless net immigration numbers were to increase very substantially. Most would also experience rapid shifts (at least by the standards of demographic change, which is usually gradual and incremental) in their age composition toward higher percentages of older age groups (often termed "demographic aging"). Such trends, in turn, have evoked rising expressions of concern and alarm. Due to a variety of factors – some anticipated, some not – some of the countries with the earliest contemporary experiences of lowest-low fertility, and Italy and Spain in particular, showed clear signs of fertility increases between 1995 and 2005 (Billari 2008: 4–16), although the economic crises that have befallen both countries since 2008 may have counteracted such trends.

M.S. Teitelbaum (✉)
Labor and Worklife Program, Harvard Law School, Harvard University, Cambridge, MA 02138, USA
e-mail: teitelbaum@sloan.org

D.L. Poston, Jr. (ed.), *Low Fertility Regimes and Demographic and Societal Change*, DOI 10.1007/978-3-319-64061-7_11

The Modern History of Population Growth and Decline

On the whole, human populations have mostly been increasing, and at unprecedented and accelerating rates, for much of the past 2–3 centuries. This modern expansion of human populations began in Europe, as high mortality rates declined while high fertility rates continued for many decades, but European growth later waned as fertility rates declined. During the twentieth century population growth rates accelerated to even higher levels in much of Asia, Africa and Latin America. Indeed, it was the very rapid pace of global demographic increase, especially in the decades after World War II, that was widely seen as the most vexing of global demographic challenges until at least the 1980s and 1990s.

Because recent centuries have been periods of substantial population growth, declines in population lie outside the experience of all who now are alive in most societies – with some notable exceptions such as Russia since the collapse of the USSR. Somewhat surprisingly, the issue of national or sub-national population decline (whether actual or prospective, whether absolute or relative to other nations or groups) also has been one that has been inadequately attended by objective scholarship. That is not to say that it has not been a topic of debate and contention. To the contrary, there is a history of passionate ideological debate, though often uninformed by credible evidence and driven instead by exaggerated claims and existential fears.

Such contentions actually go back at least a century, and were especially prominent in France following the disasters of the Franco-Prussian War of 1870–71. During the ensuing decades politically-active champions of the defeated French Republic (called "Republicans," not to be confused with the members of the U.S. Republican Party) agonized about what might explain the collapse of France before the armies of the Prussian Kaiser and the resulting loss of Alsace and Lorraine. Many of them focused, oddly enough, on the fact that France had experienced the first fertility declines in Europe.

This was quite true – fertility rates in France (along with those in parts of Hungary) began to decline during the latter half of the eighteenth century, fully a century earlier than in Germany and Great Britain (Coale and Watkins 1986). French intellectuals and other members of the "political class" deployed energetic rhetoric to argue that the fact that French fertility rates were lower than those of Great Britain and Bismarck's rapidly-consolidating German Empire underlay the relative decline of French military power and economic dynamism. Much of this came from conservative perspectives, such as the 1873 writings of Pierre Toulement, a Jesuit priest who described the French collapse before the Prussians as divine chastisement for the French sin of contraception. In 1881 the influential French conservative Paul Leroy-Beaulieu, professor at the Collège de France and editor of *L'Économiste francais,* invoked France's low fertility relative to Germany's as requiring French colonial expansion. It takes courage, he wrote:

> …to tell the truth to one's country and to destroy those illusions that will bring us new reverses and new catastrophes. In the presence of a Germany of 45 million inhabitants who

will be 60 million in 20 years and 80 million in 50 years, and who can count on the loyalty of the Austrian populations, all the hopes of armed revenge are chimeras, sentimental and patriotic delusions, singularly dangerous for our country (Teitelbaum and Winter 1985: 18–20).

But concerns about low French fertility were hardly limited to conservatives. Arsène Dumont, a leading demographer and Republican polemicist who coined the concept of "social capillarity," wrote in 1890 that "a nation must have a population dense enough to keep stable an equilibrium with her neighbors," a task for which France was manifestly unable due to its "disease" of low fertility (Dumont 1890; Teitelbaum and Winter 1985). René Goblet, a center-left French politician who at the time was Minister of the Interior and who later became Premier, issued a report in 1882 to the French President on the 1881 French Census. As summarized in the Times of London, Goblet's report highlighted the relative decline of French population compared with those of Russia, Germany, the USA, the UK, and other "great powers," and emphasized that the decline was due not to higher mortality rates or lower marriage rates in France, but instead to lower fertility within marriage. Here is a portion of a summary of Goblet's report that was published in the Times of London:

> Before 50 years are over, France will, at her present slow rate of increase of population, have sunk, if not to the level of a second-rate, at least to the bottom of the list of the great powers. If we suppose the population of the United States and of the various countries of Europe are decimated by no wars or exceptional maladies and still preserve their present frontiers and go on increasing at the present rate of increase, their populations will by the year 1932, a time which our children will see, be as follows: United States, 190,000,000; Russia, 158,000,000; Germany, 88,000,000; Great Britain, 63,000,000; Austria-Hungary, 44,000,000, and Italy, 44,000,000. So that France, which a century ago was really *La Grande Nation*, having still the largest population in Europe, will be but the sixth in rank in point of numbers.
>
> Will France, with her diminished numerical importance as a great power, make up for her deficient numbers by that public spirit and genius for enterprise which has raised so many small powers to a level in point of influence with the greatest? This, also, if we consider the causes with led to the increasing sterility of the country, may also be doubted. In fact, there are not wanting Frenchmen who look on this decreasing population as but one among many signs of national degeneracy, and are ready to exclaim hopelessly, "Finis Galliae!" (Times of London 1883).

As early as the 1890s, influential French Republicans such as Emile Zola had joined together to establish a National Alliance for the Growth of the French Population, a group that advocated measures they believed would reverse the rot.

In actuality there was no demonstrable causal relationship between the early decline in French fertility rates and the relative weakening of the French state, whether Republic or Empire. By the time these Republican pro-natalist efforts became politically influential there was evidence that fertility declines were well underway in Great Britain and Germany. Powerful concerns about low French fertility rates continued right up to the onset of the disastrous Great War (later called World War I) in 1914. During this prewar period similar concerns about military manpower relative to that of Germany also resonated in Great Britain, though in this case focused more on "quality" than quantity (Teitelbaum and Winter 1985: 30–35).

The disastrous bloodletting of World War I – for France, Germany, Great Britain, and many other parts of Europe – may actually have increased concerns in France about low fertility. The French Premier Georges Clemenceau, a principal architect of the Treaty of Versailles at war's end, spoke as follows in the Senate debate on the Treaty in October 1919:

> The treaty does not say that France must undertake to have children, but it is the first thing which ought to have been put in it. For if France turns her back on large families, one can put all the clauses one wants in a treaty, one can take all the guns of Germany, one can do whatever one likes. France will be lost because there will be no more Frenchmen (Clemenceau 1919).

With the onset of the Great Depression, fertility rates declined to previously unknown levels. European autocrats of the 1930s, including Hitler, Stalin and Mussolini, all responded to low fertility rates as political threats to their aspirations. All adopted energetic public policies, advocacy, and nationalistic propaganda designed to increase fertility. Mussolini's fascist government in Italy actually was one of the first to adopt such measures. Beginning in 1925, the Italian fascist state increased welfare benefits, lowered taxes on families with children, improved maternal and child healthcare, and provided widely-promoted medals and other recognition to women who bore more than five children (Forcucci 2010: 4–13).

The Nazi government under Hitler that took power in Germany in 1933 copied many of these initiatives, pursuing a variety of pro-natalist policies which it described as for the "relief of family burdens" (Bock 1994: 110–140). These included marriage loans to husbands whose wives had previously been employed; substantial tax exemptions to men with wives and children; tax increases imposed upon childless couples and individuals; monthly state child allowances; full-wage paid maternity leaves for women for 6 weeks before and after birth; and awards such as the "Mother Cross" for women with 4 or more children.[1] In 1936 the Stalinist leadership of the USSR banned abortion (an early Leninist commitment) and sharply increased support for maternal and child welfare. Within a few months of the German invasion of the Soviet Union in June 1941, the USSR government created special taxes on celibates, the childless, and those with only a single child, and in 1944 special titles of "Mother Heroine" were created for women with large families.

Nearly everything in this domain changed after World War II. Postwar fertility rates rose in many of the Western countries in which the loudest concerns about low fertility had been expressed during the 1930s. In some (especially the U.S., Canada, Australia, and New Zealand) these postwar "baby booms" proved to be large and long-lasting, stretching well into the 1960s; in others the postwar booms were more short-lived. The high fertility rates that had prevailed in Japan declined very sharply while economic growth rose, muting widespread concerns during the late 1940s about the risks of widespread malnutrition and epidemic – postwar concerns that

[1] The core racism of the Nazi regime meant that such policies were provided only to "valuable" recipients, not to "inferior" (*minderwertig*) categories: the "eugenically unfit"; Jews; Gypsies; handicapped; "asocials"; political opponents; laborers from Eastern Europe; etc. Moreover, most of the benefits that were provided went to men rather than to women. (Bock 1994: 128).

have long been forgotten following the dynamic economic rise of Japan in subsequent decades.

Meanwhile, in the developing countries of Asia, Latin America, and Africa, mortality rates declined rapidly while high fertility rates continued, leading to accelerating rates of population growth that evoked new concerns about an emerging population "bomb" or "explosion." In East and Southeast Asia, the governments of South Korea, Hong Kong, Taiwan, and Singapore adopted effective interventions to promote voluntary family planning and smaller family norms. Over the subsequent decades, rapid declines in fertility, coupled with strong economic growth rates averaging over 7% per year, combined to transform these "Asian Tigers" or "Dragons" into advanced economies with high levels of per-capita income. (Similar patterns appeared later in countries such as Indonesia, Thailand, and Malaysia.)

By the 1990s, the cycle of alarm about fertility rates that were too low, then too high, had come full circle. Anxieties about unsustainable "baby booms" were replaced by anxieties about unstainable "baby busts," especially in Europe, in Japan, in the former Soviet Union, and among some U.S. ideological groups especially on the right. Once again rates of demographic increase were described as alarmingly low, with lugubrious population projections pointing to the perceived threats of insufficient economic demand, declining labor forces, and trends toward demographic aging that would render public pension systems unsustainable and weaken national competitiveness and security.

Some Political Consequences of Demographic Change

The above discussion makes clear that ideological and political perspectives and policies have been important contributors to demographic change itself and to the ways it has been perceived. To what extent have demographic trends in turn been important factors in political perspectives and behavior?

The first point is that compared with the rapid and sometimes destructive discontinuities of economic and political change, demographic trends usually proceed in slow and undramatic ways. Barring convulsions such as wars, earthquakes/tsunamis, pandemics (such as Black Death or the 1917–18 influenza pandemic), or massive pulses of desperate migrants or refugees, demographic change has generally been incremental and frequently in the background. Even the historically rapid population growth of the 1960s progressed at annual rates far below the most rapid growth in economic activity – "natural demographic increase" (i.e. the excess of births over deaths, excluding migration) has rarely exceeded 3% per annum, whereas economic growth rates three or four times higher have been achieved during the past 50 years in many countries including South Korea and China.

Yet it is also true that during the last century the rates of demographic change accelerated sharply from those seen throughout much of human history. The same period also saw significant reversals in direction of demographic variables — mortality and fertility rates both declined and increased, and although on average increasingly large pools of migrants were on the move, there were periodic upward and downward flows of refugees.

Many of these demographic shifts and accelerations/decelerations have carried with them significant political consequences. Some of these are relevant for South Korea; some are not.

Population Size

In international affairs, the most commonly perceived political consequences of demographic change relate to aggregate population size. In particular, some commentators express concerns about shifts in the "demographic balance of power," as the populations of some countries continue to expand rapidly while others experience slow growth or decline. There is a long tradition of belief, going back to the Ancients, that states with larger populations and hence larger potential armies have greater capabilities of projecting military power than do those with smaller populations.

There is of course some truth to this belief – most hegemons or super-powers in history have been able to mobilize large populations, either domestically or via their control of far-flung empires. Yet the rising military importance of advanced technologies has greatly changed the significance of the raw size of potential military forces – countries with some of the largest populations today are not among the most powerful in military terms, and some small-population states (especially in Europe and the Middle East) have deployed high technology, political confederations, and military alliances to enhance their power. A related but harder-to-assess issue is the speculation that low fertility societies tend to be less aggressive in military terms, due to political opposition from parents with only 1 or 2 children.

This naturally leads to consideration of whether demographic trends have important implications for the national security of countries such as South Korea. In other words, are countries with smaller populations more vulnerable to the depredations of larger neighbors? Here much depends upon the vagaries of geographic location and boundaries. Some countries (consider Poland, Ukraine, and the Baltic states of Estonia, Latvia and Lithuania) are situated in what we might call "dangerous neighborhoods." Their locations lie between the formerly expansive empires of Germany and Russia; moreover their political boundaries are generally lacking in natural barriers such as the mountain ranges of Switzerland and Austria or bodies of water that border the United Kingdom and the United States. Similarly, the modern states of the Balkan region (including Serbia, Croatia, Bosnia-Herzegovina, Kosovo, Albania, Montenegro, Macedonia, Greece, Bulgaria, Romania) occupy territories along the fissures and long-contested boundaries of Catholic, Orthodox and Muslim cultures and empires.

What about South Korea? Some of its neighbors have very large populations and in the past have conquered and ruled large empires (including Korea's own colonial rule by Japan). Its population is much smaller than those of China and Japan. But population size does not determine national power, as demonstrated by tiny but relatively secure countries, such as modern Sweden, Norway, Denmark, or Luxembourg. Size may matter in some sense, but so too do location; economic dynamism; technological competence; and political alliances and defense treaties.

However South Korean security is unusual, even unique, in its exposure to events in its neighbor to the north. Developments within North Korea are fiendishly difficult to understand, and hence refractory to credible predictions. It is difficult to think of other advanced societies with similar vulnerabilities to such an opaque and unpredictable neighbor.

More generally, political tensions seem to have been increasing in the East Asian region, with the rapid economic rise of China. China may achieve its hoped-for "peaceful rise," but contested ocean boundaries and economic zones that may be relevant to future energy resources seem likely to be continuing irritants.

Shifts in Age Structure

Shifts in age distribution are well-established effects of changing fertility rates: other things being equal, declines in fertility lead gradually to "older" age distributions, while rises in fertility such as those of the postwar baby booms lead to "younger" population distributions. That said, there are demographic realities here that sometimes are not fully understood:

- Nearly all societies, outside of parts of the Middle East and sub-Saharan Africa, have experienced fertility declines over the past half-century. This means that nearly all are experiencing "demographic aging" to some degree – those with the most rapid fertility decline most rapidly.
- The only plausible way to reverse this phenomenon would be to return to much higher levels of fertility, which has its own negative implications.
- The belief put forward by some that increasing immigration is an alternative way to move towards substantially younger age distributions is not well-founded. Immigration can affect age composition only slightly because immigrants typically comprise many age cohorts, unless entry is somehow limited primarily to children while excluding their adult parents (a policy that is difficult to imagine, although child adoption offers one partial example).

Rapid or erratic changes in fertility imply more rapid or erratic changes in age structures, although with a delay of several decades. The large and sustained U.S. baby boom from 1947 to 1965, followed by sharp fertility declines during the late 1960s, 1970s and 1980s produced rapid changes in the relative size of subsequent generations. National, state and local governments were buffeted by numerous and vexing challenges as they sought to adapt to a pulse of first-rising then declining sizes of school-age cohorts. The same pulses later appeared for young adult cohorts, and later for those of retirement age. In many cases these challenges were not well handled, resulting in costly over-expansion followed by politically difficult efforts to downsize.

The concept of demographic "aging" is a shorthand term – a metaphor really – applied to the shifts in population age structure toward higher percentages in older age groups that follow declines in fertility from high or moderate levels to low levels. Usage of the English word "aging" in this shorthand term has proved to be unfortunate, in that "aging" as normally applied to individual people[2] carries with it connotations of physical deterioration, illness, loss of energy, cognitive decline, and so forth. This can lead to connotations for "aging populations" drawn from aging individuals – that aging populations necessarily demonstrate less energy, nimbleness, openness to new ideas and technologies – generally less dynamic and more boring. A leading French demographer, Alfred Sauvy, memorably characterized an aging population as consisting of "old people, living in old houses, ruminating about old ideas" (Teitelbaum 1978). However, demographic aging actually refers only to the age distribution of a large population of individuals across a large range of ages. These individuals do age, but age distributions are not really subject to the depredations of the same physiological and cognitive aging that usually afflict individuals.

Considerable confusion also arises from the common use of measures of demographic aging that demographers recognize as increasingly out-of-date. In particular, the standard "old-age dependency ratio" is expressed as the ratio of the "old-age dependent population" (typically defined as age 65-and-over; sometimes 60-and-over) to the "working age population" (defined as 15–64.) This boundary of age 65 between "working age" and "old-age dependent" was established during the 1930s, 1940s, and 1950s for purposes of pension eligibility. Since then life expectancy at age 65 has risen substantially. Indeed in less than two decades, from 1990 to 2008, life expectancy at age 65 for South Korean women rose 29% from 16.3 to 21.0 years, and for men rose 34% from 12.4 to 16.6 years (U.S. Census Bureau 2012). Moreover, increasingly larger numbers of persons continue working after reaching age 65.

Over the same period the proportion over 65 that is truly dependent in physical/health terms has declined, as more generally have the proportions of the workforce engaged in heavy physical labor for which physical strength and agility are essential. A countervailing trend is that the costs of healthcare that are disproportionately used by older cohorts have been rising. Meanwhile, increasing fractions of those in their 20s have pursued higher education rather than entering the workforce.

Taken together these shifts mean that in advanced societies such as South Korea the definitions embodied in the traditional "dependency ratio" have been diverging from reality, as larger fractions of young adults over age 15 are still "dependents" engaged in education and training, while larger fractions of those 65-and-over are far from "dependent." The traditional measures that hold constant a "dependency" boundary based on chronological age from birth may well be misleading us. Additional measures have been proposed based on "prospective age," defining the boundary of old-age dependency as a constant number of years (such as 15) of

[2] Similar connotations apply to inanimate objects such as "aging" machinery, cars, manufacturing plants, and housing stock.

remaining life expectancy (Sanderson and Scherbov 2008: 7). These alternatives provide additional insights into what is actually happening, and deserve assessment by governments of countries such as South Korea.

Most official reports and commentaries however continue to use only traditional measures such as the old age dependency ratio. In part this is due to the understandable preference to maintain continuity of measurements over time and across societies. Yet this rigid adherence to out-of-date measures may also be attributable in part to fierce political opposition to any changes in the historical boundary for pension eligibility – a hot political topic in most advanced economies.

Shifts in Composition (Ethnic/Religious/Racial/Linguistic/ National Origin)

Large demographic differentials among such groups living within a given country can result in substantial shifts over several decades. This applies particularly to societies that have long included diverse populations; have experienced large fertility differentials among such groups (e.g. Lebanon); or have experienced high volumes of in-migration from non-majority groups (U.S., Canada, Australia, New Zealand, and many European countries). In the latter case of large-scale immigration, the rate of change in demographic composition is amplified when domestic fertility rates are low.

For historical and other reasons, South Korea (and North Korea too) today are among the most homogeneous national populations in the world, with little experience as yet of substantial shifts in composition of this type. However, should low fertility rates among South Koreans continue, and be accompanied by substantial increases in international migration (of non-Korean ethnics), significant shifts in population composition should be anticipated. This will require policy attention in advance of such changes, in the interest of minimizing any resulting social or political turbulence in the transition from a homogeneous to a diverse population.

Divergent views prevail as to the political implications of demographic homogeneity or diversity. Some politicians in politically stable countries with longstanding population heterogeneity (such as Canada and the U.S.) believe their demographic diversity is a source of strength and stability, while others differ. Some political leaders in countries with longstanding ethnic, religious or linguistic tensions (such as Lebanon, Syria, Iraq, Estonia, Latvia) see their countries' demographic diversity as a potential source of instability. Such differing points of view may be driven more by the specific composition of diversity within national populations, as well as by the flexibility of domestic political systems and the attitudes and actions of neighboring states.

Can Policies Have Significant Effect Upon Demographic Change in South Korea?

As noted earlier, South Korea has a history of success in policies to modify (or "engineer") its demographic rates, especially in terms of reducing both mortality and fertility during the second half of the twentieth century. The Korean experience in this area is similar in many ways to the experiences of the other three Asian Tigers, in Japan, and more recently in China. However, more recent efforts to increase very low fertility rates to more moderate levels have proved challenging.

Policies to Raise Korean Fertility

Over three-quarters of the decline in South Korean fertility rates between 1965 and 1985 was attributable to adoption of smaller family size norms, i.e. fertility declines within marriage. Since then, however, continuing fertility declines to today's very low levels have been due more to changes in marriage behavior, what some have termed the "flight from marriage" (Jones 2007: 458, 468). As of 2000, an estimated 38% of South Koreans aged 25–34 were single (and 48% of those living in cities). This was comparable to figures for Singapore, but lower than those for Japan (49%). European countries such as the Nordics and France reported even higher percentages single in these age group, but such comparisons can be misleading because in these countries cohabitation outside of marriage is far more common than in most of Asia, where such behaviors are culturally discouraged and are relatively rare. Making adjustments for this difference (necessarily crude in the absence of needed data) leads to the conclusion that in 2000 East Asian countries including South Korea had higher percentages single than even the percentages "effectively single" in northern and western Europe (Jones 2007: 457–458 and Table 3).

Some leading experts on fertility in Pacific Asia believe that deeply cultural norms and practices loom large in these trends:

> …Patriarchal attitudes among employers and in government, resulting in poor workplace provision for the needs of working mothers, and the reluctance of husbands to share most of the housework and childrearing tasks of working wives, add considerable stress to the lives of women with children. The extreme pressures in countries such as Japan, South Korea, and Singapore to raise "high-quality" children, and the unequal role given to mothers in achieving this goal, are additional strong deterrents to family building (Jones 2007: 470).

Other factors affecting marriage trends in South Korea include the unfavorable marriage prospects experienced by male farmers and fishermen in rural areas, which have led to rising numbers of marriages with foreign brides especially from Southeast Asia and China (see below).

In addition to these trends in marriage patterns, South Korean couples have opted for small, often single-child, families. Indeed the Korean government has long encouraged one-child families for the urban population, propagating slogans such as "have a single child and raise it well." This trade-off between quality and quantity of children, coupled with other norms of Korean society, has produced its own dynamics. For example, Korean children demonstrate very high levels of performance on international comparative tests such as the OECD's Programme for International Student Assessment (PISA). At the same time there is concern about the high degree of pressure felt by Korean children, especially from their mothers (sometimes portrayed unflatteringly as "Tiger Moms"), the common use of "cram schools" *(hagwon),* and the high-pressure entrance exams to leading Korean universities. Some Korean commentators worry that these pressures upon Korean teenagers are destructive, even a kind of "child abuse," contributing to a high incidence of serious psychological problems and even suicide (Koo 2014). Whatever may be the validity of such concerns, such cultural elements would seem to make it far more difficult to increase Korean fertility from currently low levels than it was to lower fertility by facilitating voluntary family planning during the postwar period.

Policies Regarding Out- and In-Migration

South Korea experienced substantial out-migration during the 1950s and 1960s. It is unclear whether Korean government policies facilitated such out-movements, as was the case with the government of Japan. Official and family encouragement offered to Korean students to undertake university education abroad may have stimulated permanent out-migration, although the intent may have instead been to generate a Korean population with more advanced education.

In-migration to South Korea has long been sharply constrained, although it has been increasing in recent years. One of the most visible types of in-migration has been by women from Southeast Asia and China for purposes of marriage to Korean men, especially in rural areas, facilitated by an active industry of international marriage brokers. This pattern was driven by higher rates of rural-to-urban migration by young Korean women than men, and by a combination of modern reproductive technologies and small family norms with traditional Korean cultural preferences for male children. In both cases these forces now appear to be waning, as the sex ratio at birth (SRB) has become more balanced and as fewer Korean men have been marrying non-Korean women – down from about 31,000 in 2005 to 18,000 in 2013 (Economist 2014a). Nevertheless, South Korea did experience a seriously unbalanced sex ratio at birth from around 1985 to around 2002 or so, during which time the ratio reached a high of 117. By 2012 it was back to more normal levels. But during the almost 20 years of unbalanced sex ratios at birth, upwards of as many as 1 million boys were born who if they wish to marry will need to seek out younger Korean women or non-Korean women, most likely from other Asian countries.

South Korea is the first East Asian country to adopt a formal refugee law. In July 2013, the country created a Refugee Division in the Korea Immigration Service.

The government of South Korea has also been increasing its financial support for the UN High Commissioner for Refugees. However the number of refugees and asylum-seekers settled in South Korea remains very small relative to its substantial population – a total stock of just over 3000 (United Nations High Commissioner for Refugees 2014). In addition South Korea has a longstanding policy of settling North Koreans who are able to exit that repressive country, although such migrants are not considered migrants or refugees but instead defined as Koreans falling under the "unification" policies of the government (Borowiec 2013) — a practice similar to that long followed by the government of the Federal Republic of Germany ("West Germany") with respect to exiles from the German Democratic Republic ("East Germany") before the two states were unified.

Long-Range Demographic Projections

Those sounding alarms about too-low fertility in 1930s Europe made effective use of long-range demographic projections to illustrate the catastrophic implications if then-current low fertility rates were to continue. Projections of a near-disappearance of Italian, British, or Swedish people undergirded books with evocative titles such as *Twilight of Parenthood* and *Race Suicide* that proliferated during this period. Similarly, in the US during the 1980s an influential book entitled *The Birth Dearth* (Wattenberg 1987) made use of long-range demographic projections to show how NATO (or sometimes "the West") would ineluctably fall behind the Warsaw Pact in strategic and economic power if over the coming century there continued to be higher fertility rates in Warsaw Pact countries than among NATO countries. The book, described by its own author as a an "alarmist tract" and a "provocation" (Wattenberg 1987: 1, 10), predicted the political and economic withering away of the West — a forecast that quickly proved to be embarrassingly wrongheaded when the Warsaw Pact imploded only 4 years later, and fertility rates in the successor states plummeted.

Given this sad history of failed foresight from long-range projections, it is surprising to read recent headlines in the Korean press such as "Koreans 'to Become Extinct in 2750'" (Chosun Ilbo 2014), with derivative articles later appearing on international sites such as NBC News (Gandhi 2014). Such stories were based on a long-range simulation projection – in this case stretching more than 700 years into the future – that reportedly was produced by the National Assembly Research Service at the request of Mr. Yang Seung-jo, a lawmaker in the New Politics Alliance for Democracy. The key assumption of the simulation was that Korean fertility would remain constant at the 1.19 children per woman reported in 2013. Under this assumption, the population of South Korea would decline to 40 million by 2056; 20 million in 2100; 3 million in 2200; and 1 million in 2256. Ultimately, according to this projection Koreans would gradually become extinct over the subsequent 500 years.

It may be that such exaggerated prognostications are necessary to capture political and public attention, given the many other issues on the agenda of Korean opinion-leaders. Of course these forecasts may well turn out to be as embarrassingly inaccurate as were those of the 1930s, although given their long-range nature no one responsible for them would be alive by the time this would become obvious.

An Agenda of Sensible Policy Responses and Adaptations

It is possible to consider judicious responses to recent very low fertility rates without resorting to such alarums. A substantial research literature in both East Asian and European countries over the past two decades now points to a number of common if not universal factors underlying such instances of low and very-low fertility. It is important to note that some of these factors are more susceptible to policy responses than are others. It is also useful to distinguish between those that are driving the *postponement of fertility* and those affecting *the "quantum" of fertility*, specifically the propensity of couples who do have children to have 1, 2, or 3.

Postponement

Analyses of recent cross-national experience show common tendencies toward postponement of both marriage and childbearing (Billari 2008, p. 4), with sometimes substantial declines in the proportion of births borne by younger women in their teens and twenties accompanied by an increased proportion borne by women in their thirties and later. To some (unknown) degree such shifts represent global diffusion among industrialized countries of "ideational" change toward the "post-modern fertility preferences" of the "Second Demographic Transition" (Lesthaeghe 1995; van de Kaa 2001). The ideas include increased emphasis upon individual autonomy on fertility decisions with declining influence of social institutions such as family, clan or village. Such changes are typically accompanied by increases in gender equality and attention to individuals' "higher order needs."

A second related but distinct trend is widespread *increases in educational attainment by women*, which usually leads to rising ages of both marriage and reproduction. Higher levels of women's education and later ages of reproduction in turn tend to increase the opportunity costs of childbearing.

Third, the *increasing economic and career uncertainties* that commonly have been experienced over the past decades by young adults in industrialized countries are thought by many analysts to be leading to delayed transitions to adulthood and hence to the deferment of adult behaviors such as family formation. Of these three factors tending toward fertility postponement, this third is the only one that seems susceptible to policy interventions, to which we shall return later in this section.

Quantum Effects

To some extent the postponement of fertility can itself contribute to declines in the proportion among those who once having had a first child decide to have a second or third. In addition, however, there are factors that seem to affect this "quantum" of fertility more directly (Billari 2008, pp. 7–9).

Some research studies suggest that the *strong family ties* ("familistic") found in Southern Europe (and perhaps also in East Asia) may favor lower fertility by emphasizing the importance of the quality rather than the quantity of children, and by paying less attention in public policy to the welfare of young adults and their children and to "the compatibility of parenthood with other choices (i.e., education, work)."

A second finding emerging from the research literature is that very low fertility regimes are often associated with sustained *low levels of gender equality within households in the context of rising gender equality in education and work*. Put simply, societies in which traditional expectations prevail about women's primary responsibilities for family and childrearing even as female education and labor force participation have risen substantially are settings in which work and family are most incompatible and the opportunity costs of childbearing are higher for increasingly well-educated women. Such circumstances arguably can be found in very low fertility countries in both Southern Europe and East Asia. Like the increasing uncertainties faced by young adults, this too is an area susceptible to thoughtful policy experimentation.

Finally, some governments appear to have decided that increased immigration can counteract the effects of low fertility rates on the dynamics of the workforce and age composition. For a decade or more after the mid-1990s, some of the lowest fertility countries in Southern Europe such as Spain and Italy followed policies – sometimes explicit, often implicit – that had the effect of enabling very large increases in net immigration. Such policies have become more politically controversial with the more recent onset of deep economic recession and very high unemployment rates, and it remains to be seen how sustainable such policies will prove to be.

Policy Developments in South Korea

Some of these factors have usefully been highlighted by the Presidential Committee on Aging and Future Society established by the Korean Government in 2004, and the Government has promulgated two Five Year Plans for responding to low fertility and an aging society (2006–2010 and 2011–2015). These plans are broad-based and include a wide range of efforts that, to paraphrase their official description, seek to do the following:

- strengthen societal responsibility for childbearing and childrearing;
- foster a family-friendly and gender-equal culture;
- raise future Korean generations in a wholesome way;

- stabilize income and health security for an aging society;
- encourage greater labor force participation by women and the elderly;
- encourage life-long learning to improve the quality of an aging workforce;
- increase admission of skilled workers from abroad (including "Korean brotherhood with foreign nationality"); and
- facilitate immigrant integration of the resulting increasingly multicultural society (Cho n.d.).

A related and also sensible array of policy responses to the "aging" demographics and retirement policies of South Korea has also been discussed in detail by a U.S. think tank, the Center for Strategic and International Studies (CSIS), with support from the insurance company MetLife, Inc. (Howe et al. 2007). As noted earlier, conventional conceptualizations of "old age" and its related "old-age dependency" warrant thoughtful assessment. If we view "old age dependency" as beginning at a fixed chronological age, then persistent low fertility rates clearly imply rising magnitudes of such dependency. If we view the age boundary of "old age dependency" as unfixed and tending toward increase with improving conditions of health, mortality, morbidity, and cognitive ability, the trend lines of "old-age dependency" emerging from our measurements might look quite different.

It is hardly possible to summarize all of these discussions in this chapter, but they do warrant serious attention by Korean leaders and citizens. In so doing it would be wise to recognize two key realities: first, that there has been much international experience with efforts to raise fertility from low levels, many of which have proved to be insufficient to the task and from which much could be learned by careful analyses; and second, that any such efforts can be expected to be effective only over a period of decades rather than years, and hence patience and sustained attention will be necessary.

The policy agenda already laid out by South Korea's Presidential Committee on Aging and Future Society is very broad and ambitious, perhaps overly so. It will likely prove very challenging to effect change in all of the domains highlighted in the report. Indeed, the prospects of success might be enhanced by focusing on a smaller range of efforts. Similar trends being experienced widely among OECD countries may be having significant impacts upon the decisions about marriage and family formation being made by young adult cohorts, and therefore might warrant assessment in the Korean context.

In particular, career and related experiences of young adult generations in OECD countries have been relatively unfavorable when compared with those experienced at the same ages by the older generations of their parents. As young adults these older cohorts were beneficiaries of postwar economic growth rates that were far higher than those experienced more recently in many OECD countries. Relative to their expectations, which likely were affected by their own childhood experiences, substantial fractions of these older generations were able to achieve levels of economic security and prosperity that they may not have expected.

Yet the offspring of these older cohorts, who as children were beneficiaries of their parents' unexpected prosperity, may in turn have incorporated higher expectations than they now are finding to be attainable in terms of career prospects, job stability, income, and housing. Unemployment and underemployment rates among young adults in many of these countries are far higher than those of the older cohorts, many of whom are protected by labor laws and contracts that critics decry as limiting needed labor market flexibility. In many OECD countries, the costs of the kinds of housing already owned or stably occupied by older cohorts have risen well beyond the financial capacities of younger cohorts.

Some of these outcomes are inherent in the market dynamics of mixed economies and globalization, but others seem more likely to have been driven by traditional cultural norms and by electoral politics and institutions such as unions and professional societies that understandably are more committed to protecting the interests of their current members (who are concentrated in older cohorts) than the aspirations of younger adult cohorts.

Yet of course the fundamentals of human physiology mean that it is precisely these often economically-challenged cohorts of young adults who are responsible for nearly all the fertility outcomes in all human societies. Postponements of both marriage and childbearing among these younger adult cohorts may in part derive from the relatively high risks they have been experiencing in labor and housing markets in particular (Winter and Teitelbaum 2013). Lutz and his colleagues speculate that this and other phenomena may contribute to a kind of "low fertility trap" for such countries that complicates any efforts they may consider to encourage somewhat higher fertility (Lutz and Skirbekk 2005).

This naturally suggests that attention should be paid to the particular labor and housing market circumstances being faced by Koreans in the primary ages of reproduction, e.g. 25–34. Is Korea similar to many other OECD countries in the adoption of strong statutory and contract protections for older and already-employed workers, but with far weaker protections for new labor force entrants? In other countries the unintended effects seem to be reduced prospects for younger adult cohorts at the beginning of their careers. Indeed differentially high rates of youth unemployment and underemployment seem to be nearly universal among OECD countries, and they are especially severe in the aftermath of the economic and fiscal crises that have appeared over the past two decades. These risks, combined with other challenges commonly being experienced by young adult cohorts, such as substantial real increases in housing prices and limited access to secure social housing, may pose substantial conflicts for young adult cohorts – trade-offs between the increased risks and high costs of marriage and childrearing versus the often higher economic expectations they have incorporated from their childhood experiences,

Decisions about if and when to marry among South Korean young adults, given continuing Korean cultural resistance to the high levels of cohabitation and out-of-wedlock childbearing that now prevail in much of northern and western Europe, would appear to be highly relevant to the timing and quantum of fertility. Similar patterns can be found in other East Asian countries such as Japan. In such settings, governments might usefully assess the potential – and the political and economic feasibility — of policies configured to moderate the labor market risks and the housing markets challenges that seem to be differentially facing young adults of prime reproductive age. Put another way, are there policy innovations that might narrow the gaps between the challenges facing young adult age groups of prime reproductive age as compared with those being experienced by older cohorts?

In addition to these labor and housing market issues, there likely are less quantifiable, but no less powerful, cultural elements that affect the marriage, non-marriage, and childbearing decisions of young adult Korean cohorts, and especially of young women. Certainly there is a substantial literature arguing that well-educated young Korean women in the early stages of their careers believe they must make a choice between their career aspirations and marriage, and that young women with children are disadvantaged in the labor market and in career progression.

The Korean government has committed itself to efforts to mitigate cultural norms that pose work-family conflicts for educated and employed Korean women (Economist 2013; Song Jung-a 2013). Careful analyses are in order to consider the extent to which young Korean husbands and their employers are responding positively. It would also be useful to assess research findings that Korean women themselves may be resisting change in such norms because they view them as essential to Korean culture and "virtuous Korean custom"? (Kim 2012).

Finally, it would be valuable to understand the extent to which efforts by government and employers to mitigate such work-family conflicts may actually be counteracted by parts of the Korean mass media. In particular, we are referring to negative and positive messages about marriage and childbearing being conveyed to young adults in powerful ways by Korea's influential popular culture (including K-dramas, film, K-pop music, and video games) frequently seen as the source of a "cultural wave" *(hallyu)* that has spread across Asia over the past decade (Economist 2014b). Substantial research in Latin America and elsewhere suggests that *telenovelas* in Mexico and Brazil may have been influential in furthering smaller-family norms in high-fertility countries. Less attention has been paid to whether K-dramas and other elements of popular culture might also affect behavior in low-fertility countries such as South Korea (Basten 2009; La Ferrara et al. 2008).

References

Basten, S. (2009). *Mass media and reproductive behavior: Serial narratives, soap operas, and telenovelas*. Oxford University, (The Future of Reproduction, Working Paper #7), June 2009. https://www.spi.ox.ac.uk/fileadmin/documents/PDF/Soaps_-_Number_7.pdf. Accessed 29 Nov 2014.

Billari, F. C. (2008). Lowest-low fertility in Europe: Exploring the causes and finding some surprises. *Japanese Journal of Population, 6*(1), 1–18.

Billari, F. C., & Kohler, H. P. (2004). Patterns of low and lowest-low fertility in Europe. *Population Studies, 58*(2), 161–176.

Bock, G. (1994). Antinatalism, maternity and paternity in national socialist racism. In D. Crew (Ed.), *Nazism and German society* (pp. 110–140). London: Routledge.

Borowiec, S. (2013). South Korea: New beacon for refugees. YaleGlobal, 12 Sep 2013. http://yaleglobal.yale.edu/content/south-korea-new-beacon-refugees.

Cho, N-H. (n.d.). *New challenge for low fertility and policy responses in Korea*. Seoul: Institute of Aging Society, Hanyang University. http://www.neaef.org/public/neaef/files/documents/publications_pdf/young_leaders/4th/Population%20-%20Cho%20Nam%20Hoon%20YLP%20 paper.pdf
Chosun Ilbo (English Edition). (2014). *Koreans 'to become extinct in 2750'*. http://english.chosun.com/site/data/html_dir/2014/08/25/2014082500859.html. Accessed 6 Nov 2014.
Clemenceau, G. (1919). *Journal Officiel* (1919). *Débats du Sénat*, 11 Oct 1919, pp. 1625–1626 (cited in Tomlinson, R., 1985. The disappearance of France, 1896–1940: French politics and the birth rate. Historical Journal, 28).
Coale, A. J., & Watkins, S. C. (1986). *The decline of fertility in Europe: The revised proceedings of a conference on the Princeton European fertility project*. Princeton: Princeton University Press.
Dumont, A. (1890). Arsène Dumont on legislative measures to remedy depopulation in France. *Population and Development Review, 39*(3), 527–533. Sep 2013.
Economist (2013). In this special report A pram too far: faced with overwhelming pressures, South Korean women have gone on baby-strike. Print edition 26 Oct 2013. http://www.economist.com/news/special-report/21588207-faced-overwhelming-pressures-south-korean-women-have-gone-baby-strike-pram-too. Accessed 23 Nov 2014.
Economist (2014a). Farmed Out: South Korea's foreign brides, 24 May 2014. http://www.economist.com/news/asia/21602761-korean-men-are-marrying-foreigners-more-choice-necessity-farmed-out. Accessed 06 Feb 2015.
Economist (2014b). Soap, sparkle, and pop: South Korea's soft power — How a really uncool country became the tastemaker of Asia, 9 Aug 2014.. http://www.economist.com/news/books-and-arts/21611039-how-really-uncool-country-became-tastemaker-asia-soap-sparkle-and-pop. Accessed 30 Nov 2014.
Forcucci, L. E. (2010). Battle for births: The fascist pronatalist campaign in Italy 1925 to 1938. *Journal of the Society for the Anthropology of Europe, 10*(1), Spring/Summer 2010, 4–13.
Gandhi, L. (2014, August 27). Could South Korea's low birth rate really mean extinction? *NBC News*. http://www.nbcnews.com/news/asian-america/could-south-koreas-low-birth-rate-really-mean-extinction-n190151. Accessed 4 Nov 2014.
Howe, N, Jackson, R., & Nakashima, K., with contributions by Kwon, H., & Park, J., (2007). The aging of Korea: Demographics and retirement policy in the land of the morning calm. Washington, DC: Global Aging Initiative, Center for Strategic and International Studies. http://csis.org/files/media/csis/pubs/070321_gai_agingkorea_eng.pdf. Accessed 6 Nov 2014.
Jones, G. W. (2007). Delayed marriage and very low fertility in Pacific Asia. *Population and Development Review, 33*(3), 453–478.
Kim, Y. (2012). *Women, television and everyday life in Korea: Journeys of hope*. London: Routledge. Chapter 1.
Kohler, H.-P., Billari, F. C., & Ortega, J. A. (2002). The emergence of lowest-low fertility in Europe during the 1990s. *Population and Development Review, 28*(4), 641–680.
Koo, S-W. (2014August 1). South Korea's education system hurts students: An assault upon our children. *New York Times*. http://www.nytimes.com/2014/08/02/opinion/sunday/south-koreas-education-system-hurts-students.html?_r=0. Accessed 8 Nov 2014.
La Ferrara, E., Chong, A., & Duryea, S. (2008, October). *Soap operas and fertility: Evidence from Brazil*, ms. http://www.iadb.org/res/files/WP-633updated.pdf
Lesthaeghe, R. (1995). The second demographic transition in western countries: An interpretation. In K. Oppenheim Mason & A.-M. Jensen (Eds.), *Gender and family change in industrialized countries* (pp. 17–62). Oxford: Clarendon.
Lutz, W., Skirbekk, V., & Testa, M. R. (2005). *The low fertility trap hypothesis: Forces that may lead to further postponement and fewer births in Europe.*. http://www.oeaw.ac.at/vid/download/edrp_4_05.pdf. Accessed 9 Nov 2014.
Sanderson, W., & Scherbov, S. (2008). Rethinking age and aging. *Population Bulletin, 63*(4). Washington, DC: Population Reference Bureau.

Song Jung-a, S. (2013, June 12). South Korean women face glass ceiling in workforce. *Financial Times*. http://www.ft.com/cms/s/0/50242166-ce60-11e2-8313-00144feab7de.html#axzz3Jw1bdQyg. Accessed 23 Nov 2014.
Teitelbaum, M. S. (1978). Aging populations. In *Encyclopedia Britannica Yearbook 1978*. New York: Encyclopedia Britannica.
Teitelbaum, M. S., & Winter, J. M. (1985). *The fear of population decline* (pp. 18–20). New York/London: Academic.
Times of London. (1883). *Population in France: Striking decay there as compared with other lands*. Reprinted in New York Times, 7 February 1883.
U.S. Census Bureau. (2012). Table 1340. Life expectancy at birth and at age 65, by sex—selected countries: 1990 and 2008. https://www.census.gov/compendia/statab/2012/tables/12s1340.pdf
United Nations High Commissioner for Refugees. (2014). 2014 UNHCR regional operations profile – East Asia and the Pacific: Republic of Korea. http://www.unhcr.org/pages/49e489036.html. Accessed 6 Nov 2014.
Van de Kaa, D. (2001). Fertility preferences: From changing value orientation to new behavior. *Population and Development Review, 27*(supplement), 290-331.
Wattenberg, B. J. (1987). *The birth dearth: What happens when people in free countries don't have enough babies?* New York: Pharos Books.
Winter, J., & Teitelbaum, M. S. (2013). *The global spread of fertility decline: Population, fear, and uncertainty*. New Haven: Yale University Press.

Chapter 12
Exploring the Effects of Fertility Change on Religiosity in the Twenty-First Century: A Cross-National Analysis

Christopher G. Ellison, Xiaohe Xu, and Andrea L. Ruiz

Introduction

A wealth of theoretical and empirical literature has focused on contemporary fertility trends in advanced industrial or post-industrial societies, especially with regard to what has been termed the Second Demographic Transition. As the various contributions to this volume make clear, fertility rates in many developed countries have dropped to remarkably low levels. Rates vary significantly across European countries, remaining comparatively high–but still below replacement rate—in Anglo-Saxon and Northern European countries, plunging to "lowest-low" fertility levels–rates of 1.3 or less–in southern European nations, and in Germany and Austria (Kohler et al. 2002; Morgan and Taylor 2006).

Scholars continue to debate the relative impact of cultural factors, as opposed to material factors and increasing female labor force participation, in shaping these population dynamics (Adsera 2014). Many investigators have pointed to the role of significant value shifts, such as the growth of anti-authoritarian and egalitarian values, the increased emphasis on self-actualization, individualism, and expressiveness, and the rise of post-materialist orientations. In industrialized societies, it is increasingly common to postpone marriage and parenthood in favor of educational attainment, career achievement, consumerism, personal fulfillment, and other individualistic and expressive values. Rates of non-marital cohabitation have been on the rise, accompanied by rises in the rates of childlessness and in the percentages of births to unmarried mothers (Lesthaeghe and Neidert 2006; Thornton et al. 1992). The result of these trends appears to be long-term sub-replacement cohort fertility

C.G. Ellison (✉) • X. Xu
University of Texas-San Antonio, San Antonio, TX, USA
e-mail: christopher.ellison@utsa.edu

A.L. Ruiz
Penn State University, Old Main, State College, PA 16801, USA

D.L. Poston, Jr. (ed.), *Low Fertility Regimes and Demographic and Societal Change*, DOI 10.1007/978-3-319-64061-7_12

in a wide array of societies. Recent evidence indicates that the Second Demographic Transition is well underway throughout much of industrialized East Asia (e.g., Japan, Korea, Taiwan), and that it may also be spreading to other regions as well (e.g., Lesthaeghe and Neidert 2006; Morgan and Taylor 2006).

One important issue concerns the role of religion in these transformations. Although there is considerable debate on this point (Stark and Finke 2000), many observers have called attention to widespread declines in religious practice and belief that typically accompany economic development and prosperity (Bruce 2011; Norris and Inglehart 2011). Analyses have often treated secularization (defined mainly in terms of declines in religious practice) as an antecedent factor, and have assumed (explicitly or implicitly) that secularization has been a contributing factor to other value shifts (e.g., rising social and gender egalitarianism, and individualism) that may be implicated in the turn toward sub-replacement cohort fertility (Lesthaeghe and Surkyn 1988; Surkyn and Lestaeghe 2004). This has also figured prominently in debates about whether the United States—with its comparatively high fertility rates, and its relatively high levels of religiosity—is an exception to the patterns and processes of the Second Demographic Transition (Lesthaeghe and Neidert 2006).

This treatment of secularization as a possible antecedent, or cause, of other value shifts and fertility changes fits well with the broader scholarly literature on religion and fertility, which has often assumed that religious institutions, values, and practices tend to shape fertility (Lehrer 1996, 2004; McQuillan 2004). However, some have suggested that the religion-fertility connection may be bidirectional, i.e., that fertility may also impact levels and patterns of religious involvement. At least three lines of argument have expressed this view. For example, some conservative social commentators have argued that declines in the nuclear family, including reduced levels of fertility, have contributed to secularization in the West (e.g., Eberstadt 2013), as follows: …[Observers] have simply assumed …that the decline in the natural family was a mere consequence of the shrinking of belief …the reverse is also true …[However] the ongoing deterioration of the natural family itself has both accompanied and accelerated the deterioration in the West of Christian belief (p. 22, italics added).

From another vantage point, some scholars have discussed the long-term implications of differential fertility among religious groups for the religious, social, and political futures of various societies, including those in Western Europe and the United States (Kaufmann 2010, 2014; Skirbeckk et al. 2010). Yet another strand of work has centered on individual-level patterns especially, but not exclusively, in the United States (e.g., Uecker et al. 2016). Briefly, researchers in this tradition have argued that it is fertile families that tend to be attracted to religion, especially institutional religion, whereas families (and individuals) without children are more likely to detach (or to remain disengaged from) religious pursuits. The impact of fertility on religion may be amplified for certain types of persons and families (e.g., for new fathers, and for those who bear children at certain normative stages "on the social clock"). To be sure, some scholars have cast doubt on the argument that fertility begets religion (Adsera 2014; Berghammer 2009), but it appears that there is at least some theoretical and empirical basis for investigating these connections further.

Although theorists and researchers have focused primarily on the *positive* associations between fertility and religion–that is, the link between *higher* fertility and *higher* religiosity–the logic of their arguments also helps us to understand why declines in fertility might undermine levels of religious participation, and why long-term, large-scale reductions in fertility rates at the societal level could affect patterns of religious affiliation, participation, salience, and belief in important ways. Building on these lines of argument–in essence "reverse-engineering" some of the theoretical claims developed in individual-level studies—we examine in this chapter the association between country-level fertility decline and subsequent patterns of individual religiosity.

Theoretical and Empirical Background: Religion and Fertility

A long tradition of scholarship has explored the complex relationships between religion and fertility. Much of this work has centered on shifting fertility differentials among religious groups and traditions, and on associations between religious participation levels and fertility (Frejka and Westoff 2008). A significant body of work in this domain has focused on the United States (Goldscheider and Mosher 1991; Hayford and Morgan 2008; Mosher et al. 1992). Although secularization, i.e., declining levels and salience of religious practice and belief, has been raised as one type of value change that has contributed to the large-scale fertility declines (e.g., Surkyn and Lestaeghe 2004), fewer studies have explored religious variations in fertility in specific European contexts (Adsera 2006a, b; Philipov and Berghammer 2007; Frejka and Westoff 2008). Researchers have also highlighted the role of religious influences on fertility in a range of non-Western contexts, with particular attention to the comparatively high fertility among Muslims in several Asian and African nations (Dharmalingam and Morgan 2004; Morgan et al. 2002; Westoff and Bietch 2015).

For much of the twentieth century, U.S. studies tended to concentrate on Catholic-Protestant fertility differentials (Frejka and Westoff 2008; Westoff and Jones 1979). U.S. Catholic fertility levels began to decline disproportionately after the 1920s. Despite some reversal due to the sharp rise in Catholic fertility during the post-World War II baby boom, Catholic-Protestant differences had nearly disappeared by the end of the 1970s. These patterns have largely been attributed to increases in the access to, and use of, various forms of contraception among most segments of the U.S. population (Westoff and Jones 1979). Contemporary analyses of religion and fertility in the United States have noted comparatively high (though declining) fertility rates among Mormons, conservative, i.e., fundamentalist, evangelical, and charismatic, Protestants, and first-generation Catholics, particularly those from Latina/o backgrounds. Fertility rates are much lower among the non-religious and liberal Protestant groups (Mosher et al. 1992). Wide fertility differentials exist among Jewish groups, with high rates among Orthodox and (especially) Hasidic Jews and rates that are well below replacement levels among Conservative, Reform, and (especially) secular Jewish elements (Stark 2012).

Research using combined data on all OECD countries has reported comparatively low fertility among religiously unaffiliated and liberal Protestants, declining fertility among Catholics, and comparatively high fertility among conservative Protestants (Adsera 2014). In an important comparative analysis of the role of religious factors in shaping fertility in the U.S. and in Europe, Frejka and Westoff (2008) found that (1) Catholic and Protestant women have higher fertility than their non-religious counterparts, and (2) across the U.S. and all regions of Europe, and among all religious denominations, more devout women, i.e., those who attend services more often and who rate religion as more important, tend to have higher fertility. They concluded that, if Europeans were as religious as Americans one might theoretically expect a modest fertility increase of 15% or less for Europe as a whole, but a more dramatic fertility boost, perhaps 30%, for Western Europe (Adsera 2014; Frejka and Westoff 2008).

In a well-known formulation, McQuillan (2004) assessed the circumstances under which religion might be expected to have the greatest impact on fertility. He argued that religious influences will be most evident when the following occur: (1) religious groups and traditions hold distinctive theological beliefs regarding ideal family size, contraception, and other relevant factors; (2) religious institutions have sufficient cultural and organizational strength to enforce these norms and to impose sanctions on those who deviate; and (3) religion is an important component of the social identities of individuals, thus decreasing the likelihood that they will violate religious norms. Others have expanded on these ideas, calling attention to the ways in which religion may operate differently across temporal and spatial contexts, and underscoring the roles of familial, political, and other factors in moderating the links between religion and fertility (Goldscheider 2006; Kertzer 2006).

Although much of the literature has focused on the influence of religion on fertility behavior, there are sound reasons to believe that fertility can affect religion as well. As we noted earlier in this chapter, several strands of recent theory and research have taken this view. One example is work by conservative social critics, who have asserted that changes in family life–including rising divorce rates and reduced fertility rates–have undermined the strength of religious institutions and values in the contemporary West, and in other societies throughout history (Eberstadt 2013). A second example consists of theory and research by Kaufmann (2010, 2014) and others, arguing that (a) low and declining fertility rates among secular and marginally religious Protestants and Catholics in some European societies, along with (b) the high fertility rates of non-Christian, especially Muslim, immigrants, may dramatically alter the religio-cultural makeup of the United Kingdom and other European societies, leading to major changes in social life and potential spikes in political tension and conflict within these countries.

However, the most relevant body of work investigating the effects of fertility on religion comes from individual-level studies conducted primarily, but not exclusively, in the United States. Although some researchers have dismissed this argument, a number of studies have reported positive links between the presence and number of children in families and the likelihood of religious affiliation, as well as levels of religious attendance, salience, and belief, among adults (Argue et al. 1999; Myers 1996; Petts 2009; Stolzenberg et al. 1995; also see Uecker et al. 2007). Recent work using longitudinal data sources has clarified these patterns further, revealing that the presence of school-aged children is especially important in shaping increases in religious involvement among parents, even predicting the return of parents who were previously disengaged from institutional religion (Schleifer and Chaves 2014; Uecker et al. 2016).

Why might this be the case? Uecker et al. (2016) have helpfully distinguished among four classes or genres of explanations for these patterns. First, the experience of childbearing and childrearing may enhance the appeal of religious beliefs and practices. This may occur because parents want their children to receive religious training and moral socialization, and to participate in major rituals and life cycle events such as baptism, confirmation, or bar mitzvah (Ingersoll-Dayton et al. 2002; Manning 2013; Petts 2007; Sullivan 2008). Parents may also maintain or increase their religious involvement in an effort to serve as good role models for their children (Sherkat 2006; Uecker et al. 2016).

Second, religious congregations are network-driven institutions (Ellison and George 1994; Olson 1989). On one hand, recruitment into religious communities often occurs through pre-existing social ties; on the other hand, because religious groups bring together persons who share common values, interests, and activities, these communities offer fertile ground for the cultivation and maintenance of new friendships (e.g., Ellison and George 1994). The social dynamics of religious congregations are often more welcoming for traditional nuclear families than for persons from other family backgrounds, or for single individuals, because they provide manifold opportunities for couples to interact with like-minded congregants (Argue et al. 1999; Stolzenberg et al. 1995). Moreover, the programming of many religious communities tends to serve families with young children more than others (Wilcox et al. 2004). Taken together, this suggests that one possible appeal of religious communities for parents is the opportunity to interact and bond with fellow parents. This may help to explain why parents with school-aged children and those who have children during normative childbearing years, i.e., on the "social clock," are more likely than others to remain in, or to join, religious groups (Schleifer and Chaves 2014; Stolzenberg et al. 1995; Uecker et al. 2016).

Third, religious communities can also provide an array of formal and informal supports for parents (Chaves 2004; Edgell 2006). Specifically, studies have shown that many congregations offer babysitting and day care services, parenting classes, discussion groups, and other resources that can assist parents (Becker and Hofmeister 2001; Edgell 2006). In addition, parents can gain from their engagement with coreligionists, who may also be parents and may have considerable insight about childrearing issues, such as discipline, moral training, and education. Thus, parents may receive help from their fellow church members, in the form of shared childcare, advice and information, and other practical resources. Further, parents in religious groups may benefit from these social relationships in other important ways. For instance, interaction with others who share their values and worldview can strengthen faith commitments and can crystallize shared definitions of parental and familial roles, thereby affording valuable moral support and encouragement (Petts 2007, 2009).

Fourth, there may be broader cultural explanations linking fertility and childbearing with religious involvement. For example, many religious communities promote an ideology of "religious familism," focused on pronuptiality and pronatalism, and committed to the view that the traditional nuclear family is the central unit of the social order (Edgell and Docka 2007; Sandomirsky and Wilson 1990; Wilson and Sherkat 1994). Many parents, especially married parents, may see religious involvement as a key element of having a "good" family life (Edgell 2006; Mahoney 2010). In addition, religious engagement and family formation may be regarded as part of a common script of settled-ness and establishment (Becker and Hofmeister 2001; Wilcox et al. 2012). Childbearing and childrearing may also foster religious involvement among parents by keying expectations about parenting roles (Uecker et al. 2016). Some observers have suggested that these dynamics may be particularly evident among fathers, who may reexamine their priorities, focus their attention on family life, and accord a greater role to religious practices and beliefs (Petts 2007).

These four sets of argument help to explain why some studies often report positive empirical associations between parental status and religious affiliation, practice, and belief. More importantly for present purposes, however, they offer valuable hints concerning how and why decreases in fertility within and across societies could result in diminished religious involvement over time. Specifically, fertility decline may reduce the imperative of religious and moral socialization for children, and may undercut the social relevance of certain religious rituals and life cycle events, e.g., baptism, bar or bat mitzvah. In addition, lowered fertility may limit the centrality of congregational social bonds among parents; religious contexts may become less important as sources of friendship and social solidarity. Further, reductions in the numbers of children in religious communities may well impinge on family programming, which in turn could undermine the attractiveness of religious congregations. Taken together, these dynamics could eventually result in an overall loss of resources such as financial giving and volunteers for religious institutions, which would diminish their social visibility and influence.

The cumulative effect of such forces, animated in significant degree by fertility declines, could well impair the intergenerational transmission of faith, making religious institutions less successful in retaining the next generation of potential members. In terms of broader cultural patterning, it is conceivable that through some or all of these mechanisms fertility declines could undermine the influence of normative facets of religion, including norms that encourage religious affiliation and identity, participation, and doctrinal fidelity. To the extent that these dynamics are underway, they raise the possibility that irreligion will become more common and more widely accepted. In such a climate, religious effects on politics, culture, and institutional life would almost certainly wane, perhaps leading to the kinds of religious "privatism" and "fuzzy fidelity" that secularization theorists have long anticipated, and that some researchers have observed in parts of the developed West (Bruce 2009; Tschannen 1991; Voas 2009; Voas and Crockett 2005).

Taken together, these lines of theory and research give rise to several hypotheses, which will be tested in this chapter. The first will be tested at the aggregate, i.e., cross-national, level: Country-level fertility decline will be inversely associated with average levels of religious attendance, salience, and belief. The remaining hypotheses will be tested using multi-level models, in which individual- and national-level factors are used to predict individual-level variation in religious involvement. In these analyses, the number of children will be positively associated with organizational religious involvement, i.e., frequency of religious attendance, non-organizational practices, i.e., frequency of prayer, religious salience, and religious belief, i.e., belief in God. In addition, also among individuals, national-level fertility decline will be inversely associated with individual-level organizational and non-organizational religious participation, religious salience, and belief. It is expected that these patterns will persist despite controls for individual-level demographic characteristics, religious tradition, social and family values, and contextual factors such as country-level economic development.

Data and Methods

Multilevel data for the analyses we will undertake in this chapter came from several sources. The country level data came primarily from two databases maintained by the World Bank and the United Nations. In the case when a particular measure was not available for the countries analyzed, the statistical yearbooks were consulted. The individual level data came from the World Values Survey (WVS), which began in 1981 and collected nationally representative samples from over 100 countries. The WVS covers such topics as economic development, religion, gender equality, social capital, and subjective wellbeing. Given the goals and objectives of the present study, the pooled 1981–2014 longitudinal WVS data were utilized. This longitudinal public-use dataset was downloaded from the WVS website at http://www.worldvaluessurvey.org/wvs.jsp.

Our country level analysis included the aggregated average frequency of worship service attendance (coded on a 1–7 scale) and religious salience (coded on a 1–4 scale) as well as the aggregated percentage of religious belief, i.e., belief in God which was dummy-coded with 1 = yes and 0 = no, reported by the WVS respondents from 54 countries. Even though these three religious measures are available for more than 60 countries, we restricted our analysis to 54 countries by omitting several countries that had extremely high total fertility rates in 2000. It should be noted that these three aggregated WVS religious measures served as the dependent variables in our country level analysis. Although the frequency of prayer was included in our individual level analysis (see below), this measure was not included in the country level analysis due to the fact that it was only available for a smaller number of countries. To make sure that there was enough variation in TFR and country level religiosity, the frequency of prayer was excluded from our country level analysis.

Moreover, to explore the association between country level fertility and religiosity, the country's TFR for 2000 was utilized as a key independent variable. In addition, the gross domestic product per capita (GDP) in US$ in 2000 and the WVS year served as statistical controls. To overcome high skewness and kurtosis, GDP 2000 was log-transformed.

For our individual level analysis, there were four WVS religious measures, serving as our dependent variables. The first dependent variable captured attendance at religious services. Respondents were asked how often they attended religious services. Responses were reverse-coded into 7 categories ranging from 1 = practically never to 7 = more than once a week. Two categories that recorded religious attendance only on specific holidays were combined. The second dependent variable was religious salience. Respondents were asked how important religion was in their life. This variable was also reverse-coded ranging from 1 = not at all important to 4 = very important. The third dependent variable gauged religious belief. Respondents were asked if they believed in God, coded as a dummy variable with 1 = yes and 0 = no. The final dependent variable measured private religiosity, indicated by the frequency of prayer. Respondents were asked how often they prayed. This measure was reversed-coded into a new variable with response categories ranging from 1 = practically never to 8 = several times a day.

The focal independent variable for our individual level analysis was a fertility measure from the WVS that asked respondents how many children they ever had. This measure was recorded as a count variable ranging from 0 = no child to 8 = 8 or more children. We also experimented with a desired fertility variable measured by desired number of children. However, because these two variables were highly correlated with each other, the actual number of children was used.

Individual level statistical controls included (1) gender (dummy-coded with male as the reference), (2) age, (3) marital status (dummy-coded with never married serving as the reference), (4) educational attainment (8 ordinal categories from low to high), (5) employment status (dummy-coded with not working as the reference), (6) household income (10 ordinal categories from low to high), (7) traditional gender ideology as indicated by a survey question that asked respondents if they agreed with the statement "Men should have more right to a job than women" (dummy-coded with non-traditional serving as the reference), (8) importance of family (reverse-coded such that it ranged from 1 = not at all important to 4 = very important), and (9) abortion attitudes (reverse-coded ranging from 1 = always justifiable to 10 = never justifiable). In addition, denominational affiliation was dummy-coded into a series of variables: not affiliated, Orthodox, Buddhist, Muslim, mainline Protestant, conservative Protestant, and other faith traditions with Catholic serving as the reference category; the classification of Protestants follows closely the scheme developed by Steensland et al. (2000). Finally, the WVS year was included as a control variable.

Our statistical analyses began with three country level Ordinary Least Squares (OLS) regression models to linearly regress the aggregated frequency of worship service attendance and religious salience and the aggregated percentage of religious belief, respectively, on TFR 2000, net of GDP per capita 2000 and year of the WVS for 54 countries. These regression models were designed to estimate and test for the positive associations between fertility levels and varying degrees of religiosity at the country level.

Next we estimated four multi-level regression models, in which four individual level religious variables, namely, worship service attendance, religious salience, religious belief, and prayer were regressed, respectively, on two focal independent variables, namely, individual level fertility, i.e., number of children, and country level fertility, i.e., the TFR in 2011, net of statistical controls. For worship service attendance and prayer, linear regression models were specified and unstandardized regression coefficients were reported. By contrast, for religious salience and belief, ordered and binary logit models were estimated and odds coefficients were reported. In these multilevel models, both the intercept and the slope of the individual level fertility measure were allowed to vary across the countries. In order to control for a wider array of covariates, the number of countries included in the multi-level analysis was reduced to 38 for religious attendance, salience and belief, and to 23 for prayer. At the individual level, the sample sizes varied across the dependent variables: 47,880 for religious attendance and salience, 47,844 for religious belief, and 29,593 for prayer. Multiple imputation techniques were used to estimate and replace missing values. Unless otherwise indicated, the mixed models for multilevel modeling in both SPSS and Stata were used.

Results

Table 12.1 reports the country level OLS regression parameter estimates. The regression results show that the TFR in 2000 is positively and significantly associated with religious attendance, salience, and belief at least at the .05 level. More specifically, for each one-unit increase in the 2000 total fertility rate, the predicted worship service attendance, salience, and belief increase by a factor of .50, .19, and 4.48, respectively, net of the log-transformed GDP per capita in 2000 and year of the WVS. The R squared statistics indicate that TFR, along with the control variables, primarily GDP, accounted for 61, 41, and 21% of variance in the dependent variables, respectively. To visualize the estimated linear regression relationships, Figs. 12.1, 12.2 and 12.3 display scatter plots using the standardized predicted values (y-axis) and TFR 2000 (x-axis) based on the above regression models. As anticipated, a strong linear association pattern is observed for all three dependent variables, namely, religious attendance, salience, and belief.

Table 12.2 presents descriptive statistics for all the variables used in the multilevel regression models. It is observed that on average respondents reportedly attended religious services at least once a year and prayed almost once a week. Additionally, about 55% of respondents reported that religion was important in their lives and nearly 78% said that they believed in God. As far as the focal independent

Table 12.1 OLS regression models to predict country-level religiosity[a]

	Attendance		Salience		Belief	
TFR (2000)	0.500	***	0.193	**	4.477	*
GDP per capita (2000; logged)	−0.176	*	−0.117	*	−1.912	
Year of survey	−0.001		−0.004		−0.178	
Constant	5.854		11.346		447.527	
F	26.199	***	11.503	***	4.358	**
R^2	61.10%		40.80%		20.70%	
n	54		54		54	

*$p < 0.05$; **$p < 0.01$; ***$p < 0.001$

[a]The following countries are included: Albania, Argentina, Armenia, Australia, Belarus, Bosnia, Brazil, Bulgaria, Canada, Chile, Colombia, Cyprus, Ecuador, Estonia, Finland, Georgia, Germany, Ghana, Hungary, India, Japan, Korea, R., Macedonia, Malaysia, Mexico, Moldova, Netherlands, New Zealand, Nigeria, Norway, Peru, Philippines, Poland, Puerto Rico, Romania, Russia, Rwanda, Serbia, Singapore, Slovenia, South Africa, Spain, Sweden, Switzerland, Taiwan, Tanzania, Trinidad and Tobago, Uganda, Ukraine, United States, Uruguay, Venezuela, Vietnam, and Zimbabwe

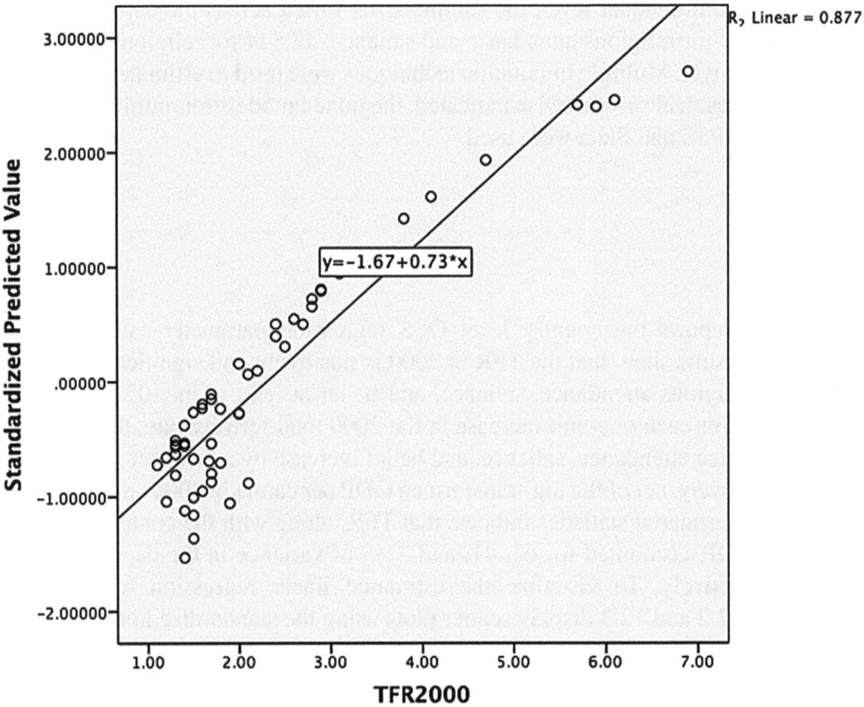

Fig. 12.1 *TFR* (2000) and predicted mean levels of attendance at religious services controlling for GDP per capita (2000) and world values survey year ($n = 54$)

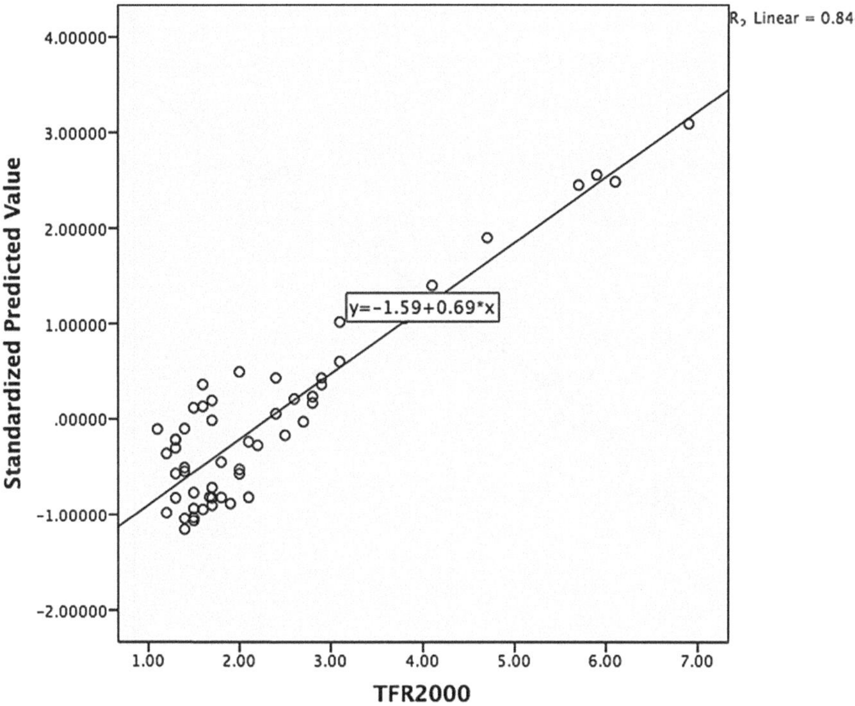

Fig. 12.2 *TFR* (2000) and predicted mean levels of religious salience controlling for GDP per capita (2000) and world values survey year ($n = 54$)

variables are concerned, on average, respondents reported less than two children, and since 1960 the TFR has declined by about 48–49% across the dependent variables.

Turning to Table 12.3, it can be seen that net of statistical controls, both the individual level and country level fertility variables are significantly associated with all individual level religious variables in the anticipated directions. At the individual level, all else being equal, for each additional child respondents reportedly have, their expected frequency of worship service attendance and prayer increase by a factor of 0.059 and 0.080, respectively. In a similar fashion, for each additional child, the expected odds of viewing religion important and believing in God increase by 7.6 ([1.076 – 1] × 100) and 5.8 ([1.058 – 1] × 100) percent, respectively. These regression slopes vary across countries while predicting the individual level religious variables. For the country level fertility variable, each percentage point drop in the TFR since 1960 is associated with decreased frequency of religious attendance and prayer by a factor of 0.015 and 0.025, respectively, holding all the other covariates constant. Likewise, each percentage point drop in the TFR is associated with decreased odds of viewing religion important and believing in God by 1.8 ([0.982 – 1] × 100) and 2.9 ([0.971 – 1] × 100) percent, respectively, all else equal. These results were highly anticipated.

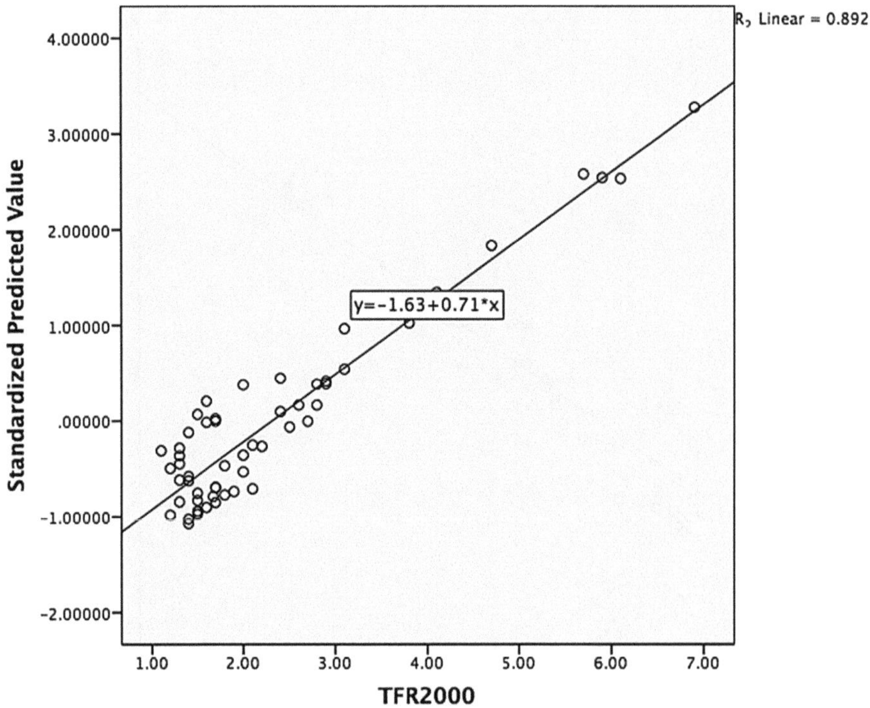

Fig. 12.3 *TFR* (2000) and predicted percentage of belief in god controlling for GDP per capita (2000) and world values survey year ($n = 54$)

Discussion

A long tradition of theory and research has explored the complex relationships between religious factors and fertility. Much of this work has focused on religion's influence on fertility attitudes and behavior, and has investigated variations in fertility, measured usually by the total fertility rate, by religious group or degree of religious commitment (e.g., Adsera 2014; McQuillan 2004; Westoff and Bietch 2015). Although there is much to be learned from this body of research, and ample additional work to be done along those lines, we have taken a different direction in this chapter. We have essentially reversed the causal arrow of this common conceptual model, arguing that fertility declines may lead to eventual reductions in religious participation, salience, and belief. In a sample of 54 countries, we determined that the rate of fertility change, i.e., decline, is clearly and consistently associated with aggregate religiosity. Then we estimated multi-level models combining pooled data from the World Values Surveys with country-level data from various other sources. These models gauged the effects of country-level fertility change on individual-level religious attendance, prayer, salience, and belief in God, controlling for country-level economic development and a host of individual-level covariates.

Table 12.2 Descriptive statistics for the variables in the multilevel models

	n/Mean	%/ SD	n/Mean	%/ SD	n/Mean	%/ SD	n/Mean	%/SD
Dependent variables								
Attendance	3.34	1.93	–	–	–	–	–	–
Salience								
Not at all important	–	–	8949	18.70	–	–	–	–
Not very important	–	–	12,641	26.40	–	–	–	–
Rather important	–	–	12,830	26.80	–	–	–	–
Very important	–	–	13,460	28.10	–	–	–	–
Belief in god								
Yes	–	–	–	–	37,504	78.39	–	–
No	–	–	–	–	10,340	21.61	–	–
Prayer							4.32	2.63
Independent variables								
Denominational affiliation								
No religious affiliation	12,734	26.60	12,734	26.60	12,419	25.96	8914	30.12
Orthodox	12,691	26.51	12,691	26.51	11,161	23.33	7029	23.75
Buddhist	2202	4.60	2202	4.60	2105	4.40	1949	6.59
Muslim	1891	3.95	1891	3.95	1881	3.93	1100	3.72
Mainline protestant	4626	9.66	4626	9.66	5980	12.50	3054	10.32
Conservative protestant	3446	7.20	3446	7.20	2325	4.86	1919	6.48
Other faith tradition	3198	6.68	3198	6.68	2592	5.42	2041	6.90
Catholic (reference)	7092	14.80	7092	14.80	9381	19.60	3587	12.12
Number of children	1.66	1.45	1.66	1.45	1.66	1.47	1.60	1.38
Changes in TFR (1960-most recent year)	−49.54	15.68	−49.54	15.68	−49.30	15.65	−47.93	16.71
Control variables								
GDP (2011; logged)	9.72	1.104	9.72	1.104	9.74	1.09	10.01	0.86
Gender								
Female	25,709	53.69	25,709	53.69	25,692	53.70	16,108	54.43
Male (reference)	22,171	46.31	22,171	46.31	22,152	46.30	13,485	45.57
Age	46.38	17.31	46.38	17.31	45.73	17.29	47.63	17.50
Marital status								
Ever married	37,865	79.08	37,865	79.08	37,725	78.85	23,419	79.14

(continued)

Table 12.2 (continued)

	n/Mean	%/ SD	n/Mean	%/ SD	n/Mean	%/ SD	n/Mean	%/SD
Never married (reference)	10,015	20.92	10,015	20.92	10,119	21.15	6174	20.86
Education	5.08	2.19	5.08	2.19	5.02	2.17	5.26	2.15
Employment status								
Working	25,854	54.00	25,854	54.00	26,017	54.38	16,500	55.76
Not working (reference)	22,026	46.00	22,026	46.00	21,827	45.62	13,093	44.24
Household income	4.68	2.13	4.68	2.13	4.57	2.22	4.71	2.03
Gender ideology								
Traditional	12,000	25.06	12,000	25.06	13,294	27.79	6919	23.38
Nontraditional (reference)	35,880	74.94	35,880	74.94	34,550	72.21	22,674	76.62
Importance of family	3.89	0.37	3.89	0.37	3.89	0.37	3.89	0.38
Antiabortion attitude	6.70	2.97	6.70	2.97	6.68	2.97	6.53	2.99
Year of survey	2009	3.46	2009	3.46	2007	6.59	2011	0.70

SD standard deviation

Consistent with our central hypotheses, number of children is positively associated with each indicator of individual religiosity, whereas country-level fertility decline is inversely associated with each aspect of religiosity. Importantly, these observed effects of country-level fertility on individual religiosity withstand statistical controls for country-level factors such as economic development, e.g., GDP per capita, individual-level demographic characteristics, and ideological variables, e.g., family-centered values, gender egalitarianism, that were measured at the individual level. It appears that country-level factors other than economic development and growing existential security may affect religious patterns (Norris and Inglehart 2011).

Drawing on multiple literatures, especially individual-level research on the fertility-religion connection, we have identified several reasons why residing in contexts of declining fertility may impact religious practice and belief. Specifically, over time, it is plausible that diminished fertility can: (a) limit the significance of religious groups and traditions as socialization mechanisms for children; (b) reduce or eliminate the appeal of religious rituals and life cycle events; (c) undermine the role of religious communities as sources of social ties for parents; (d) undercut the importance of religious congregations as sources of formal and informal social support in childrearing; and, consequently, (e) decrease the programming and resources of many religious communities, thereby limiting their visibility and potency within the public sphere. Overall, these dynamics may erode social norms that encourage and reward religious involvement, culminating in cultural shifts that foster religious privatism and "fuzzy fidelity" (Voas 2009), ultimately legitimizing irreligion. Taken

Table 12.3 Multi-level regression models to predict individual-level religiosity

	Attendance[a]		Salience[b]		Belief[b]		Prayer[a]	
Individual level variables								
Female	0.320	***	1.487	***	2.061	***	0.742	***
Age	0.003	***	1.008	***	1.000		0.011	***
Ever married	−0.005		0.949	*	0.993		−0.039	
Education	0.030	***	0.993		0.952	***	0.019	**
Working	−0.048	**	0.890	***	0.994		−0.091	***
Household income	0.010	**	0.983	***	1.006		−0.021	***
Tradition gender ideology	−0.002		1.067	***	1.136	***	0.095	***
Importance of family	0.131	***	1.501	***	1.303	***	0.182	***
Antiabortion attitude	0.099	***	1.150	***	1.116	***	0.127	***
No religious affiliation	−1.787	***	0.174	***	0.062	***	−2.403	***
Orthodox	−0.183	***	0.900	**	1.064		−0.169	***
Buddhist	−0.592	***	0.742	***	0.190	***	−0.583	***
Muslim	−0.086		1.846	***	1.678	***	−0.216	**
Mainline protestant	0.141	***	1.147	***	0.511	***	−0.066	
Conservative protestant	0.377	***	1.332	***	0.957		−0.119	
Other faith tradition	−0.152	***	1.097	*	0.477	***	−0.264	***
Year of survey	−0.026		0.975		1.001		−0.085	
Number of children	0.059	***	1.076	***	1.058	*	0.080	***
Country level variables								
Changes in TFR (1960-most recent year)	−0.015	**	0.982	*	0.971	*	−0.025	**
GDP (2011 and log-transformed)	−0.038		0.865		1.106		−0.142	
Number of respondents	47,880		47,880		47,844		29,593	
Number of countries	38		38		38		23	

$*p < 0.05$; $**p < 0.01$; $***p < 0.001$
[a]Linear model coefficients
[b]Odds coefficients

together, some or all of these processes may help to explain the impact of declining fertility on reductions in individual-level religious participation, salience, and belief that we observed in the above tests.

It is important to acknowledge several features of the data used in this study that may limit the scope and definitiveness of this work. Despite the unique strengths of the World Values Survey project, it is based on a replicated cross-sectional design, and thus is not a panel dataset, precluding a formal analysis of religious change at the individual level. Further, although the project has involved surveys of numerous countries beginning in 1981, some countries were only included beginning in the 1990s. Countries were not surveyed in the same years, and some countries were only surveyed in a small number of years. Most surveys contain only a handful of religion items, and some questions about religion were only asked in a small number of survey years for each country. Moreover, the available data do not permit us to examine directly the specific mechanisms, about which we have speculated above, that may link fertility decline with religious retrenchment. Thus, although we believe these theoretical arguments are highly plausible, given these data limitations it is appropriate to be tentative in drawing conclusions about the effects of fertility decline on religion.

Despite these constraints, the analyses reported in this chapter make several contributions to existing literatures. First, as noted, we provide at least tentative evidence that the connections between religion and fertility may be bidirectional. Although most prior work has emphasized the influence of religion and religious group differences on fertility patterns, it may be worthwhile to consider effects of large-scale fertility changes on religion. Second, over the past 15 years or so social scientists have "discovered" the value of demographic concepts and methods for the study of religion (e.g., Hout et al. 2001; Schwadel 2011; Sherkat 2014; Voas 2007). The present research augments this literature, contributing specifically to a modest body of work on demographic versions of the secularization thesis (e.g., Voas 2003, 2007). Third, our findings resonate with the claims of some western social historians and cultural commentators (e.g., Eberstadt 2013) who have argued that the decline of the primacy and integrity of the nuclear family including reductions in fertility rates has undermined the role of religious institutions, practices, and values in the contemporary West. Their significant limits notwithstanding, the empirical data presented in this chapter could be interpreted as lending at least tentative support to such claims.

What might our findings imply about the future of religion in many regions of the world during the coming decades, given projected further declines in fertility and related transformations in family structures, living arrangements, and the like? Viewed from one perspective, the continued reductions in fertility may well result in additional declines in religious participation, salience, and belief, and may further erode the visibility and impact of religion in these societies. Further, more signs of secularization may be seen, and the processes outlined here could be expected to gain traction across a wider array of societies, as the demographic transition to very low fertility continues and spreads (Kohler et al. 2002; Morgan and Taylor 2006). These effects of fertility decline could well be amplified by other contextual factors.

Although this is certainly a plausible prediction based on the findings reported here, alternative scenarios are possible as well. For example, in a number of countries with low and very low fertility, Kaufmann (2010, 2014) and others have noted that more secular and liberal religious elements tend to have particularly low fertility rates, far below replacement level. On the other hand, the most religious and conservative elements tend to have much higher fertility. The most conservative religious communities are also often characterized by comparatively low exogamy rates and relatively high rates of member retention. A number of these countries are also impacted by immigration of groups characterized by both high religiosity and above-average fertility; the continuation of these patterns could well boost aggregate levels of religiosity with respect to practice, salience, and belief, even if religiosity wanes sharply for certain subgroups of the population. Thus, in such countries secularization may be demographically self-limiting.

This raises the possibility that demographic processes may give rise to a complex and variegated set of religious trajectories within and across countries that have low or very low overall fertility at present, or will come to exhibit such patterns in the near future. In this case, these population dynamics would alter the religious composition of many such countries, making the connection between aggregate fertility decline and religiosity more difficult to predict. The effects on levels of *overall* religiosity, i.e., country-level patterns, would depend upon a number of context-specific variables, such as the initial religious composition, differential fertility across specific religious communities, migratory patterns, complex connections between religion and other social institutions, and many others.

Clearly there is a great deal of work needed to further our understanding of the links between fertility decline and religiosity and religious change. The advent of more and better longitudinal (panel) data sources, merged with country-level data on fertility and other relevant factors, will be essential to establish causal effects more clearly, and to adjudicate among the various pathways and mechanisms that have been put forth here. Nevertheless, we believe our work in this chapter casts fresh light on several specific facets of the fertility-religion connection, and it is hoped that future investigations will continue to advance our understanding of the interplay between fertility transformations and religious patterns and changes.

References

Adsera, A. (2006a). Religion and changes in family-size norms in developed countries. *Review of Religious Research, 47*(3), 271–286.

Adsera, A. (2006b). Marital fertility and religion in Spain, 1985 and 1999. *Population Studies, 60*(2), 205–221.

Adsera, A. (2014). Fertility, feminism, and faith: The influence of secularism and economic conditions. In E. Kaufmann & W. B. Wilcox (Eds.), *Whither the child? Causes and consequences of low fertility* (pp. 1–28). Boulder: Paradigm.

Argue, A., Johnson, D. R., & White, L. K. (1999). Age and religiosity: Evidence from a three-wave panel analysis. *Journal for the Scientific Study of Religion, 38*(3), 423–435.

Becker, P. E., & Hofmeister, H. (2001). Work, family, and religious involvement for men and women. *Journal for the Scientific Study of Religion, 40*(4), 707–722.

Berghammer, C. (2009). *Causality between religiosity and childbearing: Evidence from a Dutch panel study*. Paper presented at the IUSSP conference, Marrakech.

Bruce, S. (2009). Secularization and politics. In *Routledge handbook of religion and politics* (p. 145). New York: Routledge.

Bruce, S. (2011). *Secularization: In defense of an unfashionable theory*. New York: Oxford University.

Chaves, M. (2004). *Congregations in America*. Cambridge, MA: Harvard University.

Dharmalingam, A., & Morgan, S. P. (2004). Persistent Muslim-Hindu fertility differentials in India. *Demography, 41*(3), 529–545.

Eberstadt, M. (2013). *How the west really lost god*. West Conshohocken: Templeton.

Edgell, P. (2006). *Religion and family in a changing society*. Princeton: Princeton University.

Edgell, P., & Docka, D. (2007). Beyond the nuclear family? Familism and gender ideology in diverse religious communities. *Sociological Forum, 22*(1), 25–50.
Ellison, C. G., & George, L. K. (1994). Religious involvement, social ties, and social support in a southeastern community. *Journal for the Scientific Study of Religion, 33*(1), 46–61.
Frejka, T., & Westoff, C. (2008). Religion, religiousness, and fertility in the U.S. and in Europe. *European Journal of Population, 24*(1), 5–31.
Goldscheider, C. (2006). Religion, family, and fertility: What do we know historically and comparatively? In R. Derosas & F. von Poppel (Eds.), *Religion and the decline of fertility in the western world* (pp. 41–57). New York: Springer.
Goldscheider, C., & Mosher, W. D. (1991). Patterns of contraceptive use in the United States: The importance of religious factors. *Studies in Family Planning, 22*(2), 102–115.
Hayford, S. R., & Morgan, S. P. (2008). Religiosity and fertility in the United States: The role of fertility intentions. *Social Forces, 86*(3), 1163–1188.
Hout, M., Greeley, A., & Wilde, M. (2001). The demographic imperative in religious change in the United States. *American Journal of Sociology, 107*(2), 468–500.
Ingersoll-Dayton, B., Krause, N., & Morgan, D. (2002). Religious trajectories and transitions over the life course. *International Journal of Aging and Human Development, 55*(1), 51–70.
Kaufmann, E. (2010). *Shall the religious inherit the earth? Demography and politics in the twenty-first century*. London: Profile.
Kaufmann, E. (2014). Sacralization by stealth? The religious consequences of low fertility in Europe. In E. Kaufmann & W. B. Wilcox (Eds.), *Whither the child?: Causes and consequences of low fertility* (pp. 135–156). Boulder: Paradigm.
Kertzer, D. (2006). Religion and the decline of fertility: Conclusions. In R. Derosas & F. von Poppel (Eds.), *Religion and the decline of fertility in the western world* (pp. 259–269). New York: Springer.
Kohler, H. P., Billari, F., & Ortega, J. A. (2002). The emergence of lowest-low fertility in Europe during the 1990s. *Population and Development Review, 28*(4), 599–639.
Lehrer, E. L. (1996). Religion as a determinant of marital fertility. *Journal of Population Economics, 9*(2), 173–196.
Lehrer, E. L. (2004). Religion as a determinant of economic and demographic behavior in the United States. *Population and Development Review, 30*(4), 707–726.
Lesthaeghe, R., & Neidert, L. (2006). The second demographic transition in the United States: Exception or textbook example? *Population and Development Review, 32*(4), 669–698.
Lesthaeghe, R., & Surkyn, J. (1988). Cultural dynamics and economic theories of fertility change. *Population and Development Review, 14*(1), 1–45.
Mahoney, A. (2010). Religion in families, 1999–2009: A relational spirituality framework. *Journal of Marriage and Family, 72*(4), 805–827.
Manning, C. J. (2013). Unaffiliated parents and the religious training of their children. *Sociology of Religion, 74*(2), 149–175.
McQuillan, K. (2004). When does religion influence fertility? *Population and Development Review, 30*(1), 25–56.
Morgan, S. P., Stash, S., Smith, H. L., & Mason, K. O. (2002). Muslim and non-Muslim differences in female autonomy and fertility: Evidence from four Asian countries. *Population and Development Review, 28*(3), 515–537.
Morgan, S. P., & Taylor, M. (2006). Low fertility at the turn of the twenty-first century. *Annual Review of Sociology, 32*, 375–400.
Mosher, W. D., Williams, L. S., & Johnson, D. (1992). Religion and fertility in the United States: New patterns. *Demography, 29*(2), 199–214.
Myers, S. M. (1996). An interactive model of religiosity inheritance: The importance of family context. *American Sociological Review, 61*(5), 858–866.
Norris, P., & Inglehart, R. (2011). *Sacred and secular: Religion and politics worldwide* (2nd ed.). New York: Cambridge University.

Olson, D. V. (1989). Church friendships: Boon or barrier to church growth? *Journal for the Scientific Study of Religion, 28*(4), 432–447.
Petts, R. J. (2007). Religious participation, religious affiliation, and engagement with children among fathers experiencing the birth of a new child. *Journal of Family Issues, 28*(9), 1139–1161.
Petts, R. J. (2009). Trajectories of religious participation from adolescence to young adulthood. *Journal for the Scientific Study of Religion, 48*(3), 552–571.
Philipov, D., & Berghammer, C. (2007). Religion and fertility ideals, intention, and behavior: A comparative study of European countries. *Vienna Yearbook of Population Research, 5*, 271–305.
Sandomirsky, S., & Wilson, J. (1990). Processes of disaffiliation: Religious mobility among men and women. *Social Forces, 68*(4), 1211–1229.
Schleifer, C., & Chaves, M. (2014). Family formation and religious service attendance: Untangling marital and parental effects. *Sociological Methods and Research.* doi:10.1177/0049124114526376.
Schwadel, P. (2011). Age, period, and cohort effects on religious activities and beliefs. *Social Science Research, 40*(1), 181–192.
Sherkat, D. E. (2006). Preference structures and normative constraints in movements outside, between, and within religious organizations. In J. A. Beckford & J. Walliss (Eds.), *Theorising religion: Classical and contemporary debates* (pp. 149–166). Burlington: Ashgate.
Sherkat, D. E. (2014). *Changing faith: The dynamics and consequences of Americans' shifting religious identities*. New York: New York University.
Skirbeckk, V., Kaufmann, E., & Goujon, A. (2010). Secularism, fundamentalism, or Catholicism? The religious composition of the United States to 2043. *Journal for the Scientific Study of Religion, 49*(2), 293–310.
Stark, R. (2012). *America's blessings*. West Conshohocken: Templeton.
Stark, R., & Finke, R. (2000). *Acts of faith: Explaining the human side of religion*. Berkeley: University of California.
Steensland, B., Park, J. Z., Regnerus, M. D., Robinson, L. D., Wilcox, W. B., & Woodberry, R. D. (2000). The measure of American religion: Toward improving the state of the art. *Social Forces, 79*(1), 291–318.
Stolzenberg, R. M., Blair-Loy, M., & Waite, L. J. (1995). Religious participation in early adulthood: Age and family life cycle effects on church membership. *American Sociological Review, 60*(1), 84–103.
Sullivan, S. C. (2008). Unaccompanied children in churches: Low-income urban single mothers, religion, and parenting. *Review of Religious Research, 50*(2), 157–175.
Surkyn, J., & Lestaeghe, R. (2004). Value orientations and the second demographic transition (SDT) in northern, western, and southern Europe: An update. *Demographic Research, S3*(3), 45–86.
Thornton, A., Axinn, W. G., & Hill, D. H. (1992). Reciprocal effects of religiosity, cohabitation, and marriage. *American Journal of Sociology, 98*(3), 628–651.
Tschannen, O. (1991). The secularization paradigm: A systematization. *Journal for the Scientific Study of Religion, 30*(4), 395–415.
Uecker, J. E., Mayrl, D., & Stroope, S. (2016). Family formation and returning to institutional religion in young adulthood. *Journal for the Scientific Study of Religion, 55*(2), 384–406.
Uecker, J. E., Regnerus, M. D., & Vaaler, M. L. (2007). Losing my religion: The social sources of religious decline in early adulthood. *Social Forces, 85*(4), 1667–1692.
Voas, D. (2003). Intermarriage and the demography of secularization. *British Journal of Sociology, 54*(1), 83–108.
Voas, D. (2007). Does religion belong in population studies? *Environment and Planning A, 39*(5), 1166–1180.
Voas, D. (2009). The rise and fall of fuzzy fidelity in Europe. *European Sociological Review, 25*(2), 155–168.

Voas, D., & Crockett, A. (2005). Religion in Britain: Neither believing nor belonging. *Sociology, 39*(1), 11–28.

Westoff, C., & Bietch, K. (2015). *Religion and reproductive behavior in Sub-Saharan Africa*. Rockville: ICF International.

Westoff, C., & Jones, E. (1979). The end of "Catholic" fertility. *Demography, 16*(2), 209–217.

Wilcox, W. B., Chaves, M., & Franz, D. (2004). Focused on the family? Religious traditions, family discourse, and pastoral practice. *Journal for the Scientific Study of Religion, 43*(4), 491–504.

Wilcox, W. B., Cherlin, A. J., Uecker, J. E., & Messel, M. (2012). No money, no honey, no church: The deinstitutionalization of religious life among the white working class. *Research in the Sociology of Work, 23*, 227–250.

Wilson, J., & Sherkat, D. E. (1994). Returning to the fold. *Journal for the Scientific Study of Religion, 33*(2), 148–161.

About the Authors

James D. Bachmeier is Assistant Professor of Sociology, Temple University, Philadelphia, Pennsylvania, USA.

Frank D. Bean is Distinguished Professor of Sociology and Director, Center for Research on International Migration, University of California, Irvine, California, USA.

Francesco C. Billari is Professor of Demography and President of Dondena at Bocconi University, Milan, Italy.

Susan K. Brown is Associate Professor of Sociology, University of California, Irvine, California, USA.

Christopher G. Ellison is Professor of Sociology and Dean's Distinguished Professor of Social Science, University of Texas at San Antonio, San Antonio, Texas USA.

Nayoung Heo is a Postdoctoral Researcher at the Asian Demographic Research Institute, Shanghai University, Shanghai, China.

Robert A. Hummer is the Howard W. Odum Distinguished Professor of Sociology and a Fellow in the Carolina Population Center, University of North Carolina, Chapel Hill, North Carolina, USA.

Gavin Jones is Emeritus Professor, Australian National University, Canberra, Australia.

Han Gon Kim is Professor of Sociology and Director, Institute of Gerontology, Yeungnam University, Daegu, South Korea.

Juyeon Kim is Assistant Professor of Urban Sociology, University of Seoul, Seoul, South Korea.

Elizabeth M. Lawrence is a Postdoctoral Scholar at the Carolina Population Center, University of North Carolina, Chapel Hill, North Carolina, USA.

D.L. Poston, Jr. (ed.), *Low Fertility Regimes and Demographic and Societal Change*, DOI 10.1007/978-3-319-64061-7

Samsik Lee is Professor of Policy Science and Director of the Hanyang University Institute for Ageing Society Research, Hanyang University, Seoul, South Korea.

Daniel T. Lichter is Ferris Family Professor in the Department of Policy Analysis and Management, Professor of Sociology, and Robert S. Harrison Director, Institute for the Social Sciences, Cornell University, Ithaca, New York, USA.

Dudley L. Poston, Jr. is Professor of Sociology and the Abell Professor of Liberal Arts, Texas A&M University, College Station, Texas, USA.

Zhenchao Qian is Professor of Sociology, Brown University, Providence, Rhode Island, USA.

Nancy E. Riley is Professor of Sociology, Bowdoin College, Brunswick, Maine, USA.

Richard G. Rogers is Professor of Sociology and Director of the IBS Population Program, University of Colorado, Boulder, Colorado, USA.

Andrea L. Ruiz is a Ph.D. candidate in Sociology, Pennsylvania State University, State College, Pennsylvania, USA.

Michael S. Teitelbaum is Senior Research Associate, Labor and Worklife Program, Harvard Law School, Cambridge, Massachusetts, USA.

Linda J. Waite is Lucy Flower Professor of Sociology and Director, Center of Aging, the University of Chicago and the National Opinion Research Center (NORC), Chicago, Illinois, USA.

Xiaohe Xu is Department Chair and Professor of Sociology, University of Texas at San Antonio, San Antonio, Texas USA.

Index

D.L. Poston, Jr. (ed.), *Low Fertility Regimes and Demographic and Societal Change*, DOI 10.1007/978-3-319-64061-7

MIX
Papier aus verantwortungsvollen Quellen
Paper from responsible sources
FSC® C105338
FSC
www.fsc.org

If you have any concerns about our products,
you can contact us on
ProductSafety@springernature.com

In case Publisher is established outside the EU,
the EU authorized representative is:
Springer Nature Customer Service Center GmbH
Europaplatz 3, 69115 Heidelberg, Germany

Printed by Libri Plureos GmbH
in Hamburg, Germany